Wanted in America: Posters
Collected by the Fort Worth
Police Department, 1898-1903

WANTED IN AMERICA

WANTED
IN AMERICA

POSTERS COLLECTED
BY THE FORT WORTH POLICE DEPARTMENT, 1898-1903

EDITORS **LEANNA S. SCHOOLEY** | **TOM KELLAM**

A Joint Project of the Center for Texas Studies and TCU Press

FORT WORTH, TEXAS

Library of Congress Cataloging-in-Publication Data

Names: Schooley, LeAnna Starr, 1970- editor. | Kellam, Tom, 1948- editor.
Title: Wanted in America : posters collected by the Fort Worth Police Department 1898-31903 / edited by
    LeAnna S. Schooley and Tom Kellam.
Other titles: Corrected title: Wanted in America : posters collected by the Fort Worth Police Department
    1898-1903
Description: Fort Worth, Texas : TCU Press, 2019. | Includes bibliographical references. | Summary:
    "Wanted in America: Posters Collected by the Fort Worth Police Department, 1898-1908 features
    fifty posters and the fascinating true crime stories behind them. While some of the offenders are
    virtually unknown today, others, such as Butch Cassidy and the Sundance Kid, remain household
    names. You will meet fugitive pickpockets, embezzlers, robbers, kidnappers, murderers, and more,
    along with their associates and their victims. They are a cross-section of America-men and women
    of all ages, social classes, and many races and nationalities. Though the notices were assembled on a
    local level, they reflect national social and economic changes in a growing population. The fifty post-
    ers selected for publication here represent only a small sample of the hundreds available for research.
    The stories behind the posters demonstrate how twentieth-century advances in mass media distribu-
    tion, law enforcement techniques, transportation, and communication impacted the ability of lawmen
    to locate the fugitives they sought and the ability of the suspects to stay on the run. They reveal that
    the game of cat and mouse continued as both hunter and hunted found ways to use technology to
    their advantage"—Provided by publisher.
Identifiers: LCCN 2019030158 | ISBN 9780875657301 (hardcover)
Subjects: LCSH: Fugitives from justice—United States—History—20th century. | Fugitives from j
    ustice—United States--History--20th century—Posters. | Wanted posters--United States—
    History—20th century. | Fort Worth (Tex.). Police Department—History--20th century.
Classification: LCC HV6241 .W365 2019 | DDC 364.1092/273—dc23
LC record available at https://lccn.loc.gov/2019030158

TCU Box 298300
Fort Worth, Texas 76129
817.257.7822
www.prs.tcu.edu
To order books: 1.800.826.8911

Cover and Text Design by Preston Thomas

It is my belief that no crime, however cowardly and however shameless and cruel, can be imagined which there isn't somebody in Christendom willing to commit.

—Mark Twain

CONTENTS

ILLUSTRATIONS

FOREWORD

Wanted in America represents the Center for Texas Studies at TCU's guiding principles: collaborate and cooperate with other organizations whose aims converge with or are parallel to those of the Center and to present aspects of Texas life and culture in formats that are accessible to the public. The Center's efforts have often taken the form of exhibitions or books or workshops and lectures, but the goal consistently has been to make all that makes Texas distinctive approachable and enjoyable.

LeAnna Schooley and Tom Kellam's *Wanted in America* refreshingly brings to us a sliver of Texas and Fort Worth life at the turn of the twentieth century in a compelling and vivid way. The wanted posters reflect not only people pursued by law enforcement for the commission of crimes, but also lost relatives and missing children. This glimpse of the non-heroic side of Texas history situated within the broad American story adds to our understanding of social and cultural trends as well as law enforcement at the time. Thus, *Wanted in America* belongs on every coffee table to be read in snippets and to enliven a social gathering. Indeed, this volume demonstrates that life can be far more intriguing than fiction.

This project and so many others that the Center has undertaken would not have been possible without the support, financial and psychological, of many. TCU embraced the Center when it was instituted and has sustained it for nearing two decades. The following organizations have been instrumental in fostering the goals of the Center: the Burnett Foundation, the Jane and John Justin Foundation, the Lowe Foundation, and the Summerlee Foundation. We are most grateful for their support in our mission to celebrate all that makes Texas distinctive.

MARY L. VOLCANSEK

INTRODUCTION

This book is the result of a lunchtime brainstorming session between Tarrant County College archivist Tom Kellam and Center for Texas Studies at TCU Director Gene Allen Smith. The college archives held a large and fascinating collection of notices seeking wanted persons. The documents, created by law enforcement officials for their colleagues and the press, merited study and publication. Smith agreed that these stark relics should be shared with all lovers of true crime. Thus, they formed a partnership to create this volume of remarkable posters with essays detailing the intriguing stories behind them for TCU Press. The fifty posters selected by editors Tom Kellam and LeAnna Schooley to be included here represent only a small sample of the hundreds that are available for research at the archives. They were chosen to highlight the scope of crimes committed, the diversity in class, race, and ethnicity of the victims and the accused, and the stylistic nuances of the posters themselves as pieces of material culture. Over thirty professors, journalists, and local historians generously contributed their time to research and craft the accompanying essays for your perusal.

While construction of the first two campuses of what was then known as Tarrant County Junior College (TCJC) was just beginning, officials began discussing an archival collection focused on county history. Eventually, they chose the Northeast Campus library to be the home of a local history and genealogy collection. Jenkins Garrett, a prominent Fort Worth attorney and an early member of the TCJC Board of Trustees, probably urged this effort forward. He was an avid collector of books, maps, and documents relating to Texas history. In 1974, the same year the Heritage Room opened on the Northeast Campus, Garrett also helped launch the UTA Special Collections with a donation. The Heritage Room accession records show that Garrett began donating material to the college as early as 1968, six years before the Heritage Room officially opened under founding director Duane Gage.

Joe D. Galloway, retired deputy chief of police of Fort Worth, also brought an interest in history and archives to TCJC. After thirty-two years with the city, beginning in 1968 he spent four years as law enforcement coordinator for the school. While on staff, he donated a collection of records from the Fort Worth Police Department that included two scrapbook-style ledgers of wanted posters, handbills, postcards, correspondence, and newspaper clippings; a court docket book, 1873-1877; a register of prisoners in the city jail, 1886-1890; and a bound volume of *The Detective* magazine (1901-1912), a trade periodical for police officers advertising equipment, new professional techniques, and, of course, wanted persons from around the country.

The two volumes date to the turn of the century. Because the Justice Department did not receive authorization to create a Bureau of Investigation until 1908, at the time law enforcement was still primarily the realm of private agencies and local officials. Therefore, the Pinkerton National Detective Agency and other professional agencies as well as local sheriff and police departments created the advertisements, which they then distributed to cities such as Fort Worth. The first volume focuses on the written word and contains a mix of reward notices, correspondence from other agencies, and newspaper clippings on wanted persons in the city or those who might be passing through. The second volume, which spans the years 1898 to 1903, supplied the notices featured in this book. Unlike its predecessor, these pages include many more mass-produced, large-format circulars which displayed one or more photographs and included specific measurements to help identify the subject. A quick review reveals that they bear little resemblance to the modern image of the wanted poster popularized by movies and television with its old west fonts and decoratively burned paper edges. The genuine articles featured simple designs that were hastily created to convey an important message.

In the second ledger a systematic approach to criminal identification begins to emerge that demonstrates significant advances in criminology around the turn of the century. Photographs were used in criminal investigation almost immediately after the technology became readily available, but not consistently or in a standard format. The reader will note that the images that illustrate the posters in this volume range from personal snapshots or studio portraits to formal mug shots familiar to Americans today. When mug shots were not available, detective agencies and police departments turned to local photography shops, employers, clubs, and fraternal organizations or associates and relatives of suspects in search of a likeness. Many of the images on our notices are obviously cropped from group photographs or family portraits. Authorities selected an image of Kid Curry on a Pinkerton poster from a wedding picture. The most famous examples of this practice are the pictures of Butch Cassidy and the Sundance Kid pulled from their "Fort Worth Five" photograph taken in the Swartz brothers' studio.

In some instances, the issuer attached original photographic prints to notices. Over the time span of the second ledger, however, print technology improved to the point that halftone images could be easily reproduced on printing presses when large quantities of circulars were required. The Pinkerton Detective Agency saw itself as critical to the crime fighting process because they monitored technological advances in business and industry alongside the innovations developed by outlaws who wished to circumvent new security features. They standardized the use of the modern front-and-side-view mug shots originally introduced by Alphonse Bertillon, a French criminologist, and widely distributed their mass-produced posters.

Bertillon used the photographs alongside a carefully categorized system of anatomic measurements or anthropometry with an equally specific vocabulary to describe human features. Based on the idea that every person is physically unique, Bertillon went beyond height and weight to include details such as span of outstretched arms, width of skull, and length of left little finger. Influenced by his anthropologist father, he and others thought his process could also identify genetic or physical attributes that characterized persons with criminal minds. By the 1880s most police departments and detective agencies relied on his system of "Bertillon measurements," which routinely appeared on Pinkerton bulletins and were often included on notices issued by the largest police departments in the nation. Law enforcement remained focused on their use for individual identification rather than classifying criminal types.

Bertillon's careful measurements and specific terminology remained the standard in criminal identification until fingerprinting gradually proved to be a more reliable alternative in the mid-1920s. Some of Bertillon's original goals for a scientific identification system have now been achieved with the use of DNA testing. Even so, the traditional mug shot continues to play a critical role in the process.

Not all wanted notices were issued for possible criminals. Some were for missing persons, such as former bank official George Kimmel, who disappeared during a business trip in 1898. Others were prepared by worried relatives of mentally ill loved ones who had wandered off or escaped from asylums. Perhaps the most poignant are those for missing children. Posters improved the chances that law enforcement could accurately identify the persons being sought should they encounter them. They also offered the public an opportunity to get a firsthand look at the missing people they should be looking out for as well as the criminal element thought to be in their midst. Perhaps they could even participate in the hunt. Though most posters were created with law enforcement audiences in mind, average folks could read about the search and see images of the suspects in articles published in their local newspapers or in the rogues' galleries displayed in urban post offices and police departments across the US.

In addition to the photographs and "scientific" descriptions on the posters, law enforcement officers included in notices personal details that revealed prevailing social and moral attitudes of the period. Suspected murderer Charles Hadley was said to have "cohabited with a woman not his wife during one year prior to his disappearance," and "resided in questionable portions" of San Francisco. The poster for Mamie Babcock, who left Cleveland, Ohio, with her lover—an older, married father of two who absconded with all the family assets—described her as uneducated and unfashionable but a "good looking girl." Train robber Channing Barnes's poster declared that he lived among "good society," but that he was a "free drinker and an inveterate smoker of cigarettes." Comments such as these colored readers' opinions of the accused and suggested one more reason to believe in their guilt.

Taken as a whole, the collection provides a window into the operations of the police department of a mid-sized city during a transitional period of American history. In 1873, when Fort Worth incorporated, it was a village of about one thousand people. The country was in a depression. The economy of the town revolved around cattle drives coming up the Chisholm Trail and saloons and gambling halls of the rowdy red-light district known as Hell's Half Acre. The arrival of the Texas and Pacific Railroad in 1876 ushered in an era of explosive growth. The modest population of 6,600 in 1880 reached 26,600 by 1900 and a remarkable 73,000 by 1910. The city thrived as a center of industry and a regional transportation hub that attracted new residents looking for work, not only from the United States, but from around the world. For law enforcement agencies, a bustling crossroads like Fort Worth was an important locale to keep apprised about the fugitives from justice who might pass through their jurisdiction, as evidenced by the numbers of wanted notices the police received.

This pattern of population growth, internal migration, and immigration led to an intermingling of diverse languages and cultures and accompanying social strains in metropolitan areas across the United States. Though the contents of the Fort Worth wanted notice ledgers were collected on a local level, they reflect national change. Among the wanted persons are men and women of all ages, of every social class, and of most races and nationalities making up the US population in the latter part of the nineteenth and early twentieth centuries. The crimes they were accused of were blue collar and white, tame and violent, premeditated and passionate. They were presumed to be pickpockets, embezzlers, robbers, kidnappers, murderers, and more; drug-related offenses, however, are conspicuously absent from this list. This collection covers a time when opiates, cocaine, and cannabis were used in patent medicines and sold in pharmacies. While the public considered them a social and moral problem, their use and abuse had not yet been criminalized.

This volume uses surviving wanted posters to take a closer look at the deeply intertwined relationship between law enforcement officers and the fugitives they sought. Though not a comprehensive study, these fifty posters demonstrate several trends. They show that lawmen deployed the most current turn-of-the-century technology available to conduct their searches, just as those running from justice used every method at their disposal to escape capture. The stories behind the advertisements reveal that police did not always arrest the guilty party on their first attempt, and occasionally they never apprehended a suspect at all. In some cases, there is strong evidence that individuals committed the crimes of which they were accused. Yet others leave historians unsure as to whether fair judgements were reached.

Ultimately, the essays that follow will introduce the people behind the faces that peer out of these pages, along with their pursuers, victims, partners in crime, and families as well. The tales themselves run the gamut from amusing to puzzling to horrific. At some point while leafing through this book, readers are likely to shake their heads and think back to that age-old saying that applies to many true crime stories: "You just can't make this stuff up." These may not be the styles of popular wanted posters that most commonly come to mind, but they are the real thing—and that makes them all the more compelling.

LEANNA S. SCHOOLEY
TOM KELLAM

PART I

KIDNAPPERS

AND MISSING PERSONS

FRANKLIN ZIMMERMAN

Linda Barrett

MISSING SINCE 1895.

Where is Franklin Zimmerman, Formerly of Blue Ball, Penna.?

A Legacy and Accumulated Interest on Other Funds Awaiting Him—His Friends Anxious to Hear From Him - Last Heard From at Sioux City, Iowa, in January, 1895.

In the summer of 1893, Franklin Zimmerman, a well-known resident of Blue Ball, East Earl township, Lancaster county, Pa., then twenty-eight years old, went to Chicago, as thousands of others did, to visit the Columbian exposition. He stated to some of his friends before leaving that he intended to travel some throughout the west before returning home and probably would go to California. He was heard from occasionally until January, 1895, when he telegraphed from Sioux City, Iowa, to S. H. Musselman, of Blue Ball, who has charge of part of an estate of his, asking for some money. A draft was sent to him but it came back some time afterwards with the information that he had left the place and it was not known where he was. Since that time nothing whatever has been heard in regard to him, and his mother and other relatives and friends are anxious to know whether he is still living, and if so where he is.

FRANKLIN ZIMMERMAN.

There awaits him a considerable sum of interest money accumulated from the fund, already referred to, in the hands of his guardian, S. H. Musselman, and besides there is awaiting him another legacy which is ready to be paid this spring, and those having charge of these moneys are anxious to get them off their hands.

Mr. Zimmerman, when he left home, was a stoutly-built, robust looking man weighing about 185 pounds. He was about five feet six inches high, had dark hair and a mustach. His eyes were grayish-blue and the left eye was slightly crossed or turned inward. He had a slight impediment in his speech and was somewhat eccentric in some respects.

The above picture was taken several years before he left home.

Any information leading to a knowledge of his whereabouts will be well rewarded.

S. H. MUSSELMAN,
Blue Ball, Lanc. Co., Pa.

April 2, 1902.

In the spring of 1902, newspapers throughout the western United States published a plea for assistance in locating Franklin Zimmerman of Blue Ball, Lancaster County, Pennsylvania. The puzzling story began in 1893, when Zimmerman went to Chicago to attend the World's Columbian Exposition, a six-hundred-acre extravaganza which hosted over twenty-seven million people during its six-month run. Before leaving, he indicated to friends that after his visit to the fair he planned to spend some time traveling in the West, perhaps as far as California. Indeed, they heard occasional news from him over the next couple of years as he journeyed around the country. In January of 1895, he sent his guardian, Samuel H. Musselman, a telegram from Sioux City, Iowa, to request money from the estate left to him by his father. Musselman responded, but Zimmerman had reportedly departed town before the funds arrived, and they reverted back to the sender. He left no forwarding address and did not contact his guardian again. After seven years passed with no further missives from his ward, Musselman involved local police and the national media hoping to locate the missing man.

Though Franklin Zimmerman was raised in a tightly knit Mennonite community, he had never known his father, Francis. His mother, Anna Martin Zimmerman, gave birth to the boy three months after his father died while serving as a bugler in Company G of the Fourteenth Pennsylvania Cavalry in September 1864. He left about $300 in property to his young family, and they began receiving his pension benefits in 1865. That fall, the court appointed his mother's uncle, Samuel Martin, guardian of Franklin Zimmerman at a time when a male relative was most likely to be selected to manage the estate of a minor child. By the time the census taker visited in 1870, Franklin Zimmerman lived with his widowed maternal grandmother, Leah Martin, and his mother's younger siblings. Meanwhile, his mother Anna Zimmerman resided with relatives of her deceased husband, Abraham and Mary Weaver, where she helped around the house. It was not unusual for families to assist each other when the need arose. Ten years later she listed her occupation as a servant in the home of the Gehman family, but Franklin's whereabouts at the time are unknown.

In the Orphans' Court of Lancaster County, Pennsylvania, in 1883, Samuel S. Martin relinquished his guardianship of Franklin Zimmerman's inheritance, which amounted to $665.84, in favor of another relative, John S. Martin. Normally, under Martin's watchful eye at least, the nineteen-year-old Franklin would have to spend his funds judiciously until he reached twenty-one, the age of majority at the time. In Zimmerman's case, however, supervision continued. Over the years, Franklin's guardianship passed to a paternal uncle by marriage. The appointee, Samuel H. Musselman, was a dedicated member of the Mennonite church in Lancaster County, and served in many leadership positions in later years.

When Franklin Zimmerman headed for Chicago in 1893, he was twenty-eight years old, far beyond the need for a guardian, and there is no evidence of a trust in his name. The specifics about the young man found on the wanted poster and in newspaper articles may provide some clues to illuminate the situation. His family described him for the poster as slightly cross-eyed, with a "slight impediment in his speech and [being] somewhat eccentric in some respects." It seems possible that he may have struggled with impaired cognitive function, and if so, that would explain why a guardian was still required. Advertisements seeking Zimmerman indicated that he had access to the interest on a substantial estate, and that as of 1902 he was due to receive another legacy from his grandfather, Peter Zimmerman.

Speculation on the rest of Franklin Zimmerman's life produces a variety of scenarios. It is possible that he met his end in an accident or illness with neither a witness to report the incident nor any friend to identify him. Alternatively, he may have chosen to take on a new identity. Perhaps he fell into the company of an unscrupulous person or persons, and it was they who precipitated the request for funds that Musselman received in January of 1895. Should that have been the case, they did not receive the reward they hoped for, since the money was returned to Musselman. Even so, they may have caused harm to Zimmerman. If he suffered from a cognitive disability—or someone perceived he did—that would have placed him at an increased risk of someone attempting to take advantage of him. Unfortunately, no one ever discovered the truth.

Zimmerman's mother did not remarry. She lived near her relatives and worked in the homes of others until she died of cancer at the age of seventy-seven in 1917. Throughout her life she remained the eternal optimist in regard to her boy. When the census taker visited her in 1900 and in 1910, she reported that she had one child, and he was living. Her obituary explained that in addition to the two sisters and brother who survived her, she had "one son, Franklin Zimmerman, whose whereabouts are unknown."[1]

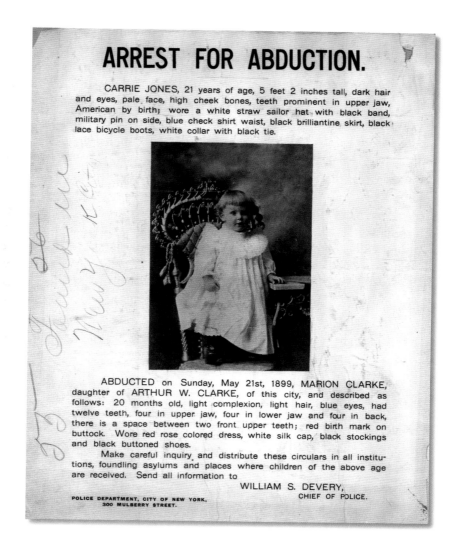

ARREST FOR ABDUCTION.

CARRIE JONES, 21 years of age, 5 feet 2 inches tall, dark hair and eyes, pale face, high cheek bones, teeth prominent in upper jaw, American by birth; wore a white straw sailor hat with black band, military pin on side, blue check shirt waist, black brilliantine skirt, black lace bicycle boots, white collar with black tie.

ABDUCTED on Sunday, May 21st, 1899, MARION CLARKE, daughter of ARTHUR W. CLARKE, of this city, and described as follows: 20 months old, light complexion, light hair, blue eyes, had twelve teeth, four in upper jaw, four in lower jaw and four in back, there is a space between two front upper teeth; red birth mark on buttock. Wore red rose colored dress, white silk cap, black stockings and black buttoned shoes.

Make careful inquiry and distribute these circulars in all institutions, foundling asylums and places where children of the above age are received. Send all information to

WILLIAM S. DEVERY,
CHIEF OF POLICE.

POLICE DEPARTMENT, CITY OF NEW YORK,
300 MULBERRY STREET.

CARRIE JONES AND MARION CLARKE

Jensen Branscombe

On a spring day in May 1899, a young mother in New York City grew frantic waiting for the return of her daughter, Marion, only twenty months old. A recently hired nurse named Carrie Jones had taken Marion for a stroll in Central Park on the morning of May 21 but was late returning home. When the father, Arthur Clarke, arrived home hours after his daughter's expected return, he immediately went searching for the missing pair. Upon discovering an empty baby carriage in the park, the parents notified the police. Not long after, a young boy delivered a ransom note to their doorstep that read: "Mr. Clarke—Do not look for your nurse and baby. They are safe in our possession, where they will

remain for the present." The note issued a chilling warning that the matter should be kept out of hands of the police and press, or "we will see to it that you never see her alive again." The note, signed "Three," assured the parents that their baby was "safe and in good hands," and explained that unemployment and desperation were what drove the kidnappers to their action.[2]

Despite the "Three's" warning, the police and press were heavily involved in the case from the beginning. The investigation centered on Carrie Jones, as she was the only known suspect. A wanted poster issued by the New York City Police Department included a thorough description of Jones, but the picture on the poster was of the missing girl. Within hours of the abduction, thousands of police from the city and surrounding areas were out looking for Clarke and Jones. After a week, searchers' spirits were low. "The mother was gradually sinking to her grave under the shock," one reporter observed, and "the hearts that beat in unison with those of the parents grew heavy and sick." Leads emerged, then faded, directing the search "into a hundred false channels."[3]

As the search dragged on into an eighth, ninth, and then tenth day, Captain George McClusky, the chief of the detective bureau, was busy following a report from a local landlady that only hours after the abduction she had rented a room to two women with a child who matched Clarke's description. Upon seeing reports of the kidnapping in the newspapers, the landlady claimed, the women disappeared. At some point after fleeing the city, Jones left the child in the care of the other woman, one of her accomplices in the crime. McClusky, meanwhile, was still tracking Jones's trail on the eleventh day of the disappearance when the case broke open due to another eyewitness account.

A postmistress in a small town near Sloatsburg, New York, about forty miles from the Clarke home, reported to the local sheriff that she had seen a girl in the post office matching the picture of Marion published in the *New York Herald*. Following up on the new lead, Sloatsburg authorities found the child in good health in a farmhouse and detained the woman caring for her. Arthur Clarke arrived later that day, June 1, to confirm that his daughter had been found alive and well.

Clarke's picture in the *Herald* and the role it played in her recovery suggests that perhaps press coverage of the case was more important than the police work. In the height of sensationalized yellow journalism, the kidnapping case was covered thoroughly by the papers. The press "turned itself into a wanted poster" with information, pictures, and reward offers, making the crime a huge story in the city. Although it certainly helped draw attention to the case and undermined the kidnappers' cause, there was some criticism of the coverage by skeptics of sensationalism in the news. Some went so far as to claim newspaper editors orchestrated the abduction just for the story. "Baby writings were appeals to female readers, appeals to sentimentality, and ultimately appeals for circulation," one scholar of the press at the time concluded.[4]

Even with the questionable motives and sensationalism in the media, it was the widespread publication of Marion Clarke's image that brought about a successful resolution of the case and reunited Clarke with her parents. One paper reported at the time that a crowd as large as two thousand people was waiting at the Clarke home when father and daughter returned, revealing just how closely the city was following the story. The papers, of course, also covered the subsequent arrests of the "Three," who turned out to be the nurse Carrie Jones—whose real name was Bella Anderson—and a married couple, George and Addie Barrow, who also used assumed names.

The focus of the investigation for much of its duration had been on Anderson, aka Jones, the hired nurse. It was confirmed in the aftermath of Clarke's return home that Anderson had been working with the Barrows, who plotted the kidnapping in hopes of making easy money. The plan, which ultimately failed, was not well-conceived. Contemporary descriptions of the Clarkes' wealth range from them being very poor to having moderate means, but it seems in any case the family was not in a strong position to pay a ransom, reported to be $300.

It is unclear in the existing record which one of the Barrows was the mastermind behind the abduction, though most of the evidence implicates George. George Barrow, aka James Wilson or Mark Beauregard, had a violent past that involved torturing animals, and had kidnapped before. Anderson was adamant in her confession that she was just a tool in her accomplice's plans. George convinced her that "it was the easiest thing in the world to make money by kidnapping children," Anderson admitted in her confession. Though she "begged him not to persuade" her, he was successful in securing her role in the plot. Addie Barrow, aka Jennie Wilson or Jennie Beauregard, was the woman detained by police when Marion was found, and for a time the authorities viewed her as the primary culprit in the plot. Subsequent investigations, however, brought to light George's criminal past. He was arrested shortly after his wife, and both were sentenced to prison. He received close to the maximum sentence for kidnapping (fifteen years); the courts sentenced Addie to twelve years and ten months behind bars after she changed her plea to guilty.[5]

Bella Anderson, aka Carrie Jones, remained at large for a short period of time, but she, too, was found and arrested for her crime. After her confession she agreed to serve as a state's witness against her accomplices and received a reduced sentence of four years for her role in the abduction of Marion Clarke.

$50,000 Reward!

An Additional Reward of $5,000 for the Arrest of Pat Crowe.

Taken 1893.   Taken 1894.   Taken 1900.   Taken 1900.

The above cuts are likenesses of Pat Crowe, supposed to be the leader of a gang of men who kidnapped Edward A. Cudahy, Jr. in this city on the night of Dec. 18, 1900, and held him for a ransom of $25,000.00, which was paid in $5, $10 and $20 gold pieces.

Three men were implicated in the kidnapping, and are described as follows:

No. 1. Pat Crowe. Aged 33: height 5 ft. 10½ in.; weight 155 to 165 lbs.; brown hair, mixed with gray at sides; blue eyes of nervous expression, light sandy mustache probably dyed, may be smooth shaven or wear sandy full beard, has faint scar on right cheek, scar on inner right wrist, scar on base of left thumb, several scars at base of left index finger, three upper right molar teeth out, which causes cheek to sink, unless replaced by false teeth, left eyetooth out, which may have been replaced by a false one. Bertillon measurements, ht. 1m79-4. O. A. 80-0. Tr. 93-6. H. L. 19-3. H. W. 15-4. Ch. 14-1. R. E. 6-8. L. F. 26-4d2. L. M. F. 11-9. L. L. F. 9-4. L. F. A. 48-5.

* * By a resolution of the Mayor and City Council of the city of Omaha, passed January 22, 1901, I was authorized to offer an additional and direct reward of **$5,000** for the arrest and delivery into the custody of an officer of this department, in any jail in the United States or Canada, of Pat Crowe, alias Frank Roberts, alias John Wilson, alias James Martin, alias Frank J. Murphy, alias Harris. The cut showing him as he appeared in 1894 is said to be the best likeness of him as he appeared when last seen here.

No. 2. Aged 32 to 37, height 5 feet 9 or 10, weight 150 to 160, dark hair, dark complexion and dark mustache if any.

No. 3. Aged about 40, height 5 feet 10 inches to 6 feet, rather stout build, weight 185 to 190, dark hair and complexion, dark mustache, speaks with Irish dialect in gruff voice, is a heavy drinker and cigarette smoker.

* * There is also a woman remotely connected with the case, she having been with No. 1 at the time negotiations were being made to rent the house which was afterwards used as young Cudahy's prison. She is described as being aged 20 to 23 years, height 5 ft. 4 to 6 inches, weight 130 to 135 pounds, very heavy dark brown hair, one front tooth gold plated, which is noticable when she speaks, and has the resemblance of being solid gold, pale complexion, of delicate appearance, wore an imitation Astrakan black cape, black winter hat with long black feather, and she will likely be found in company with Pat Crowe.

In affecting a trade for the pony used by No. 1, a Hunter case, gold filled watch, was given as part payment. The watch is an Elgin Giant, case No. 46614 horse's head with bridle engraved on back, and a shield on front case around which are floral engravings, has a cheap Elgin movement No. 5017624.

The $50,000 is offered as follows: $25,000.00 by the city of Omaha and $25,000.00 by Mr. E. A. Cudahy, to be distributed as follows, the city of Omaha and Mr. Cudahy having agreed each to pay, $5,000.00 for the arrest and conviction of any one of the kidnappers, $15,000.00 for the arrest and conviction of any two of the kidnappers, and $25,000.00 for the arrest and conviction of all three of the kidnappers of E. A. Cudahy, Jr.

To avoid any unnecessary commotions, I would suggest that photographs be sent to this office, of any suspects who may be arrested for the above crime, as the only way we have of identifying No. 2 and No. 3 will be by photographs.

Address all communications to

J. J. DONAHUE,
Chief of Police.

Omaha. Nebraska, January 22, 1901.

PAT CROWE

O. K. Carter

Based on the $50,000 reward offered for his capture, Pat Crowe should have been one of the star desperadoes of twentieth-century America. After all, when law enforcement posted it in early 1901, that amount was equivalent to more than $1.4 million today—a desperately wanted man indeed when compared to, say, future Public Enemy No. 1 John Dillinger, who merited a $25,000 reward, or George "Baby Face" Nelson, for whom a comparatively paltry $5,000 was offered.

The difference? Dillinger and Nelson were killers

who also robbed banks. Though Crowe involved himself in a variety of criminal activities, mostly involving stickups, his claim to lasting fame was that on December 18, 1900, in Omaha, Nebraska, he and an accomplice kidnapped sixteen-year-old Edward Cudahy Jr., the son of Edward A. Cudahy Sr., the wealthy owner of Cudahy Packing, which was then one of the four largest meat packing companies in America along with Armour, Swift, and Morris.

In a vicious note, Crowe threatened to throw acid in the boy's eyes if the senior Cudahy did not pay $25,000 ransom in gold coins. The elder Cudahy loved his son and heir and capitulated immediately. He followed the kidnappers' instructions to the letter, and they released his son unharmed. Everything was over and done in a few hours.

That would have been the end of the drama but for the fact that the angry millionaire meat packer then hired the famed Pinkerton Detective Agency to identify and track down the kidnappers. He sweetened the offer with the $50,000 reward, half from him and half from the City of Omaha. Before long, Pinkerton's identified Crowe as the chief suspect. But it would take five long years before he surrendered and threw himself upon the mercy of the courts—not once but twice. During that time, sightings of Crowe were reported from a variety of states, as well as England and South Africa.

The size of the reward alarmed Crowe so much that he sent Cudahy a letter threatening his entire family with vengeance if he did not instantly withdraw the reward offered for his apprehension. "If you value the boy's life at the price of a bullet you will withdraw the reward at once. And let well enough alone," the letter said. "If you don't we will finish the job with a bullet. And if any man whether guilty or innocent is ever arrested a bullet will close the boy's mouth." The senior Cudahy declined to rescind the reward, and Crowe never followed up on his threat. Astonishingly at his two trials he was found not guilty both times, despite not providing a single witness in his defense.[6]

Who was Pat Crowe? Born on an Iowa farm, he was young when his mother died. He had more bad luck and sorrow in his marriage. First, all three of his children died as youths. Then his wife left him. In Omaha, he opened a small butcher shop that went under when the Cudahy Packing Company began selling meat retail. Crowe went to work in one of those establishments but soon developed a self-confessed habit of skimming dollars from sales. When he was caught, fired, and blackballed by the company, his animosity toward the

Cudahys grew. He then moved to Chicago, where he participated in several thefts, including a jewelry heist and train robbery. It might have been during his brief stint in Joliet prison for those crimes that Crowe developed his kidnapping plot to enrich himself and to retaliate against Cudahy Packing. The actual abduction turned out to be astonishingly easy. Crowe and accomplice James Callahan grabbed the teenager as he was returning home from running an errand. Moreover, the distressed father responded just as they had hoped— that is until he hired Pinkerton's.

Once authorities identified Pat Crowe as the kidnapper, the media began embellishing his reputation. A *Baltimore Sun* article described Crowe as a "Western bandit and daring gunfighter," while the *Weekly Times* went lowbrow by describing him as "a kidnapper, a thief and a rascal of the first order." Those who knew Crowe described him—apparently inaccurately—as outwardly meek in appearance and mild in demeanor.

Investigators caught Pat Crowe's accomplice, James Callahan, and tried him in 1901. Because Nebraska at the time had no kidnapping laws that applied to the case, a jury acquitted Callahan on related charges. After he had been on the run for five years, officers finally arrested Crowe. After the shock of Callahan's acquittal in the face of overwhelming evidence, however, Crowe's results were hardly unexpected. Unable to try him directly for the kidnapping, they charged him with attempting to kill a policeman in an escape attempt during his time on the lam. The jury acquitted him after eighty minutes of deliberation. A new charge of grand larceny for the theft of the ransom money sent Crowe to trial again in February 1906. After ninety-two witnesses for the prosecution, and no witnesses for the defense, the jury again acquitted Crowe.

What happened? The trial took place as the Progressive Era unfolded. Writers like Upton Sinclair exposed unscrupulous practices in the meat packing industry, among others, that included everything from price fixing, to providing abhorrent working conditions, to eliminating competition, to forcing workers to become "wage slaves." At that time Cudahy would have been one of the most unpopular men in Omaha at least, perhaps in the country. Soon, reformers like President Teddy Roosevelt instituted numerous reforms that dramatically altered many industries for the better.

After his trials concluded, Crowe wrote a lengthy half-biography and half-philosophy piece headlined "How and Why I Kidnapped the Cudahy Boy" in the *Philadelphia Inquirer*, in which he admitted to the kidnapping, saying it was his idea alone. "If they (jurors) leaned in my favor they did it for the same reasons that led me to the kidnapping—a belief that the law of our land has ceased to be a thing of strict justice and right for all the people," he wrote. "The big fortunes that have been made in this country have been made mostly by men who have broken the criminal law—the same law that was used against me. The owners of these fortunes are called successful and are held up as models for our sons because they have been able to find safe ways of getting around the law." Crowe claimed to still have $20,000 in gold coins of the ransom buried, but he pledged that he'd had enough of the criminal life. He wrote, "I have never really enjoyed a dollar of what I have stolen and I haven't enjoyed a minute's real peace." Crowe lectured on the evils of crime for the remainder of his life and wrote an autobiography titled *Spreading Evil*. When he died in New York in 1938, he was destitute.[7]

As for young Edward Cudahy Jr., he seemed to suffer no ill effects from the kidnapping. He served with distinction in World War I, eventually ran the family business, and prospered for many years despite tougher governmental requirements. Though business declined severely after World War II, he died in 1966 still a wealthy man.

OFFICE OF SUPERINTENDENT OF POLICE,
Cincinnati, O., Sept. 8, 1899.

$100.00   REWARD.

Chief of Police,

   Sir:-

        We have a warrant charging Charles O. Winold with kidnap-
ing the following described children:

        No. 1.   Harold Aiken Winold, 5-1/2 years of age; slen-
der; light golden curls, may be cut off; light blue eyes; long
black lashes; one lower double tooth gone; peculiar habit of moving arms up and down when happy or excited.

        No. 2.   Frances Louisa Winold, 2-1/2 years of age; very
chubby and large for age; light brown hair, naturally straight;
large deep blue eyes; long brown lashes; peculiar habit of pulling
or twisting lock of hair on left side, front.

        Charles O. Winold, wanted on charge of "Kidnaping" is
5 ft. 11 in. tall; stooped shouldered; light brown hair, slightly
bald; heavy light mustache, may be cut off or may wear full beard;
deep set light blue eyes; very nervous in action.

        If found, wire me at once at my expense, and I will send
the necessary papers.

                        Respectfully,

                        PHIL. DEITSCH,

                            Sup't of Police.

CHARLES, HAROLD, AND FRANCES WINOLD

Michael Cervantes

In September 1899, Cincinnati Police Superintendent Philip Deitsch issued a bulletin to police departments across the United States alerting them to be on the lookout for Charles, Harold, and Frances Winold. He accused forty-one-year-old Charles O. Winold, a traveling salesman, of kidnapping his two children, aged five and two, respectively, from their Cincinnati, Ohio, home where they resided with their mother, Susan. The kidnapping was one part of a longer feud between Charles and Susan that provides insight into how family law functioned at the turn of the century.

Charles and Susan married in Cincinnati in 1892. It seemed that initially they were happy and actively involved in the Methodist church. Not long after the birth of their second child, however, an unknown scandal prompted charges and countercharges that resulted in a separation. Susan sought a "Dakota Divorce" in May 1898 to quickly dissolve the union, the Dakotas being a popular destination for divorce-seekers at a time when Americans still frowned upon it in most cases. Claiming her divorce decree awarded the children to her, she moved them to Minnesota.

The first reported kidnapping of Harold and Frances Winold occurred in early 1899, after the divorce was final. According to the July 21, 1899, *Stark County Democrat*, Charles allegedly took the children to an unknown location, and in response Susan sued for their return. The attorneys for both Winolds reached an agreement on behalf of their clients which confirmed Susan's custody. It required Charles to provide child support and allowed periodic visits with the children.

Charles broke the terms of the settlement almost immediately. He repeatedly kidnapped the children, one instance of which resulted in the creation of the aforementioned police bulletin. After a chase that lasted several months and crossed multiple state lines, the authorities found Charles and the children in Hoboken, New Jersey, and they sent Harold and Frances back to their mother. Later, Susan moved back to Cincinnati to live with her father and stepmother, Charles and Fannie Aiken, in hope of providing more stability for herself and the children. Instead, things took a shocking turn for the worse for all involved.

On March 30, 1900, Susan, her two children, her stepmother, and a live-in nurse became violently ill after eating their morning oatmeal. Suspecting poisoning, an investigation by the local police discovered that the household servant, eighteen-year-old "Fatha" Gilliam, under the pseudonym Lena Heigh, had purchased a half-ounce bottle of arsenic at a nearby drug store. To make matters more confusing, Gilliam told authorities that her name was Violet Foster, the alias she had apparently given Susan Winold upon being hired. Gilliam admitted that she was, in her own words, "infatuated" with Charles Winold and that "he had told her he would marry her if his wife was out of the way."[8]

Upon further questioning, Gilliam confessed that Charles sent her to answer Susan's recent advertisement for domestic help. In the short two weeks that Gilliam worked in the household, Charles visited her in the kitchen, "plotting against the life of Mrs. Winold." In addition, she claimed that he appeared the morning of the attempted murder, and that he personally put the poison in the oatmeal which she only delivered to the table after he threatened her life.[9]

But where did Charles go after the crime? Gilliam explained that he ran from Susan's home that morning upon hearing the family come down the stairs for breakfast. His flight took him all the way to the East Coast, where he was arrested by Baltimore police on April 10. According to some reports, he told arresting officers, "I understand that my former wife is to be married again. I would rather kill my children than to allow them to be placed under the care of a stepfather." The *Baltimore Sun* reported otherwise, stating that Winold "claimed the charge is all bosh and the result of spite on the part of his divorced wife and her family and that he can easily prove he was not in Cincinnati when the alleged poisoning took place."[10]

In an effort to ferret out the truth, Cincinnati Chief of Police Phillip Deitsch brought the two alleged perpetrators together in his office, where Fatha Gilliam reportedly recoiled at the sight of Winold though he claimed to have never met her. "You are accused of poisoning the Winold family. Did you do it?" the Cincinnati police chief inquired. She responded in the negative. When asked who did commit the crime, she pointed to Winold, who maintained to the end that he was innocent and that he did not know Gilliam. Indeed, the grand jury that heard the case concluded that Winold could prove he was not present in the kitchen the morning of the crime and refused to indict him. Gilliam, however, was charged with attempting to poison the family. She pleaded guilty in exchange for a lighter sentence and received four years in the penitentiary.[11]

Charles Winold, meanwhile, went on with his life. He remarried and had another child, Gilbert, in 1906. He ran a dry goods store in Massillon, Ohio, for several years before he died in 1914. After surviving the poisoning attempt, his former wife, Susan Winold, lived with her parents in Cincinnati until their deaths. In the 1930s, she moved to Monmouth, New Jersey, where she lived in the Bancroft Taylor Rest Home until her death in 1949.

After her release from prison, Gilliam always appeared in public records under her given name, Ella Fay. After a brief first marriage, she married farmer Edward Keel in 1911, and the couple remained together for over fifty years. Fay died in her nineties in 1976.

HAROLD F. EASTMAN
At 12 years of age.

MISSING BOY!

HAROLD F. EASTMAN,

Since Jan. 6th, 1900. He is 14 years of age, but would pass for 17 or 18 years, being very large for his age, and well matured. Light complexion; blue eyes; light brown hair; very poor black teeth. He wore a soft brown hat, light overcoat, dark blue coat and vest, and gray pants. He plays the Piano well for his years, "Clayton's Grand March," "Old Kentucky Home," and other old airs, with variations by Ryder, being favorites. Should this meet the eye of the beloved son, may he think of the anguish and desolation caused by his absence to fond father and mother, whose nights are passed in tears and wakefulness, crying, "Where is our darling boy to-night? Is he dead?" All charges and expenses will be paid. Hold him and telegraph at my expense.

Address,   DR. CHAS. A. EASTMAN,
461 WASHINGTON ST., BRIGHTON, MASS.

HAROLD F. EASTMAN

Jamalin R. Harp

Youthful tramp. Boston's champion runaway. Boy wanderer. Harold F. Eastman earned several titles, bestowed by various newspapers, as he spent much of his adolescence at the turn of the nineteenth century absconding from his parents' New England homes. From ages ten to sixteen, Eastman traveled illicitly not only throughout the region but along the Eastern seaboard and to the American Midwest, becoming a reoccurring figure in American newspapers. He was born in 1886 in Calais, Maine, to Charles, a physician, and Cora Eastman. The couple already had a six-year-old, Herbert. Harold grew into a precocious and charming adolescent, blue-eyed, brown-haired, with poor teeth and a large build for his age. Throughout his many travels he exhibited a thirst for independent adventure, a relative disregard for financial and physical security, and a talent for coercion and trickery that grew with experience.

It was possibly during the family's tenure in Exeter, New Hampshire, that Harold began his career of absenteeism. During one of his first ventures away from

home, in 1897, he made it to Philadelphia. Shortly after his return, he ran away to Worchester, Massachusetts. In September that year, he borrowed a classmate's bicycle and traveled to Portsmouth, New Hampshire, where he stole numerous items, including three boats. He was found when Orin Gerry, a whaler, spotted him alone in a sailboat that was in danger of overturning. Gerry secured the boat and escorted the youth to the authorities. The incident was the second time in two weeks that Harold had run away. Not long after reclaiming him, the Eastman family relocated to the Boston, Massachusetts, area, first to Charlestown and then to Brighton, perhaps hoping to better their youngest son's behavior through a change of environment.

Such measures proved ineffective. Harold ran away five more times in 1898 alone. It seems he escaped from the family's Boston home first on July 12, 1898. He was spotted two days later in the eastern part of the city, at Jeffries Point, when he inquired about renting a rowboat from Charles Murphy. Murphy, perplexed by the boy's ragged appearance, interrogated Harold, who provided a few vague answers before departing. The Eastmans, in an effort to deter their son from running away, had reportedly divested him of his nicer clothing. Murphy, who happened to look at a newspaper just moments after his encounter with the boy, recognized him and called his father.

Harold was home less than a month before he left again on August 8. Police spotted him two days later in Portland, Maine. He had procured a bicycle and claimed that he was on his way to visit relatives in Bath, Maine. Shortly after hearing what the police learned, Cora Eastman traveled to the home of Harold's grandmother in Augusta, Maine, as it seemed a likely destination for him. Police in Harold's birthplace of Calais, however, reported on August 17 that they had apprehended a boy matching his description for stealing a set of clothing and a bicycle in Eastport. Harold stated he was visiting a wealthy uncle in the area. Charles Eastman, upon hearing of his son's whereabouts, traveled to Bangor, Maine, to retrieve him.

On September 4, Harold, whose parents believed him to be asleep, climbed out the bathroom window and down a grapevine trellis. He left again at the end of September, when he supposedly persuaded train conductors to grant him passage from Boston through to St. Joseph, Michigan, half way across the country. His next escapade led him to Washington, DC. Leaving Boston on November 16, he traveled for three days by freight train and arrived in the capital on Friday. Unlike on his previous trips, he presented himself to the police, asking how far he was from Boston and informing them he had not eaten since the previous day. His parents were notified of his whereabouts, and Cora Eastman came to retrieve him. After taking in some of the sights in Washington, the two returned home.

On his next publicized outing, Harold left August 26, 1899, paid for train passage to Washington, then secured the help of a vagabond to make it to Richmond, Virginia. Upon arriving at his destination, he contacted his father, who told the police to have his son detained until Cora Eastman arrived to take him back to Boston. Just five months later, in January 1900, he embarked on his longest journey yet. News of his parents' search appeared in papers as far as St. Paul, Minnesota, likely due to his extended absence and the impressive number of times he had wandered from home. The Chicago police also began actively searching for him. The date and circumstances of Harold's return to his family are unknown, but he was gone for several weeks. He was back with his family by

June of that year, however, because he ran away again while his family stayed at a hotel in Old Orchard, Maine.

By 1902, the frequency of Eastman's antics, and the resulting expense and effort expended by his family, pushed his father to a shift in mentality and approach. That August, the sixteen-year-old once again left home. His father, as usual, issued notices to newspapers. While expressing a desire for information concerning his son, Charles Eastman also made it clear that he would not be covering any of his son's debts, and people should not "harbor or trust" the adolescent.

This habitual delinquent's story slips into obscurity for much of the first decade of the twentieth century. Charles and Cora Eastman appeared in newspapers for a brief period in 1904 and 1905, when the doctor was accused of performing a "criminal operation," meaning abortion, on a patient, Edith McIntyre, who subsequently died. Eastman was convicted of manslaughter and sentenced to a year in jail. It is unclear whether Harold still lived with his family at the time.

In 1907 the wanderer married Anna Isabel Tabor, and the couple had two daughters, Florence and Anna. They lived with his wife's family in New York City. Somewhat predictably, Harold left between 1907 and 1917 and moved to New Hampshire. There, he met Mary "Jennie" Frazier and the two married in February 1917, six days before his divorce from Anna Tabor Eastman was finalized. Harold and Jennie's first son, Charles, was born May 1917. The family later added Catherine, Harold, and Lucy. Harold and his second wife lived in New Hampshire and Vermont, where Harold worked as an engineer and a crane operator at a paper mill.

The driving force behind Harold's habit of running away as an adolescent remains a mystery. Rather than the hardships of an abusive or difficult home, which prompted some children to run away, Harold conveyed to the world a rootless spirit and desire to travel, perhaps encouraged by his parents, whom newspapers labeled "kind and indulgent." His relationship with his father was presumably good enough for Harold to name his first son Charles, after his father. Harold's August 1898 trip to Calais might have been a wish to return to his hometown to see relatives. His leaving Old Orchard in June 1900 possibly was, as his mother believed, to cure his homesickness for Boston. No matter his motivation, Harold F. Eastman's behavior followed the form of many young runaways, who not only worried and vexed their family members but also stole and conned strangers to support them while on the road.

GEORGE A. KIMMEL

Quentin McGown

On August 25, 1898, the Pinkerton National Detective Agency issued thousands of flyers across the country seeking information on a missing Arkansas City, Kansas, banker. More often than not, a missing person in such a position would have absconded with bank funds or committed some other crime worthy of running from the law. The disappearance of George A. Kimmel, however, was different. He was not accused of a crime, and his upstanding life offered no clues. He simply vanished. What began as a confusing puzzle got even stranger as the decades passed.

George Kimmel was an officer and cashier at the Farmer's State Bank of Arkansas City, Kansas, an affiliate of the First National Bank of Niles, Michigan, whose president, Charles A. Johnson, was Kimmel's uncle. Kimmel had arrived in the small town in May 1897 and quickly became a well-liked and respected member of the community. He seemed to have settled into a stable routine. He owned real estate and stock in the banks. Also, he had purchased $27,000 in life insurance, all but $2,000 of it through the New York Life Insurance Company, with his only sister named as beneficiary. On Friday, July 29, 1898, he took a business trip to Topeka to deliver some municipal bonds held by his bank. The following day, he checked into the Midland Hotel in Kansas City. He cashed a draft for about $500 at a local bank that afternoon and dined with fellow guests at the hotel. About 7:00 p.m., he bought a cigar and left the hotel in the company of three men. Kimmel was never seen again. Maybe.

Two weeks passed before anyone thought to check on Kimmel's whereabouts. He had apparently been known to take unannounced vacations in the past. When bank officials contacted his family back in Niles, Michigan, a worried Charles Johnson first called for an audit of the books at the bank. Finding nothing wrong, Johnson then contacted Pinkerton's, instructing the detective agency to "spare neither time nor money" to find his missing nephew. According to Pinkerton's, Kimmel was thirty years old, had brown hair and a mustache, was five feet eight inches tall, and

weighed one hundred and fifty-five pounds, although his hometown paper described him as slightly older, taller, heavier, and with a full head of dark brown hair and "piercing black eyes." The posters advertising the disappearance advised law enforcement agencies to search local hospitals and asylums, but the nationwide effort turned up nothing. And so it remained. Kimmel's sister assigned a $5,000 life insurance policy to the bank in Niles, either to reimburse the bank for expenses it incurred while mounting the search or to secure debts owed by Kimmel—both reasons reported at the time.[12]

By 1900, the First National Bank of Niles was in receivership due to the loss of $150,000 embezzled by Charles Johnson to cover what he called "investment losses and personal debts." He was caught a year later living in Ohio under an alias, tried, and sentenced to seven years in a Detroit prison. Then, in 1903, the trustee for the insolvent Niles bank sued New York Life for the $5,000 policy on the still-missing George Kimmel. Two years later, Kimmel's sister sought to have her brother declared legally dead, having waited the mandatory seven years. Both suits launched a series of courtroom dramas that captured the attention of the nation as New York Life resisted payment of the claims.

The first trial found in favor of the receiver now managing the Niles bank and ordered the insurance company to pay out the $5,000 on the policy. The appeals court reversed the decision on technical grounds and remanded it back to the trial court. The insurance company then dropped a bombshell. The national story caught the attention of an inmate in a New York prison, and New York Life announced that they had found George Kimmel. Hopeful friends traveled to Auburn Prison to see the inmate, whose name when sentenced was Andrew J. White. They found an old man with receding sandy hair and blue eyes, but he knew details of Kimmel's life that many felt proved he was the missing banker. One cousin stated, "It's George. He's changed. But it's George." Kimmel's own mother, however, along with his sister, were just as convinced that the aging inmate was not George. Subsequent trials pitted

Pinkerton's National Detective Agency.

=FOUNDED BY ALLAN PINKERTON, 1850.=

OFFICES.

WM. A. PINKERTON, **Chicago,**
ROBT. A. PINKERTON, **New York,** } Principals.

GEO. D. BANGS, Gen'l Sup't. **New York.**

D. ROBERTSON, Ass't Gen'l Sup't Middle Division, CHICAGO.

JAS. McPARLAND, Ass't Gen'l Sup't Western Division, DENVER.

ATTORNEYS,
SEWARD, GUTHRIE & STEELE,
New York.

CONNECTED BY TELEPHONE.

KANSAS CITY, 622 MAIN STREET.
J. H. SCHUMACHER, Sup't.
BOSTON, 30 COURT STREET.
NEW YORK 57 BROADWAY.
PHILADELPHIA, 441 CHESTNUT STREET.
CHICAGO, 201 FIFTH AVENUE.
ST. PAUL, GERMANIA BANK BUILDING.
DENVER, OPERA HOUSE BLOCK.
PORTLAND, ORE. MARQUAM BLOCK.
SAN FRANCISCO, CROCKER BUILDING.

$500 REWARD!

MISSING!

GEORGE A. KIMMEL,

BANKER, OF ARKANSAS CITY, KANSAS.

DESCRIPTION: 30 years of age, 5 feet 8 inches high, weight 155 pounds, medium complexion, brown hair and mustache. Wore when last seen light brown suit of clothes, straight brim straw hat, Knight Templar's charm, heavy band gold ring, double eagle and small diamond in center, emblem of 32d degree Mason.

Five Hundred Dollars Reward

is offered by Chas. A. Johnson, banker at Niles, Mich., for information leading to the discovery of his whereabouts and placing him in the hands of his friends. He was last seen in Kansas City, Mo., on Saturday, July 30th, 1898, at the Midland Hotel, about 7:15 P. M., where he received a package of money containing $530.20.

Officers receiving this circular will please search hospitals and asylums. He has committed no crime and his business is in a prosperous condition. His friends are very anxious about him.

Wire all information to Chas. A. Johnson, Niles, Mich., or to the undersigned at the nearest of its offices as listed above.

PINKERTON'S NATIONAL DETECTIVE AGENCY,

622 Main Street, KANSAS CITY, MO.

Or, J. H. SCHUMACHER,
Resident Superintendent.

Kansas City, August 25, 1898.

the "Kimmelites" against the "Anti-Kimmelites," and the insurance company against the claimants. A judge finally ruled in 1912 that George Kimmel was dead and that the insurance policies should be paid.

Yet the story didn't end there.

Rumors of how Kimmel may have met his demise abounded during the trials. One story suggested that the three men seen leaving the hotel with Kimmel had lured him away with tales of a Colorado treasure hunt, then murdered him. Another version claimed Kimmel had been kidnapped, robbed, and then beaten so severely that he lost his mind. Andrew White, the prisoner who created the confusion, had a deep scar on the back of his head. In an attempt to explain away the difference in the eye color of the two men, one doctor testified that he had seen similar trauma cause eye color to change. Someone else speculated that Kimmel's uncle masterminded the disappearance to stop him from revealing details about the elder banker's malfeasance. In the end, after countless theories, allegations, and testimony from both Andrew White and George Kimmel's mother, among others, the judge declared that White was not Kimmel. White said that his "mother" and "sister" had disowned and discredited him, leaving him "an outcast, an alleged impostor." After his own release from prison, he vowed to fight on.[13]

Following the 1912 trial, White underwent an operation to relieve pressure on the brain. Afterward he appeared to recall the smallest details of Kimmel's life. He returned home to Niles to prepare for a final trial on the insurance policies, but he left town before the judge ruled. The judgement was against the insurance company, yet again demonstrating that the court did not believe White's story. Whoever the man was, he continued to write to his supporters as he made his way around the country. He sent his last letter to a Kimmel cousin postmarked from San Francisco in 1928. And then he disappeared for good.

Was he Kimmel? Many people fervently believed him to be. Just as many did not. Even the mighty Pinkerton's could not solve the case of the missing banker, whose own mother, while proclaiming on the stand that White was not her son, consistently referred to him as "George."

GEORGE R. BOYD

Amanda Milian

On September 15, 1899, Richard Sylvester, major and superintendent of the Metropolitan Police, issued a notice to law enforcement agencies around the country that George R. Boyd, a fourteen-year-old African American boy, had run away from his home in Washington, DC, a week earlier. He was described in his wanted poster as "bright and intelligent." He could read and write and had attended school. He kept his hair and nails neatly trimmed. Boyd's description indicated that he came from a family of some means. He "wore [a] dark striped suit, knee pants, tan shoes, black stockings, old white straw hat, [and a] ring with set out on little finger." This last detail foreshadowed Boyd's future.

George R. Boyd had grown up just blocks from the White House at 1742 K Street Northwest in Washington, DC, with "respectable parents." Born in July of 1885, he was the only child of Russell Nathan Boyd and his first wife, Tulip V. Cook. Russell Boyd, who was born enslaved in his native Georgia, had built a substantial career by the time George was born. Having worked his way northward after the Civil War, he found employment in the household of Admiral John Dahlgren, designer of the Dahlgren gun used by the US Navy. Later, the senior Boyd, who was literate, took a position at the State Department that he parleyed into a long and illustrious career. He served as a messenger, and for many years he also boarded with the chief messenger of the department, who was prominent in African American social and religious circles. Thus, he met George's mother who descended from a local family so elite that the description of their elegant church wedding and sumptuous reception feast filled several paragraphs in the black newspaper.[14]

Unfortunately for Russell and his son, Tulip died before George turned two. The Cook family surely helped to raise the boy until his father remarried some eight years later. His second wife, Cordelia Syphax, came from an even more illustrious pedigree than Tulip Cook. The Syphax family's ancestors were slaves who had worked in the household of George and Martha Washington and were by family tradition descended from the Washingtons' grandson, George Washington Parke Custis. By the late nineteenth century, their number included many well-known African American community leaders.

Ten-year-old George Boyd experienced an avalanche of change beginning in 1895. First, he had a new stepmother, and the next year a baby sister named Edna arrived. It is difficult to say whether he was unhappy with the new arrangements from the beginning or if becoming a teenager influenced his desire to run away in 1899. His father wondered out loud if he was trying to make his way to the Philippines to join the war, since the boy had expressed an interest in it. Nevertheless, his parents obviously missed him, or they would not have reported his disappearance to the police. To their great relief, he soon returned home and back to his school routine.

Less than six years after running away from home, police arrested George R. Boyd for the theft of property belonging to Thomas F. Marshall, US Representative from North Dakota. On February 5, 1904, the Washington, DC, *Evening Star* ran a short story about Boyd's arrest the previous day, when he was accused of stealing four rings. The jewelry had disappeared from the representative's rooms at Stoneleigh Court, a new upscale apartment building located at the southeast corner of Connecticut Avenue and L Street, a block from Boyd's childhood home. He worked there on the date the rings disappeared and "accidently got possession of the key to the apartments of the North Dakota representative." Although accounts of the worth of the items ranged between $1,000 and $1,500, the accused reportedly received $40 when he pawned one of the rings in Baltimore. He was caught while trying to unload another, and "relieved of the rings" by the police. His family could not have been happy when the Baltimore papers published their address along with George's name and his admission of guilt in their report on the crime. Even so, they may have been the reason he went free.[15]

The following year, authorities arrested Boyd again. This time he was the prime suspect in the theft of $3,000 worth of jewels from Bessie A. Patterson of the Mount Royal Flats in Baltimore. They did not catch him with any of the jewelry, however, and he proclaimed his innocence. Soon, some of the jewelry was found floating around Jones Falls, a nearby water feature, but no physical evidence linked Boyd to the crime. The officer based his arrest solely on the descriptions given by the two black servants and his memory of the previous incident involving Boyd. After hearing the description given by Jane Sherrod of a man seen outside of Patterson's apartments, the detective showed the woman a picture of Boyd to confirm that was the man she saw. The second witness established Boyd's connection to the building by noting that he had worked as a waiter in the café there three years ago, but that fact did not cement his guilt. Boyd's earlier trouble with the law might have made him a target of false accusations or mistaken identity. In any event, it is unlikely that Boyd served time for this incident either, but his parents had to fear the damage to his reputation and what could turn into a pattern of irresponsibility— especially considering their boy was now a married man.

In April 1903 George Boyd had married Florence Payne in Washington, DC. Whether Boyd was guilty or not, their union must have gotten off to a rocky start, but he eventually found some stability, or at least managed to keep his name out of the papers and off the minds of the local lawmen. He took a job as a porter for a grocery store, then as a Pullman porter at Union Station, and later followed in his father's footsteps at the State Department, though the older man had long since been promoted. George's career there was cut short by his death in 1923, at only thirty-seven years old. He had one daughter, Gursta, who became a school teacher.

Headquarters of the Metropolitan Police
WASHINGTON, D. C.

SEPTEMBER 15, 1899.

Runaway Boy!

GEORGE R. BOYD,

Colored; light brown skin; 14 years old; large for his age; dark brown eyes; dark brown knotty hair, cut short; weighs about 110 pounds; finger nails cut close; wore dark striped suit, knee pants, tan shoes, black stockings, old white straw hat, ring with set out on little finger; had an extra light faded blue suit of clothes, with white buttons, with him; ran away from his home in this city September 7, 1899; is a bright and intelligent boy.

Please cause diligent enquiry to be made, and should he be found arrest as fugitive from parents, and telegraph

RICHARD SYLVESTER,
Major and Superintendent of Police.

THOMAS L. PHILLIPS AND ELLIE GARNER

Elizabeth Moczygemba

Dr. Thomas L. Phillips, the physician for the third ward in the city of Atlanta, abruptly sold his drug store and "left for parts unknown" in January 1901. A doctor selling his practice and abandoning both his patients and wife would hardly alert the police, but the same day Dr. Phillips disappeared, Ellie Garner, the wife of a well-known bartender, also went missing. People acquainted with Garner and Phillips implied that the two not only knew the whereabouts of one another but had been having an affair. Now the two married runaways faced charges of abandonment. Atlanta Chief of Police W. P. Manley said that Phillips left his wife, his practice, and wrecked another man's home while Ellie Garner deserted her husband and her two-year-old daughter, Velma. He sent wanted posters to police departments across the South to locate the runaways. Even a South Carolina newspaper picked up the couple's story. The blurb stated that the local chief of police received a circular concerning Dr. Phillips and Mrs. Garner, who were said to "have eloped from Atlanta" and caused "quite a sensation." A local Georgia newspaper article about the disappearances noted that in their neighborhood, "the affair was all the talk" and the incident "was food for the gossips for many hours."[16]

Ellie Garner was born in February 1880 and married Jack Garner in 1898. She was twenty years old and had been married for about two years when she and Phillips disappeared. The wanted poster issued for the pair featured two square photographs, one each of Phillips and Garner, and explained their crime. She is described as having a fair complexion, blue eyes, moles on her face, and she weighed approximately one hundred and twenty-eight pounds. The circular noted that he was thirty-seven years old, stood five feet eight inches tall, weighed approximately one hundred and fifty pounds, had black hair and a moustache. Phillips, who was up for reelection as city physician, was also the Garner family doctor, which is how he became acquainted with Ellie. When he sold his drugstore, he claimed he did so in order to join his wife in the city of Norcross, Georgia. In the week prior to the disappearances, Jack Garner heard rumors of an affair between his wife and Dr. Phillips. He actively sought a confrontation with the doctor, to the point that his friends and family would not leave Garner alone for fear of violence and bloodshed. Two weeks before she disappeared, Ellie Garner had shot a pistol off her back porch. At the time, she told her husband there was a burglar, but with the revelation of an affair it was suspected that she had fired the pistol as a signal to Phillips that her husband was home.

What would have been only the rumor-filled disappearance of two married people in the middle of an affair took an interesting turn when Ellie Garner returned without Phillips. She granted the local newspaper, the *Atlanta Constitution*, an interview to clear up the confusion surrounding her disappearance. Garner claimed that she had been in New Orleans since she left Atlanta and had no knowledge of Phillips's whereabouts. She told reporters that "my mind was in a perfect cloud and since that time it has been so. It seems that some great, terrible, mental disability has just thoroughly destroyed all my reasoning powers and all control of myself."[17]

Once he saw his wife's condition, Jack Garner believed she was innocent and professed that she was in no way connected with Phillips or his disappearance. The interview paints her departure in a completely different light. Instead of being an adulterous woman who vanished with her lover, it appeared that she was a mentally ill woman who wandered away from her family. The notion that Ellie Garner was mentally disturbed was further confirmed by relatives who told reporters that she had attempted suicide at least four times by taking morphine, most recently on the Wednesday before they discovered she was missing.

Two years after this strange episode, in October of 1903, Ellie Garner was once again the subject of newspaper headlines. She had attempted suicide again, but this time with a gun. She was in declining health and told her husband many times that she would rather be dead than continue to suffer as she had been. After Jack Garner left for work, she placed a revolver to the left side of her chest and pulled the trigger. Neighbors,

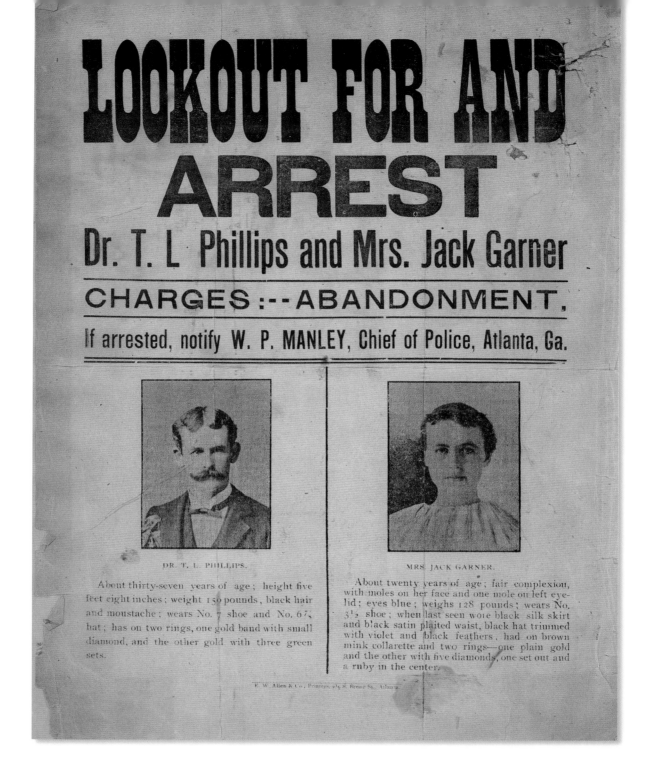

LOOKOUT FOR AND ARREST

Dr. T. L. Phillips and Mrs. Jack Garner

CHARGES :--- ABANDONMENT,

If arrested, notify W. P. MANLEY, Chief of Police, Atlanta, Ga.

DR. T. L. PHILLIPS.

About thirty-seven years of age; height five feet eight inches; weight 150 pounds, black hair and moustache; wears No. 7 shoe and No. 6⅞ hat; has on two rings, one gold band with small diamond, and the other gold with three green sets.

MRS. JACK GARNER.

About twenty years of age; fair complexion, with moles on her face and one mole on left eyelid; eyes blue; weighs 128 pounds; wears No. 3½ shoe; when last seen wore black silk skirt and black satin plaited waist, black hat trimmed with violet and black feathers, had on brown mink collarette and two rings—one plain gold and the other with five diamonds, one set out and a ruby in the center.

E. W. Allen & Co., Printers, 24 S. Broad St., Atlanta.

alerted by the gunshot, found her on her bed and rushed her to a hospital. After this report, Ellie Garner disappeared from the public record. Jack Garner lived to be seventy-seven years old and died in Tampa, Florida, in April 1950.

Based solely on the information in her wanted poster, Garner abandoned her family and ran away with her lover, Dr. Phillips. As her story emerged, however, it became much more complicated. Ellie Garner did disappear but returned to her husband and child, claiming she was delusional and knew nothing about Dr. Phillips or his whereabouts. Combined with the revelation that she attempted suicide a number of times, she indeed appears to have been a mentally ill woman whose disappearance happened to coincide with that of Dr. Phillips. One can only speculate about whether anyone was able to help her with her illness or if, instead, she finally succeeded in one of her suicide attempts.

ALBERT EDWARD CURTIS AND MAMIE BABCOCK

Jessica Webb

On the first day of November 1900, Albert Curtis left his office at the Empire Fast Freight Line in Cleveland with all of the money he had and disappeared into the night. When he did not arrive home, and remained absent for a few days, his wife Clara and their children began to assume the worst, believing foul play could be involved. After a few days, regional newspapers like the *Norwalk Daily Reflector* published articles on his disappearance, reiterating the suspicion that something bad had happened to Albert. Their worries were for naught, however, as Albert was very much alive and in fine health. He had not been kidnapped, assaulted, or murdered. Instead, Albert had decided to take every penny he had and flee with a woman twenty-four years his junior.

Albert Curtis was born in Ohio in January 1854 to Edward H. and Louisa Curtis. He had one sibling, a little sister named Ina. Albert grew up in Fairfield, Ohio, where his father worked as a carpenter. He moved to Cleveland at age seventeen and found employment as a clerk for a railroad, the Empire Transportation Company, where he stayed until he left the city in 1900. After living and working in Cleveland for six years, Albert met young socialite Nettie Maud Young, the daughter of well-known railroad man Levi S. Young. They married in a sumptuous and elegant ceremony on November 13, 1877. For Albert and Nettie, marital bliss was short-lived. Less than a year after marrying, on October 4, 1878, a notice was published in the *Cleveland Leader* claiming

Nettie had been granted a divorce. Albert's rebuttal came the following year, on November 10, 1879, when he announced in the *Plain Dealer* that Nettie's statement was fraudulent in nature, as they were not divorced at the time. Instead, Albert went to the Cuyahoga County Court earlier in November and obtained a divorce on the grounds of adultery. Presumably, Nettie had an affair with Captain Asael Booth, whom she married that same year. While Albert's first marriage ended badly, he got another chance when he met Clara L. Marshall, who would become his second wife.

Clara was born on September 25, 1856, in Cleveland, to Franklin Marshall, a bricklayer and stonemason, and Mary A. Marshall, a homemaker. She had two sisters, Sarah and Kate, both older. Clara and her sisters were at least middle-class and enjoyed active social lives. She married Albert Curtis on September 6, 1881, after courting only a few months. The new Mr. and Mrs. Curtis settled down in Cleveland at 256 Pearl Street, but they moved around quite a bit during their marriage. Eventually, they made 64 Beechwood Street their permanent residence. Clara had their first child, a son named Ralph, in April 1889. Four years later, they welcomed a daughter, Edna. The four Curtises seemed to be living a happy, peaceful life, which soon changed when Miss Mamie Babcock entered the picture.

Babcock was born in 1877 in Medina, Ohio, to Cyrus S., a liveryman and Civil War veteran, and Helen, a homemaker. She was the fourth of five children, with three sisters and a brother: Grace, Bertha, Harry, and Gertrude. In the late nineteenth century, she left her family home in Medina to live in Cleveland with her older sister, Grace. There, she found employment as a dressmaker, thanks to her exceptional skills. In 1900, twenty-three-year old Babcock joined the family at 64 Beechwood Street. Her move into the Curtis household implied that she was either employed there as a nanny or housekeeper, or perhaps she simply rented a room. Her presence there would eventually cause significant emotional and financial loss for Clara and her two children.

To the outside world, Albert and Clara seemed to have a happy marriage. The newspapers noted their movements as a couple. For example, in January 1894, she threw him a surprise fortieth birthday party that was reported on in the *Plain Dealer* society pages as offering a bountiful, sumptuous spread and having several of Cleveland's finest citizens in attendance. They also appeared to be capable parents. Both Ralph and Edna

attended school. Furthermore, the *Norwalk Daily Reflector*, a regional paper, noted that Albert and Clara, worried about Edna's health deteriorating in the city, had her stay with Albert's parents in Norwalk, a small rural town. After three months, they went together to fetch Edna and bring her back to Cleveland in September 1900, merely two months before Albert left his family for good.

Clara's entire life changed on November 1. When Albert did not come home from work that day, she was concerned. Her worries multiplied every day he did not return and were compounded by the fact that all of their money, along with their roomer, Miss Babcock, had disappeared with her husband. Eventually she discovered that Albert had borrowed money, refused to pay any of their bills for several months, and transferred ownership of their property and home to a relative of his. She realized that Albert was not the victim of foul play. Instead, he and Babcock had absconded with every penny they had. The Cleveland police stepped in to help Clara and bring him back to the city to answer for what he did. On August 1, 1901, they created a wanted poster with both Albert and Mamie's photos. Newspapers across the country like the *Seattle Daily Times* and the *Minneapolis Journal* printed articles seeking their whereabouts. These efforts, however, were for naught. Albert and Mamie disappeared. Presumably, they moved to another state, changed their names, and lived as a married couple. Clara never saw her husband again. And yet, she continued on, creating a new life for herself and her children.

In March 1903, Clara Curtis filed for divorce from Albert. She moved her family to 2212 E. Eighty-Sixth Street, where she set up a boarding house and rented rooms to four boarders, providing an income for herself and her children. Ralph found employment as a bookkeeper at a Cleveland bank. Edna followed in her mother's footsteps and developed a wide circle of friends in Cleveland. The *Plain Dealer* printed articles discussing parties Edna threw and her travels to Chicago, Minneapolis, and Canada. In 1916, Ralph married Florence, a stenographer, and moved to Chicago to be with her. Two years later, Edna and Clara followed him, and Edna married Albert J. Gossmiller Jr., a piano salesman. Clara passed away soon after. Both Ralph and Edna stayed in Chicago and never returned to Cleveland. While Albert's choice to run away from his family had immediate and awful consequences for Clara, Ralph, and Edna, they were able to rebuild their lives and move on. Albert and Mamie's fate is unknown.

PART II

ROBBERS, THIEVES, EMBEZZLERS, AND FORGERS

EMILE BECKER AND ELIZABETH KAMBEITZ BECKER

Shirley Apley and Tom Kellam

WANTED FOR LARCENY
— OF —
$20,000 Worth of Diamonds.

EMILE BECKER, *alias* BAUMSTARK; 38 years, 5 feet 10 inches, 185 pounds, well built, fair complexion, good color, brown hair and eyes, heavy, dark-brown moustache (may shave off moustache), dark clothes, grayish-brown mackintosh, brown Fedora hat (worn student style), very nervous, and when spoken to "blinks" his eyes and hesitates before replying, walks very quick, with a slight swagger, is a German and a waiter by occupation; speaks English, German and French fluently. Is accompanied by his wife.

ELIZABETH BECKER, maiden name KAMBEITZ; 23 years, 5 feet 9 inches, medium build, light complexion, blue eyes, dark blond hair, eyelids somewhat inflamed; wore a green skirt, brown golf cape, lined with red woolen material, plaid hood, black sailor hat, trimmed with brown feathers. She is a native of Durlach, Karlsruhe, Germany.

Notify, GEORGE W. McCLUSKY, CAPTAIN,
DETECTIVE BUREAU,
300 MULBERRY STREET, NEW YORK CITY, N. Y.

Meet the Beckers: charming, refined, bourgeois jewel thieves. Emile Becker was born September 26, 1864, in Pforzheim, Baden, Germany. He spoke German, French, and English fluently when he arrived in the United States in 1885. Though he maintained contacts in Europe and frequently traveled there, Becker became a naturalized citizen on October 5, 1892. In the summer of 1898 he married Elizabeth Kambeitz, aged twenty-four, also an immigrant from Germany. He worked as a hotel waiter on and off throughout his life, but claimed to be an expert in the jewelry business. In fact, he was a professional thief who preferred to ply his legitimate trade in upscale establishments that catered to wealthy guests. Thus he could discreetly scope out the possessions of potential victims when he delivered room service.

In January of 1899, world-famous soprano Frances Saville resided at the Madison Avenue Hotel in Manhattan, Mr. Becker's current employer, while performing for the Metropolitan Opera House. Born Fanny Martina Simonsen in San Francisco in 1862, she changed her name after a brief marriage to her father's secretary. Saville's parents owned and managed their own opera company and shortly after her birth moved the family to Australia, where her mother trained her to sing and nurtured her early career. By the mid-1890s, she lived in Austria where she performed with the Vienna Court Opera and worked with Mahler and Puccini, among others.

Like Becker, Saville was fond of jewels. Unlike Becker, she could afford them. In her room in the Madison, her jewelry box contained over thirty diamond-encrusted pieces including rings, pendants, necklaces, gold chains, broaches, watches, and bracelets. Two of the bracelets were made of six US five-dollar gold pieces. Appraisers estimated the collection she kept with her at the Madison to be worth about $20,000—equivalent to about $500,000 in 2018.

By the time he encountered Frances Saville, Emile Becker had been a career criminal most of his adult life. Between 1885 and 1910, he traveled extensively between the United States and Europe, refining his skills as a confidence man with every successful rip-off. In one of his favorite schemes, he presented himself to diamond merchants as an expert in precious stones and appeared to be a sharp well-connected businessman capable of turning a quick profit.

Admittedly, this part of his schtick was not *entirely* false. He persuaded his marks to front him some of their stock to sell on consignment, whereupon he promptly unloaded the cache on the black market and skipped town. Becker moved across the US from New York to Chicago, on to San Francisco, and then back again. He always worked in hotels between scams while he lay low and plotted more criminal mischief. He did time in the 1890s in California, and later in New York State, where he attempted to steal $1,200 worth of diamonds from the wholesale jewelry firm of Schuman Brothers. During his trial, he claimed to suffer from kleptomania.

By 1898, Becker was back in New York City, employed by the Madison Avenue Hotel, and poised to make a major score at the expense of Frances Saville. As she came and went from the hotel dressed for social gatherings and gala performances, his trained eye could not possibly miss her sparkling accessories. He positioned himself to oversee Saville's room service needs during her stay, which allowed him to become familiar with her schedule and to perhaps gain a degree of trust as a dutiful attendant. He must have seen his encounter with her as the opportunity of a lifetime.

On the afternoon of New Year's Eve 1898, Saville left her rooms to perform in the Saturday matinee at the Metropolitan, where she was singing the role of Elsa in Richard Wagner's *Lohengrin*. When she returned to her rooms around 7:30 p.m., she discovered that her jewels had been stolen. Coincidentally, Mr. and Mrs. Becker had disappeared. Investigators quickly determined that Becker, assisted by Elizabeth, had absconded with the jewels. Saville was distraught. Two months later, with law enforcement officials worldwide no closer to finding the Beckers or the jewels they had liberated, she threatened to sue the owners of the Madison for $20,000—her loss at the hands of their employee.

They must have breathed a sigh of relief, however, when French authorities apprehended Becker near Monte Carlo in September 1899. He had pawned Saville's treasures, but with the receipts in hand the authorities were able to reclaim most of the missing pieces. Even so, the police refused to return the evidence until the courts closed the case against Becker. Finally, almost two years after the theft, Saville was reunited with her jewels while on a European tour in November 1900.

Though Elizabeth Becker's fate is unknown, her husband resurfaced a few years later while skillfully executing yet another con. He and a supposed Mexican associate named Don Ciriolo Jose de Elorduy attempted to swindle $37,500 from Bavarian court jeweler Otto Koch by passing a forged check in exchange for some of his most spectacular pieces, which included bejeweled scarf pins, a diamond ring, and a seventy-six-carat diamond necklace. Had they succeeded, the two might have retired on their ill-gotten gains. Instead, authorities tracked De Elorduy to New York, where he was arrested with a portion of the jewelry in his rooms in December 1910. Becker was captured a short time later in Germany, where a Munich judge sentenced him to five years in jail. When he returned to America after serving his time, he appears to have abandoned his life of crime. He settled in Chicago, where he worked in the hotel business for the rest of his life.

Frances Saville retired from opera in 1903 after a distinguished career. She suffered several emotional blows in retirement. Her son died in 1911, and she was forced to leave her beloved Austria three years later with the outbreak of World War I. She relocated to California, where she lived with her niece, Daisy, until her death in 1935.

MOE COHEN AND JOHN MACKIE

Kendra K. DeHart

HEADQUARTERS OF THE POLICE DEPARTMENT,
BOSTON, MASS.

SUPERINTENDENT'S OFFICE, 37 PEMBERTON SQUARE.

Moe Cohen, alias Joseph Phillips.

BERTILLON MEASUREMENTS.

Height........1m. 74.1	Head, length ..18.5 L. Foot 27.2
Eng. Height, 5ft. 8¼in.	Head, width ...15.4 L. Mid. F. 11.8
Outs, A.....1m. 80.0	Cheek......... L. Lit. F....9.6
Trunk.........92.8	Rt. Ear, length ..5.6 L. Fore A. 47.4
Curv...........	Rt. Ear, width

ENGLISH MEASUREMENTS.

Age................30	Complexion..........Dark
Height.......5ft. 8¼in.	Weight 140
Hair.........Brown	Eyes.............Brown

Scars at base of left thumb and over left eyebrow; mole on jaw under right ear.

John Mackie, alias "Paddy Irish."

BERTILLON MEASUREMENTS.

Height 1m. 76.5	Head, length ...18 2 L. Foot....27.7
Eng. Height, 5ft. 9¼in.	Head, width...15.9 L. Mid. F. 12.1
Outs, A 1m. 75.0	Cheek.........14.2 L. Lit. F....9.5
Trunk.........95.5	Rt. Ear, length..6.2 L. Fore A. 47.5
Curv.............	Rt. Ear, width..

ENGLISH MEASUREMENTS.

Age 29	Complexion....... Medium
Height.......5ft. 9¼in.	Weight 138
Hair............Brown	Eyes............Gray

Scar at root of nose; mole on right of cheek; birthmark on right middle finger.

WANTED FOR PICKING POCKETS.

This Department holds indictment warrants for the arrest of JOHN MACKIE, alias PADDY IRISH, and MOE COHEN, alias JOSEPH PHILLIPS, professional pickpockets. They will be found about celebrations, fairs, horse races, etc.

If located, arrest, hold, notify me and I will send officers with necessary papers for them.

WM. H. PIERCE,
Superintendent of Police.

Boston, August 1, 1901.

Arrested in Denver about Aug the 1st in Denver and carried back to Boston

"**C**rooks with a string of aliases a yard long," reported the *Denver Post* in late July of 1901, as Moe Cohen and John Mackie sat in the Denver County Jail unsure about their prospects. Police Chief Hamilton Armstrong took the two men into custody a few weeks before he discovered their professional notoriety. Cohen—aliases Joseph Phillips, Fields, and Sellars—and Mackie—aliases Paddy Irish and Arthur Cavenaugh—were professional pickpockets with wanted posters in several metropolitan police stations. Undoubtedly, these crooks' numerous aliases made their identification challenging, as did their neat and conventional appearances.

Cohen was a year older than twenty-nine-year-old Mackie. Each had brown hair, stood around five feet eight inches tall, and weighed about a hundred and forty pounds. Cohen's eyes were a dark brown, but Mackie's gleamed gray. Cohen had a scar over his left eyebrow, while Mackie had a scar below his nose. Through their Bertillon measurements, lawmen learned of the two men's more imperceptible differences, particularly in the length and width of their heads, the size of their right ears, and the dimensions of their trunks, details that further aided in identification.[18]

Cohen and Mackie were a long way from home when they arrived in the Denver Police Station. William H. Pierce, superintendent of police in Boston, had distributed the wanted posters. Little is known about the personal lives and public crimes of Cohen and Mackie back home. Given their surnames, perhaps the two men or their families were among the thousands of Irish, Italian, German, and English immigrants who flooded into the United States trying to escape famine, to acquire land, or to meet the growing labor demands prompted by the country's rapid industrialization between 1850 and 1900. In the city of Boston alone, the population nearly quadrupled, radically transforming the cityscape.

Cohen and Mackie did what many cunning criminal entrepreneurs did in such changing times—they found a way to use the situation to their advantage. Pickpocketing is neither a new profession nor is it gender specific. Historically, both men and women engaged in larceny. The rapid urbanization of the United States in the late nineteenth and early twentieth centuries provided new opportunities for pickpockets who found innovative ways to capitalize on technological advancements.

The exploding population of urban areas didn't just provide crooks with more victims, it also offered new spaces to work, especially where crowds gathered for entertainment, labor, and commerce. These tactics certainly did not go unrecognized by police. Superintendent Pierce advised fellow lawmen through his wanted poster that the two Boston crooks would most likely be "found about celebrations, fairs, horse races, etc." Streetcars and trains were favorite spots for pickpockets because most passengers were easy targets as they rubbed up against one another. Moreover, the constant movement of strangers made thieves harder to identify. Just as importantly, transportation networks provided an essential element for the pickpocket's success—the quick getaway.

Cohen and Mackie's experiences illuminate just how far they would go to locate victims and to avoid arrest. When Denver police arrested the two Boston crooks, they were riding the rails for a very specific purpose. The *Denver Post* reported, "They were supposed to be working the Epworth League excursion to California." Founded in 1889, the Epworth League was a Methodist organization designed to promote biblical education and piety among the youth of the church. Methodist men and women from the ages of eighteen to thirty-five were encouraged to attend the annual meetings that were hosted by major cities all over the nation. In 1901, San Francisco, California, hosted the Epworth League Convention, which thirty-thousand men and women planned to attend. In order to attract business, railroad companies offered special excursion rates to the group. For instance, the Atchison, Topeka and Santa Fe Railway Company enticed travelers by boasting that the "best way to go [was] via Santa Fe Route . . . [with its] Fred Harvey meal service [and] personally-conducted excursions" that allowed travelers to "visit Indian pueblos and petrified forest." These advertisements lured not only clients but also crooks. Cohen and Mackie, professional pickpockets extraordinaire, seized the opportunity to practice their craft on unsuspecting young evangelicals. Unfortunately, they were caught.[19]

Once Chief Armstrong learned of the suspects' reputation, he held them while Boston authorities brought the proper extradition papers. When they presented the documents to a Denver judge, however, he found some significant problems that forced him to release the two Boston crooks on writs of habeas corpus. The arresting authorities refused to give up these notorious criminals without a fight. The *Denver Post* reported, "Irish and Cohen were arrested again as soon as they got out of the courtroom. . . . The object of the arrest was to hold them until the officers could get another requisition from

Boston." What happened next is unclear, but it appears that Chief Armstrong had endured quite enough from the two gentlemen. He decided to let them go after both promised to leave the city that night. Dismayed, the Boston authorities pledged, "The chase has just begun for these crooks, and that they will follow them to other states and get them back to Boston if it takes five years."[20]

Cohen and Mackie's escape from justice was hardly rare for their sort during this period. In addition to the advantages of speedy transportation, many notorious pickpockets had a widespread underground network of support. When sitting in jail, Cohen received a package from some friends in Minneapolis with over $600 to aid in their defense and departure. A detective told Frank Loomis, the victim of a pickpocket on a streetcar in Chicago, to be aware of his accoster's many associates. "He said most professional thieves belong to some kind of a ring and have ample funds for defense. I would probably be approached, as many witnesses are, and urged for reasons of sympathy or by other methods to drop the case."[21]

Another likely reason many thieves remained free was the difficultly in securing convictions. Unlike today, all acts of larceny, from five dollars to $500, were considered acts of grand larceny, which meant that those accused of the crime had to go through a lengthy court trial that rarely resulted in mandated state sentences. Moreover, there were just too many larceny cases for lawmen to investigate. Loomis eloquently summed up other problems with convicting pickpockets: "Witnesses disappear, evidence is lost, cases are *nolle prossed*, dismissed for want of evidence, cases are finally adjusted or 'fixed' without trial, many skip bail and are not heard from again until arrested for some other crime."[22]

So it was for both Cohen and Mackie in the summer of 1901. Cohen—aliases Phillips, Fields, and Sellars—disappeared from newspaper accounts after his release. Mackie—aliases Paddy Irish and Cavenaugh—made it to San Francisco and decided to stay. Four years later, according to the *San Francisco Call*, police arrested him again at a busy streetcar intersection and described him "as desperate in a corner as he is clever with his fingers." Did he evade prosecution yet again? The answer remains unknown. What does emerge from this sordid tale of professional pickpockets is that they were exceedingly resourceful. Like most Americans in the late-nineteenth and early twentieth centuries, they used increasing urbanization and technological advances for their own personal gain.[23]

W.A.S. GRAHAM

Rene Gomez

William Alexander Stewart Graham was born in County Armagh, Ireland, in 1863. He was apprenticed to be a sailor at the age of twelve and a few years later immigrated to the United States. Once in Philadelphia he got a job as an office boy for a local newspaper, which set him on course for a new career. With some experience under his belt, he relocated to Denver to be a reporter, then moved again to take a job with the *Chicago Times*. His skills enabled him to become secretary to city Mayor Carter Harrison in 1893, and the very next year Graham was elected secretary of the Chicago Board of Education. Soon, he assumed the duties of school agent and clerk for the board. In addition to his salary, Graham made investments and sometimes speculated in stocks and real estate. He provided well for his family and was known to have many friends in Chicago.

Graham was not reelected to his post in 1899, however, and problems soon arose. When the president of the board asked him to turn over his books to be audited before his successor took office, Graham demurred. He asked for more time to make sure all was in order before he passed the torch. At first this seemed reasonable, but the longer he delayed, the more suspicions grew. An investigation determined that Graham had taken $34,500 from a $50,000 payment made by a county superintendent and meant for deposit to the city school fund.

An auditor hired by the Chicago Board of Education traced Graham's "irregularities" back a little over two months before he was discovered. The investigation revealed that he had speculated heavily in stocks that dropped dramatically in value. His method was to deposit school money collected from tenants renting school property to his personal account. In one instance, he received a check for $3,000 from a school tenant made payable to him instead of to the board of education. He then deposited the money into his personal account. To hide his criminal activity, Graham's habit was to go to the Chicago National Bank and withdraw the funds as a school agent and turn that money over to the city saying it was received from the tenant as rent. He expected to replace the money he took before

anyone realized it was missing, but when his bid for reelection failed there was no time to follow through with that plan.

Graham fled rather than face a court of law. Before he left, he prepared a statement, cosigned by his wife, which requested that his remaining property be transferred to the city to cover the amount he stole. In this way, he indirectly confessed to the crime. In the final tally, the board determined that the amount swindled was closer to $25,000 rather than $35,000, but it was still a large sum at the time. Initially, Graham's wife agreed to reimburse the school board for the loss in his absence. Soon after, she changed her mind because she claimed that officials had promised that her husband's actions would not be publicized if she returned the money. Friends of Mrs. Graham also reminded her that if she reimbursed the school board, she would be left penniless, and her husband would still be a fugitive.

On July 25, 1899, the board of education gave Graham a deadline of 4:00 p.m. to return public school funds. Newly installed secretary Louis C. Legner issued the demand, which stated that "you deliver over to me as your successor all moneys, funds, and securities which you have received as clerk and school agent and which have not been by you lawfully paid out and accounted for." According to Legner's letter, he was willing to meet Graham at a place of his choosing to receive the funds, or he could send someone to the board of education with the funds. Two days later, the board of education passed a resolution prohibiting any officer from entering into any agreement not to prosecute, even if he returned the money.[24]

A few days later, a Cook County grand jury indicted W.A.S. Graham for embezzlement. City detectives began the search for Graham. They sent circulars to officials around the country and hired the Pinkerton National Detective Agency to help find the fugitive. Rumors suggested he might be headed to Cripple Creek, Colorado.

While the authorities pursued Graham, his attorney, Donald L. Morrill, was trying to raise money to cover the shortfall. He hoped that Graham's friends would help make up the difference. When they did not,

Morrill worked with Graham's eighty-year-old father-in-law, Andrew J. Brown, a founder of Northwestern University and prominent citizen of Evanston, Illinois, who offered to give up property to help make up the deficit.

After much debate, Graham's wife, with the assistance of her father, finally repaid the money, including the principal and interest, taken from the board of education. In addition to sending a certified check in the amount of $25,598, she turned over two residences and a lot in Chicago and a house and seven lots in Evanston, Illinois. Moreover, two companies that bonded Graham, National Security Company and the Safety Deposit Company, promised not to demand he be prosecuted if he returned to Chicago.

After his family reimbursed the board, many of its members were hesitant to prosecute him. The board president said, "I think Graham has made amends. He has paid back the money and he already has been punished by three years of exile from his family. In the face of the restitution he has made I do not believe he deserves further punishment." Despite the statement, Graham did not reappear. In the fall, three men thought they saw Graham on the streets of Chicago. Two of them claimed that Graham had changed his appearance by shaving off his moustache and wearing a wig. Other reports claimed that he had fled to Colorado, New Orleans, or South America.[25]

In 1905, the board of education passed a resolution proclaiming that full restitution was made and that the state attorney should nullify the indictment. It read in part: "In view of the facts in the case, W.A.S. Graham has, in the judgement of the board of education, been sufficiently punished and a chance should be given him to return home, and, as far as may be, to rehabilitate himself." As a result of the Graham case, Mayor Harrison requested that the city develop a plan to make it difficult for any future school agent to misuse board funds. As for Graham, apparently he never returned to Chicago, and his fate is still unknown.[26]

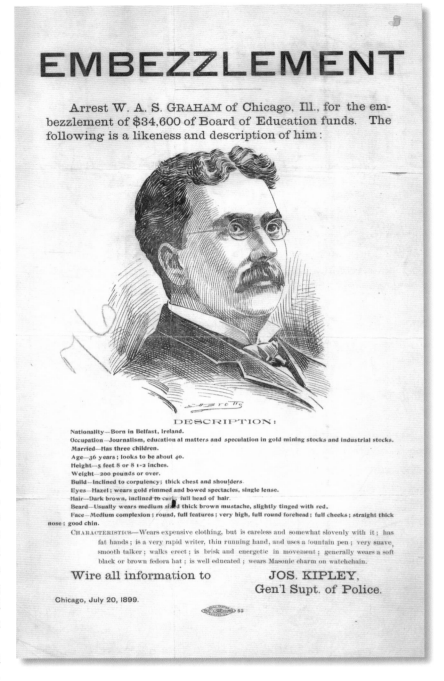

EMBEZZLEMENT

Arrest W. A. S. GRAHAM of Chicago, Ill., for the embezzlement of $34,600 of Board of Education funds. The following is a likeness and description of him:

DESCRIPTION:

Nationality—Born in Belfast, Ireland.
Occupation—Journalism, educational matters and speculation in gold mining stocks and industrial stocks.
Married—Has three children.
Age—36 years; looks to be about 40.
Height—5 feet 8 or 8 1-2 inches.
Weight—200 pounds or over.
Build—Inclined to corpulency; thick chest and shoulders.
Eyes—Hazel; wears gold rimmed and bowed spectacles, single lense.
Hair—Dark brown, inclined to curl; full head of hair.
Beard—Usually wears medium sized thick brown mustache, slightly tinged with red.
Face—Medium complexion; round, full features; very high, full round forehead; full cheeks; straight thick nose; good chin.
CHARACTERISTICS—Wears expensive clothing, but is careless and somewhat slovenly with it; has fat hands; is a very rapid writer, thin running hand, and uses a fountain pen; very suave, smooth talker; walks erect; is brisk and energetic in movement; generally wears a soft black or brown fedora hat; is well educated; wears Masonic charm on watchchain.

Wire all information to   JOS. KIPLEY,
                                   Gen'l Supt. of Police.

Chicago, July 20, 1899.

H. ST. JOHN DIX

Michael Green

Inspectors Froest and Sealfe of Scotland Yard were in London attending business when they noticed a rather short man departing from a carriage. Some weeks earlier, Froest had been tasked with tracking down a wanted embezzler by the name of Henry St. John Dix who had, among other things, defrauded banking customers in Whatcom, Washington, before fleeing to his native England. "Hallo Dix!" shouted Froest "I'd like to speak to you!" Taken by surprise, Dix turned toward the two men to inquire how they knew his name but quickly realized his mistake. Though he bolted for the nearest door in an attempt to escape, the two inspectors laid their hands on him, thus ending his flight from justice.[27]

Owing to his frequent movement and use of aliases, biographical information is somewhat sparse concerning Henry St. John Dix, and separating truth from fiction is a daunting task. He was born Henry Jenkins in England sometime around 1871. Dix claimed to be the eldest son of a British peer and told close friends that he was entitled to inherit peerage when his father passed. Whether or not this was completely true is debatable, but his movements suggested important connections in England. He married at least twice. His first wife's identity is uncertain, but his second wife was named Aida and they had a son together named Ralph St. John Dix.

Henry St. John Dix was quite the schemer. As a young man, he moved to America to pursue a literary career. This is when he first began using the alias Henry St. John (adding Dix later when he became a banker.). He spent more than a decade carousing throughout the United States and hustling wherever he could. One of his first endeavors

Pinkerton's National Detective Agency.

FOUNDED BY ALLAN PINKERTON, 1850.

ROBT. A. PINKERTON, New York,
ALLAN PINKERTON, New York, Ass't to
WM. A. PINKERTON, Chicago,
E. S. GAYLOR, Chicago, Ass't to

Principals.

GEO. D. BANGS,
General Manager,
NEW YORK.

JOHN CORNISH, Gen. Supt. Eastern Division, New York.
E. S. GAYLOR, Gen. Supt. Middle Division, Chicago.
JAS. McPARLAND, Gen. Supt. Western Division, Denver.

Attorneys, GUTHRIE, CRAVATH & HENDERSON,
NEW YORK.

Telephone Connection.

Representing the American Bankers' Association.

OFFICES.

PORTLAND, ORE., MARQUAM BLOCK
JAMES NEVINS, SUPT.
NEW YORK, 57 BROADWAY
BOSTON, 30 COURT ST.
PHILADELPHIA, 441 CHESTNUT ST.
MONTREAL, MERCHANTS BANK OF
CANADA BLDG.
CHICAGO, 201 FIFTH AVENUE
ST. PAUL, GERMANIA BANK BLDG.
ST. LOUIS, WAINWRIGHT BLDG.
KANSAS CITY, 622 MAIN ST.
DENVER, OPERA HOUSE BLOCK
SAN FRANCISCO, CROCKER BLDG.
SEATTLE, WASH., BAILEY BLDG.

$500.00 REWARD.

H. ST. JOHN, or H. ST. JOHN DIX, whose photograph and description appear on this circular, embezzled $28,000.00 by wrecking the Scandinavian American Bank of Whatcom, State of Washington, U. S. A., and the Blaine Bank of Blaine, State of Washington, U. S. A.

A warrant has been sworn out in the State of Washington, U. S. A., charging him with embezzlement.

H. St. John or H. St. John Dix is described as follows :

Age----35 years---- Height----5 feet, 1 inch
Weight----140 pounds---- Build----Medium
Eyes--- Black---- Nose----Slightly hollowed in center
Color of Hair Black----Style of Beard Small mustache----Color of Same Dark, may have smooth face now
Remarks:--Quick movements ; low soft voice ; no particular accent ; features regular ; dresses neat and often flashy; square shoulders.

HANDWRITING OF
H. ST. JOHN or H. ST. JOHN DIX.

In August, 1900, representing himself as a member of a wealthy English family named Dix, he secured control of three local banks, and subsequently wrecked the Scandinavian American Bank of Whatcom, Washington, and the Blaine Bank of Blaine, State of Washington, U. S. A. He embezzled $28,000 of the funds of these banks and left the United States, going to London, England, where he was on April 1st, 1901.

Dix came to Whatcom, State of Washington, U. S. A., in the Spring of 1899 as solicitor for the "Seattle Argus," a newspaper of Seattle, Washington. He secured a divorce from his wife, Aida Dix, in Whatcom, Washington, May 19th, 1900, and their boy was given into his custody. Shortly after his divorce he introduced another wife, who left the United States in his company and is presumably now with him. She is 28 years old, medium height, and the breadth of her nose between the eyes is very noticeable.

The County Commissioners of Whatcom County, State of Washington, U. S. A., offer Five Hundred Dollars ($500.00) Reward for the arrest and detention of H. ST. JOHN or H. ST. JOHN DIX, until properly delivered to the officer of the State of Washington, duly authorized to receive him on requisition papers issued by the Governor of the State of Washington, U. S. A.

Write, wire or cable any information to the nearest of above listed offices.

Or
Wm. A. Pinkerton,
201 Fifth Ave.,
Chicago, Ill., U. S. A.

Pinkerton's National Detective Agency,
306 Marquam Building, Portland, Oregon, U. S. A.
Portland, Ore. August 14th, 1901.

was as a "townsite boomer" in Kansas, where he operated all the major institutions in a small Kansas town, including their bank. He also spent time in Arizona, where he ran some form of scheme involving irrigation and water rights.

Two events stand out as far as his dealings go. The first is known as the Itata Affair. In 1891, Chile was embroiled in a civil war between President José Manuel Balmaceda and the Chilean congress. The congressional insurgents purchased weapons from the United States and Europe and moved them using their allies in the Chilean Navy. One of these shipments, which included over five thousand Remington rifles, was to be loaded on the Chilean steamer *Itata* and delivered to the congressional forces. The United States forbade the ship from leaving the harbor in San Diego, but the *Itata* quickly lifted anchor and made a course to rendezvous with other congressional forces to offload their cargo. The United States Navy dispatched the USS *Charleston* and USS *Baltimore* to chase the *Itata,* finally catching up with the ship on June 4 in the Chilean harbor of Iquique. Although his exact role is unclear, St. John Dix may have been aboard the ship, because he served time in a prison in Valparaiso, Chile, for his involvement. The papers described him as being one of the "principals" in the incident. He attained his release through his connections and influence with the British minister in that country.

The second event occurred when his work as a correspondent for a Chicago paper led him to become embroiled in the famous protest known as Coxey's Army. Led by Ohio businessman Jacob Coxey, the *Army of the Commonwealth in Christ* marched on Washington, DC, to protest unemployment and to push for reforms and infrastructure projects that would help embattled farmers hit hard by the financial Panic of 1893. Nominally there to cover the story for the paper, St. John Dix took a more active role by serving as the commissary general on the march. He reputedly provided beef for the march at a personal cost of $40,000.

His luck finally ran out in Whatcom, Washington. St. John Dix moved to the Pacific Northwest in 1900 and quickly initiated a plan to establish a chain of banks stretching all along the West Coast from San Diego to Vancouver, British Columbia. Of course, being a newspaper correspondent with no money to invest did little to deter him from this grandiose scheme. He began by securing a loan of three thousand dollars from a Seattle bank. He used this money to buy a controlling interest in the Scandinavian-American Bank in Whatcom. After negotiating the use of the Scandinavian-American deposits for eight days, he purchased the Bank of Blaine and the Citizens' National Bank of Fairhaven, located in neighboring towns. His plan, it seems, was to continue purchasing banks, using the deposits from one bank to buy the next. He had entered negotiations with several other banks in the surrounding area to do just that before the whole arrangement imploded.

Doubts arose over his lavish lifestyle, which caused some depositors to withdraw their accounts. It became apparent to Dix that the banks would become insolvent very quickly. Promising his investors that he was going to London to collect a $100,000 insurance policy which had just matured, he made his way to New York with his suspicious attorney trailing along behind him. Dix managed to allay his lawyer's concerns long enough to escape by offering him some paintings that he claimed to be the work of Italian masters, but that were, in fact, cheap reproductions. He eluded the authorities for some months in London before being apprehended in his encounter with Froest in November 1901. Upon capture, he fought extradition on the grounds that he was a native Englishman. This ploy failed, however, and Whatcom Sheriff William I. Brisbin returned him to the United States to stand trial for embezzlement from the now-defunct Scandinavian-American Bank in Whatcom in 1902. Despite his attempts to pass blame onto his subordinates, he received a sentence of ten years in prison. In the intervening time, however, stockholders of the bank performed an investigation which determined that he was not responsible for the collapse after all and that he stole no funds from the institution. Upon learning of their findings, Dix's wife prepared a petition requesting a pardon for her husband which she later presented to the governor. The petition succeeded, so after serving only a fraction of his sentence, Dix walked free in December 1904.

Undeterred by his brush with the law, he returned to England and in 1912 engineered a railroad plot with the Hungarian government to build an expansive railroad system in that country that connected Budapest with the surrounding countryside at a cost of nearly one million pounds. As with most things involving St. John Dix, this quickly went awry. By the next year, the British courts judged him bankrupt because of seventy thousand pounds of debt that he ran up pursuing the railroad scheme, which ultimately failed. It is unknown what happened to Henry St. John Dix after this, but his son Ralph went on to distinguish himself as a pilot in the R.A.F. during World War I. He served at the rank of captain and earned the Military Cross and Bar for gallantry during that conflict.

JOHN K. MURRELL

Peter R. Hacker

At the dawn of the twentieth century, nineteen members of the St. Louis, Missouri, House of Delegates, calling themselves the "combine," took a solemn oath. The oath said nothing about faithfully serving the citizens of St. Louis or governing in a fair and honorable manner. In fact, protecting the best interests of the city ran counter to their purpose. These elected officials, including the mayor, agreed to cut the throat, tear out the tongue, and cast into the Mississippi River any one of them who revealed the existence of the secret combine or "the fact that any person in this combine has received money." Before "Almighty God" each swore to "vote and act with the combine whenever and wherever I may be so ordered to do . . . so help me God." Little did they know that by 1902 they and their boss, a blacksmith millionaire named Edward Butler, would be exposed in the most notorious "boodling" scandal in American history.[28]

St. Louis city government was organized in a fairly typical manner: a mayor and a bicameral Municipal Assembly consisting of a House of Delegates and a City Council. The combine was a secret caucus or gang of bribe-takers in the House who sold legislation to those wishing to conduct business with the city. They even had a price schedule that varied depending on the nature and scope of the proposed bill. The process of offering and accepting bribes was known as "boodling" in St. Louis lingo. For at least twenty-five years it had greatly enriched the group, but not the city. John K. Murrell, a delegate and devoted member of the combine, was known as a "caretaker" amongst his fellow boodlers. As such, his colleagues frequently trusted him to handle the physical exchange of bribes. An undertaker by trade, Murrell was a happily married father and generally well-liked in the community. He had a conscience, but like so many other boodlers, years of corruption had desensitized him. The new circuit attorney, Joseph W. Folk, soon reminded him of the principles of right and wrong: "Bribery is treason, and the givers and takers . . . traitors!"[29]

Folk first caught wind of scandal when a reporter, James M. "Red" Galvin, repeated a rumor concerning unhappy boodlers in connection with expansion efforts of the St. Louis & Suburban Railway Company. In a nutshell, the Suburban wanted to extend some transit lines in the city. Company officials agreed to pay $60,000 in bribes to the city council and $75,000 to the House of Delegates combine to ensure that Transit Bill 44 passed. They placed the money for the combine in a safety deposit box with a company official retaining one key and a combine member holding the other. Upon passage of the legislation, the two keyholders were supposed to convene at the box and exchange the bribe. Murrell served as the key caretaker for the combine.

The trouble began when, despite the bill passing, a last-minute court ruling overturned it. The combine felt entitled to payment regardless. The Suburban resisted, saying it would only pay if granted full permission to build the new lines. When the grumbling reached circuit attorney Folk's ears, he courageously decided to prosecute not only the Suburban scandal, but a couple of other boodling cases involving combine members as well. Enlisting the help of a young journalist named Lincoln Steffens to publicize his anti-corruption crusade, Folk exposed a city government long held hostage by criminals. Facing overwhelming difficulties, he brought to trial a terrified collection of corporate millionaires and crooked politicians, garnering the much-needed support of President Theodore Roosevelt in the process.

The court scheduled Murrell among the first to be prosecuted in the St. Louis boodle cases, but the combine urged him to flee to "the land of the Montezumas," or Mexico. They realized his testimony could prove devastating to all involved, and he needed to disappear. Since Mexico had no extradition treaty with the US for bribery, they convinced him that he should hide out there for three to four years until the statute of limitations for all their crimes expired. Murrell reluctantly agreed to leave after boodlers promised to send him money and to look after his wife, Emma, in his absence.

His "disguise," a shave and a change of clothes, proved effective, and he slipped out of St. Louis on March 15, 1902. St. Louis police immediately issued wanted posters offering an $800 reward for his arrest. They described him as forty-three years old, five foot nine inches tall, and weighing one hundred and ninety-eight pounds.

St. Louis, Mo., March 18th, 1902.

$800.00 REWARD.

JOHN K. MURRELL.

WANTED FOR BRIBERY.

$800.00 REWARD will be paid for the arrest and detention of JOHN K. MURRELL, whose photograph appears above, until an officer from Missouri, with requisition papers, can reach him. Murrell was indicted on a charge of bribery in connection with a railroad franchise bill in the Municipal Assembly, he taking a bribe of $75,000.00 which was placed in a safe deposit vault, Murrell holding one key and a representative of the railroad the other.

His bond was forfeited March 18th, 1902, in Circuit Court, Division No. 8, in this city.

His description is as follows:

Age, about 43 years; about 5 feet 9¼ inches tall; weight about 198 lbs.; figure, medium; fair complexion; dark brown hair, thin on top; dark brown heavy moustache; might have had moustache cut off; can raise heavy beard; grey eyes; nose, aqueline; long face; voice, medium; occupation, undertaker; habits, drinks, smokes and chews tobacco; also uses profane language at times. He was a member of the House of Delegates, this city, in the years 1900 and 1901.

If arrested or located, communicate immediately with the undersigned.

MATHEW KIELY,
CHIEF OF POLICE,
ST. LOUIS, MO.

Reportedly, he had a dark brown heavy moustache, drank, smoked, chewed tobacco, and used profane language. Despite such detail, Murrell escaped recognition and made it to Mexico. Much to the consternation of the combine, Murrell returned to St. Louis after only six months to turn state's evidence.

Murrell was tracked down by Frank O'Neil, a legendary newspaperman best known for convincing the fugitive Frank James, brother of Jesse James, to surrender and stand trial after a lengthy interview. Talking sense, O'Neil persuaded Murrell to surrender unconditionally without guarantee of immunity. Once back in St. Louis, Murrell was assigned a bodyguard and stated publicly, "I could no longer stand the agony I endured as a fugitive from justice, and the wrong done me by the parties [combine] just as guilty as I, who made me their catspaw." He seemed surprised that the gang of boodlers failed to honor their commitments to him. Although they often made contact through messengers and by wire, he complained that "they did not send me money as promised." In fact, Julius Lehmann, a boodler go-between, borrowed ten dollars from him while touching base in El Paso, "and he has never returned it." Most upsetting, he accused the gang of deserting his wife and leaving her in a "desperate plight." He claimed that many "letters which my wife would write were destroyed" because they feared she would implore him to come home. Feeling lost, abandoned, and bitter, Murrell concluded, "I will do all I can to aid the circuit attorney in breaking up the boodle gang that has so long controlled the affairs of this city."[30]

As a star witness for the prosecution, Murrell testified twice against the boodlers in 1902. He described in shocking detail the brazen way the combine operated, named its members, and confessed his role in the $75,000 Suburban bribe and in a prior $47,500 street light scandal. His riveting testimony put him in the national spotlight as he exposed unthinkable depths of municipal corruption. He told of boodlers who would meet after lump sum bribe payments to distribute the "pieces of the pie," ensuring that each got "his'n." Murrell's statements, in conjunction with others, resulted in sixty-one indictments against twenty-four individuals, eight of whom went to prison. Although several convictions were overturned by the Missouri Supreme Court, the St. Louis boodling cases resulted in a sweep of city governments by Progressive politicians nationwide. The public relished the belief that corporate millionaires might have to atone for their sins. A Seattle editorial urged the "necessity of cultivating a public sentiment which will punish great criminals as severely as petty criminals. . . . How can respect for the law be cultivated among poor people if law is not enforced against the rich?"[31]

Lincoln Steffens, the young journalist recruited by Folk, did such a fine job publicizing the St. Louis scandals that he unwittingly gave birth to a new genre of American literature known as muckraking. Folk, who became something of a folk hero, rode his newfound celebrity into the Missouri governor's office in 1904, where he continued to advocate for meaningful reform. Through the rest of his life, he maintained that bribery wrested government from the people and bestowed it upon an oligarchy of special interests. As for Murrell, he remained in St. Louis until his death in 1939 at the age of eighty-one. Despite the blood-curdling oath of the combine, his throat remained uncut, his tongue remained intact, and his body was not dumped into the Mississippi River. He was instead buried in an elaborate grave beneath a well-crafted headstone befitting an undertaker.

BESSIE HALL, HENRY HALL, AND J. MARSHALL BROOKE

Meredith May

Newspaper writers in California and the surrounding region often referred to the escape of Henry Hall, Bessie Hall, and Judge Marshall Brooke from the San Diego County Jail as "sensational." The trio had already been convicted for their crimes—the Halls for grand larceny and Brooke for cattle rustling. They were sentenced to serve time in the notorious San Quentin prison, and awaited appeals in the San Diego County Jail. At 7:30 p.m. on July 8, 1902, however, Henry Hall and Brooke attacked their jailer, L. C. Foster, as he locked them in for the night and beat him with the leg from an iron stove. They then freed Bessie Hall, provided her with men's clothing, and all three bicycled away to Mexico.

The stories of Henry Hall, Bessie Hall, and J. Marshall Brooke prior to their brazen escapes are convoluted and shrouded in rumor and gossip. Henry Hall claimed he was born in Herodsburg, Kentucky, where he was raised by an aunt and uncle. At age twelve he ran away to join the circus, where he stayed about three years. He later worked for a while in St. Charles, Missouri, as a messenger boy. Once he acquired enough skills to become a telegraph operator, he found steady jobs in San Antonio and El Paso, Texas. From there he enlisted in the signal corps, which sent him to Puerto Rico until his discharge in 1899. After short stints in New York City and St. Louis, the telegraph operator accepted several positions that took him back out West. While in Del Rio, Texas, he met Belle Grosh (alias Bessie Hall). Grosh was the wife of David Elmer Grosh, who worked as an engineer for multiple railroads and had lived in Del Rio almost his entire life. It seems that Hall swept Belle Grosh off her feet, seduced her, and convinced her to leave Texas with him. The jilted husband caught up to the pair in Albuquerque, New Mexico, and, allegedly, they drew weapons. At least one of them fired a shot, although there is no evidence of anyone being wounded in the altercation. Hall and Belle Grosh continued on to San Diego, where she assumed the identity of Bessie Hall and introduced herself as Henry's sister. David Grosh returned to Del Rio.

Hall went to work for the Santa Fe Railway in San Diego, but after only a month or two, complaints arose about valuable articles disappearing from passengers' trunks. The authorities arrested Hall on suspicion of petty larceny. When he pawned a $500 diamond ring to make bail, the police learned that the ring belonged to Mrs. H. H. Stowell, the wife of a New York senator, who found that $2,000 worth of diamonds was missing from her luggage. They later discovered that Bessie Hall had been involved in the theft, and the two were charged with grand larceny. At the time of the trial, which began in January 1902 and lasted more than a month, the rest of the diamonds remained missing. During the proceedings, David Grosh arrived in San Diego to convince his wife to forsake Hall. In return, he offered to get her out of prison and send her to her parents. According to the *San Francisco Chronicle,* "she did not weaken, but maintained a coolness that gave him no encouragement." Rebuffed, Grosh remained in San Diego throughout the trial, hoping to gain revenge on Hall. On February 16, the judge sentenced the couple to ten years each in the penitentiary. Because their lawyer James Callen immediately filed an appeal, their transfer was delayed.[32]

Around the same time, J. Marshall Brooke awaited the outcome of his second conviction for stealing cattle. He was born in Ohio in December of 1878 and served in the Spanish-American War as a private. After his military service, he stole cattle from a ranch where he worked as a laborer and found himself in San Quentin by the tender age of twenty-one. When released, he stole more cattle, slaughtered them, and sold the meat, only to be caught again. This crime earned him three years behind bars plus an extra ten for his prior conviction. Like Hall and Grosh, he awaited his appeal in the San Diego County Jail.

The three originally plotted an escape in March of 1902, but the sheriff discovered their plan. Officials concluded that Bessie Hall had organized most of the escape attempt. She communicated her plans to her partner and Brooke through singing, humming, and messages passed via a prisoner entrusted with sweeping the jail. Bessie

$600 REWARD

BESSIE HALL   HENRY HALL   J. MARSHALL BROOKE

ESCAPE FROM JAIL
ALSO WANTED FOR ROBBERY

Henry Hall (alias H. R. Hall), Mrs. Belle Grosh (alias Bessie Hall), and J. Marshall Brooke.

HENRY HALL is about 5 feet 9 inches tall, slim built, light complexion, brown hair, smooth face, long neck, eyes large, light (either blue or gray), boney head, ears stand well out from head; actions quick and slightly nervous, about 28 years old, and is a telegraph operator; probably wears beard now. The Halls speak a little Spanish, and formerly resided at Del Rio, Texas.

J. MARSHALL BROOKE is about 5 feet 7 or 8 inches tall, stocky build, sandy complexion, very dark hair, inclined to be curly; smooth shaven, but should his beard show it will be quite red on chin; some freckles on and about his nose; nose inclined to turn up a little; thick lips, eyes gray; will weigh about 175 pounds; is an ex-convict.

BESSIE HALL is about 5 feet 4 or 5 inches tall, dark complexion, quite heavy black hair, cut off after escape; very determined countenance, very heavy under-jaw; dark, piercing eyes; scars on one side of neck, or just under jaw; thin lips, very slim build; when escaped had throat trouble and hacked very often; also coughed considerably.

The Halls are under sentence of ten years, and Brooks for thirteen years, for grand larceny, and all are guilty of robbery and assault with intent to kill, and all are doubtless going under assumed names.

I will pay a reward of $600 in gold for the arrest of all, or $200 in gold for the arrest of each or any one of them anywhere in the United States, or other countries, before June 1st, 1903, provided they are held and legally turned over to an officer or agent of the State of California. The reward will be paid when they are turned over to the proper officers of San Diego County, in the City of San Diego, State of California.

Reference is made to any bank in the City of San Diego, California, as to my reliability.

FRANK S. JENNINGS,
Sheriff of San Diego County, California.
San Diego, September 15th, 1902.

Hall destroyed all of the messages to her from Henry, but Henry did not demonstrate the same foresight. The sheriff discovered multiple letters from Bessie in Hall's cell and a letter intended for Bessie penned on thirty to forty sheets of toilet paper. Journalists delighted in sharing the details of the romantic drama with their readers, noting Bessie's use of "My Baby" in her correspondence to Hall and his vow that "come

what might he would never leave the jail without her."

In July, the three achieved their escape and crossed into Mexico. In Tijuana, the Halls and Brooke parted company. The Halls headed farther south, first to the vicinity of Mazatlán and perhaps as far as Chiapas before they disappeared. Brooke roamed around Baja California freely until his capture in 1906 near Ensenada by the chief of police of that city and a sergeant of the *rurales*. Having stopped at a ranch overnight before taking the prisoner to jail, all three travelers joined their hosts in a game of cards before retiring. In the morning, Brooke was gone. Everyone would have believed that he had made another successful escape as his captors reported he had, but for one small detail. The lawmen were suddenly flush with cash, which they distributed liberally around town. When someone tried to spend a bill across the border, however, it was discovered that it was old Confederate money. Brooke had used it to buy his freedom from the officials—who ultimately went to jail themselves.

Henry Hall and J. Marshall Brooke had more adventures to come, as members of a group of rebels operating in Tijuana during the Mexican Revolution. In 1911, the *San Diego Union* announced that they had been identified by fellow members of the insurgent group. Given another chance to capitalize on the pair's exploits, the newspaper recounted the stories of their earlier crimes and their daring jailbreak, and provided an update on their activities in the intervening years. Hall refused to discuss Bessie's whereabouts, so her fate remains unknown. Hall did, however, declare his intention to fight to the end in Mexico.

If Brooke had a plan, he did not reveal it. In 1940, he applied for and received a pardon and returned to California. He died in 1952 in Los Angeles.

In an interesting footnote to the crime, James Callen, the Halls' attorney, was committed to an insane asylum in 1904. In his desk the guardian of his estate discovered Mrs. Stowell's missing diamonds. Callen had left a cryptic note with the packet, but it shed little light on why they were in his possession. The jewels were finally returned to the Stowells by the guardian of Callen's estate.

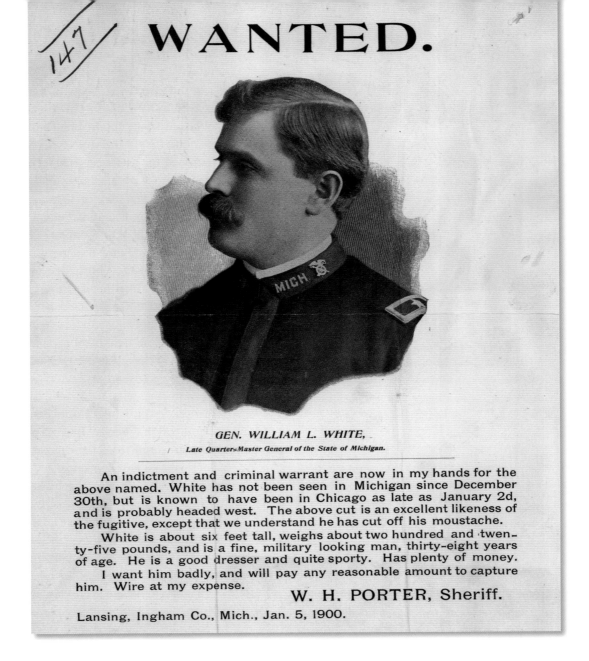

WANTED.

GEN. WILLIAM L. WHITE,
Late Quarter=Master General of the State of Michigan.

An indictment and criminal warrant are now in my hands for the above named. White has not been seen in Michigan since December 30th, but is known to have been in Chicago as late as January 2d, and is probably headed west. The above cut is an excellent likeness of the fugitive, except that we understand he has cut off his moustache.

White is about six feet tall, weighs about two hundred and twenty-five pounds, and is a fine, military looking man, thirty-eight years of age. He is a good dresser and quite sporty. Has plenty of money.

I want him badly, and will pay any reasonable amount to capture him. Wire at my expense.

W. H. PORTER, Sheriff.

Lansing, Ingham Co., Mich., Jan. 5, 1900.

WILLIAM L. WHITE

Bryan McKinney

A grand jury in Ingham County, Michigan, indicted Gen. William L. White for conspiracy to defraud the state on December 29, 1899. That same day he told everyone he was off to Chicago to spend the weekend with his mother, but instead he vanished. A successful businessman, White had risen quickly through the ranks of the Michigan State Militia, but the once-lauded soldier had been exposed as a crook, and the hunt was on to bring him to justice. Law enforcement distributed wanted posters widely, describing him as a "fine, military-looking man, thirty-eight years of age. He is a good dresser and quite sporty."

General White and his brother-in-law, William Edward White, owned several White & White drug stores in Grand Rapids, Michigan. The partnership flourished because "William L. was ambitious, aggressive, and a skilled organizer complemented by the affable personality and pharmaceutical expertise of William E." William L. also joined the state militia where he applied his organizational skills to the position of quartermaster general. In fact, Michigan troops called up during the Spanish-American War in 1898 did not have the same logistical problems that plagued other units. General White's performance was so extraordinary that leaders talked of nominating him to run for mayor of Grand Rapids on the Republican Party ticket.[33]

The trouble started when Spain's quick defeat left the state of Michigan with a surplus of military equipment and war loans to pay off. White, who ran the state military board, approved a sale of clothing and equipment valued at $65,000 to the Illinois Supply Company for $10,500. He then authorized a second purchase of $40,000 for identical equipment from another military supplier, Henderson-Ames Company of Kalamazoo. When an Ingham County impaneled a grand jury to investigate rumors of corruption in the Michigan state government, the details of these questionable transactions were exposed. The *Grand Rapids Press* reported "A check of the state armory revealed that it wasn't just the same kind of equipment, it was the actual same equipment. It had never left the state."[34]

The grand jury focused on White, Inspector General Arthur Marsh, and Colonel Eli Sutton. General White testified that he authorized the transactions, but "knew nothing of the details of either sale or purchase," and "was obliged to sell these stores to close the war loan account." An agent for Henderson-Ames confessed that the Illinois Supply Company was fictional and that there was a scheme to divide the profits between the firm and members of the war board. With the details of the plot revealed, the governor of Michigan demanded that Quartermaster General White and Inspector General Marsh both resign. When he was indicted nine days later, William White disappeared, sparking an international manhunt.[35]

Sheriff William H. Porter of the state capital at Lansing traveled to Grand Rapids on January 1, 1900, to serve a warrant on General White. He heard that White had gone to Chicago to see his mother and family, but these relatives had no knowledge of his trip. He learned that "White did not go to a family residence in Chicago, but apparently only stopped in that city for a short time and then left at once, in which direction is unknown." While passing through, White penned a letter to a friend saying, "I am thoroughly discouraged, and can't stand this any longer. Everything is working against me, and if I returned I would be in torment continually. I have suffered every minute for weeks, and I am now going away where I can get a little rest. I don't know just where it will be but I leave here at once." White's disappearance may have spared him the anguish of a trial, but others indicted in the scheme faced justice. Inspector General Marsh went on trial after White fled the country. In April 1900, Marsh was convicted of having conspired to defraud the state and sentenced to fourteen years in prison. Prosecutors also tried Eli Sutton, a member of the governor of Michigan's military staff, but he was acquitted.[36]

With Pinkerton agents tracking him both in New York and across the West, White escaped the United States on a ship sailing out of New Orleans to Cape Town, South Africa. From there he played the tourist as he hopped from Zanzibar to Cairo, Jerusalem, Marseilles, Paris, and finally London, where he took a ship to Vera Cruz, Mexico. From there he headed north and slipped back over the border into California. In the end White's convoluted journey covered a total of 35,000 miles. After a time, his sister, Mary Ellis, finally persuaded him it was time to come home and face justice. A little less than a year after his indictment, he returned to Grand Rapids. A crowd of onlookers and press greeted him. His brother-in-law, William E. White, distracted reporters while his sister went aboard the train and snuck him out the rear exit.

General White entered a guilty plea to the Ingram County Circuit Court on December 3. He was sentenced to ten years hard labor at Jackson State Prison, which he admitted "staggered him." Though he said he had "no arrangements to seek a pardon," the very next day Governor Hazen Pingree granted one to both White and Marsh on condition of payment of a $5,000 penalty. The governor reasoned that since the county failed to prosecute the conspirators from the Henderson-Ames Company, who happened to be prominent citizens, it would be unjust to only have some of the guilty parties pay for the crimes committed.[37]

After his pardon, White left Grand Rapids. He became a silent partner in White & White, and moved to Detroit, then Buffalo, finally settling down in San Francisco. After his crime, he avoided politics and military matters altogether. Upon his death in September 1933, the Grand Rapids newspapers graciously omitted any reference to the scandal in his obituary, reporting instead that he was a former druggist who left the community thirty years ago to live elsewhere.

JOHN THOMPSON HALL

William Meier

John Thompson Hall was the picture of Victorian respectability—that vital mix of moral rectitude, paternal authority, public service, and financial security that distinguished the thrusting middle class of nineteenth-century Britain from both the supposedly spendthrift working classes below and the allegedly idle and indebted aristocrats above.

His community of Darlington in northeastern England was in many ways the ideal place for a gentleman on the make in the final third of Queen Victoria's reign. This provincial market town, already bustling with prominent Quaker entrepreneurs in 1800, became the terminus of the Stockton and Darlington Railway in 1825. The railway carried inland coal to the River Tees, from where it could be shipped farther afield to fuel the industrial revolution. The line was one of those feats of engineering much celebrated by champions of British industrial genius, and it complemented nicely the local railway manufacturing and bridge-building industries. Civic pride also dwelt upon Darlington's own influential newspaper, the *Northern Echo*. Here, out in the provinces, away from the teeming metropolis of London and its centers of financial and political power, middle-class men found wide scope for self-improvement through political participation, investment, philanthropy, and public service.

In pursuit of this improvement John Thompson Hall threw himself into every imaginable activity. As a chartered accountant and stock- and share-broker, Hall was instrumental in mobilizing private savings for investment in joint stock companies that promoted economic development in industrial England. He had ample opportunity to display his moral zeal as a member of the Darlington Temperance Society and of the Society for the Prevention of Cruelty to Animals, two notable pressure groups that gave the middle classes a voice in the clamor for moral reform. He also served as a local churchwarden and was licensed by the bishop of Durham as a lay preacher for the Church of England. Hall was of sufficient local renown to be nominated to and chair the Darlington School Board and to serve on the boards of the North Eastern Counties Employers'

Liability Insurance Company and the Equitable Building Society. He joined magisterial to moral authority in his position as justice of the peace for the borough of Darlington, where he dispensed judgment from the bench on the poorer sort for their petty crimes and misdemeanors.

From such heights of respectability his fall was precipitous. On August 20, 1901, he stood arraigned in Darlington Police Court—the very chamber where he had served as a magistrate—on charges of defrauding investors of tens of thousands of pounds. Passers-by hooted Hall as police drove him to and from the court. Even before the trial Hall was big news, for, drowning in debt, he clambered aboard a transatlantic steamer, shaved his face, assumed a false name, and hoped to evade his creditors as "John Francis Harris, schoolmaster," in the USA. In a hastily written missive composed on board ship for the new world, Hall implored the chairman of the Equitable Building Society to keep his creditors from harassing his wife and children whom he was now leaving in the lurch—and perhaps leaving for good. But the trouble was that a former resident of Darlington, now also in New York City, recognized Hall and informed Pinkerton detectives, who caught him in East Orange, New Jersey. Soon, Hall was shipped back across the Atlantic Ocean to pay the piper. His malfeasance was sufficiently grave to warrant trial at Durham Assizes, where Justice Grantham sentenced Hall to five years' penal servitude. The convict then faced the additional shame of appearing before that most Dickensian of horror chambers, the Stockton-on-Tees Bankruptcy Court, to declare his debts exceeding £16,000. Newspapers up and down the country and across the Atlantic in New York, Massachusetts, and Ohio reported on the case, reflecting public thirst for stories about how the righteous had fallen.

Hall's misdeeds were part and parcel of the economic developments that had totally transformed Britain into a modern, urban, industrial society, and one in which men of capital were beginning to supplant landed elites as the richest and most powerful stratum in society. The very complexity of the British economy, which had so spectacularly expanded national wealth, was best captured in the instrument of the joint stock company. These companies provided at one and the same time an outlet for middle-class savings and a source of funding for large projects like the improvement of the River Tyne—one of the funds from which Hall misappropriated several thousand pounds. If on the one hand the joint stock company spread risk and liability very broadly among all investors, it was also open to various forms of managerial malfeasance that could ruin small shareholders. It was bad enough that Hall defrauded investors by pocketing their money and giving them bogus shares; worse that in at least one instance the shares he misappropriated from the London and Westminster Bank had been intended to support a widow's children.

Was he not the chairman of the school board? The trustee? The magistrate? The lay preacher? Hall's case reveals that beneath the veneer of Victorian respectability ran a whole host of temptations and sins. In the court of public opinion his transgression was not simply financial fraud, but wholesale deceit: Hall traded not just in shares, but on his *status*, in inspiring and then exploiting confidence among shareholders and the wider com-

TAKEN 4 YEARS AGO.

TAKEN RECENTLY.

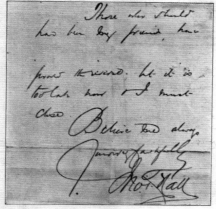

POLICE INFORMATION.

DURHAM COUNTY CONSTABULARY,

ENGLAND.

WANTED here charged on warrant with larceny and misappropriation of very large sums of money. JOHN THOMPSON HALL (portrait and fac-simile of hand writing shewn opposite), a chartered accountant and stock and share broker, late of Darlington, England, age 49 years, 5 feet 7 or 8 inches high, proportionately built, dark brown hair, bald on top of head, dark eyes, fresh complexion, had when last seen dark beard, whiskers and moustache, irregular and prominent front teeth marked with tartar, is ruptured and wears a truss, walks with a short shuffling gait, is generally dressed in dark clothes, and carries an umbrella. Is a man of pleasant manners and respectable appearance, a fluent and easy speaker, was a licensed lay preacher, sunday school teacher and temperance advocate. Is very likely to seek employment as an accountant and will probably engage himself in religious and temperance work. He sailed from Queenstown on 10th March, 1901, in the S.S. Campania, arriving at New York on 16th of same month. He booked himself as John Francis Harris, schoolmaster. Supposed to have taken with him a considerable sum of money in Bank of England Notes.

Please cause every search and enquiry to be made for the above described and should he be found or any trace of him obtained, communicate with the undersigned, who will take immediate steps to procure his extradition.

J. H. EDEN, Lt.-Col.,
Chief Constable.

Chief Constable's Office, Durham,
County of Durham,
England, 29th April, 1901.

munity. So why did he defraud? In the end, Hall did not embezzle to feed his vices. There is no evidence of gambling or overindulgence in drink. In fact, so desperate was Hall to defend his image that at his trial he reassured judge and jury that he was a total abstainer. And therein is the key: Hall stole to keep up the image of respectability that he had so diligently constructed.

At his trial he pleaded that his debts were due to his clients who failed to make good on their payments, so that he defrauded to cover up his losses. Whatever the cause, loss of financial independence simply couldn't be countenanced because it meant loss of standing as a pillar of community and paterfamilias. Hall stole to keep up appearances.

MAMIE SCULLY AND TESSIE ELLIS

LeAnna S. Schooley

Detectives caught Mamie Scully and Tessie Ellis stealing pocketbooks from unsuspecting shoppers at a large Boston department store in the spring of 1899. Officers had observed the suspects working the crowd for several minutes to confirm their motives before apprehending them. Between them the women had accumulated over $100 in cash, an expensive silk shirtwaist, and perhaps some diamonds. Scully and Ellis were arrested and charged with five counts of larceny from the person, or pickpocketing. The pair immediately hired a lawyer, and a professional bondman posted bail for them at $1,500 each. A month later, after four continuances of their case, the women failed to appear before the municipal criminal court, prompting arrest warrants to be issued for the fugitives.

Mamie Scully and Tessie Ellis proved to be elusive characters in person and on paper. As career criminals, the women protected their anonymity as best they could with a variety of aliases. Mamie Scully, reportedly the wife of notorious Chicago thief "Scully the Robber," also used the names Annie Rigby and Annie Scully. Some also suspected she was known as "Texas." Her real identity remains obscure. Similarly, Tessie Ellis went by Tessie Hamilton, Annie Evans, Mary Murray, and Miss Graham. Her maiden name was most likely Theresa Leonard, and she claimed to be the widow of Graham McCandless, a fellow pickpocket and native of St. Louis, Missouri. Though the details were sketchy, authorities thought both women originally hailed from New York City and were about twenty-four years old at the time of their Boston crime.

Only two days after the Boston police issued warrants for their arrest, photos of Scully and Ellis were added to the rogues' gallery. The authorities soon distributed wanted posters featuring their mug shots to major US cities as well. The circulars were neatly printed with a simple design. Each woman's image appeared alongside her Bertillon and English measurements, in addition to a brief description of their crime and police department contact information. They were both slightly over five feet tall with blue eyes and round faces. Scully was redheaded, while Ellis had chestnut locks. Newspaper articles declared them "young and pretty," which no doubt contributed to the interest of the media and the reading public.

Fugitive status did not impact Scully and Ellis's activities significantly. Following the Boston incident, they were arrested together in Louisville, Milwaukee, and elsewhere but managed to obtain bail and disappear before Boston police could arrive to claim them. The ease of railroad travel and improved lines of communication in turn-of-the-century America enabled the women to become "known to police around the country," as news outlets often proclaimed. Contemporary accounts suggest that their participation with a well-connected gang of thieves and murderers based in Chicago also may have helped them evade police. Local papers linked them to the case against Chicago Chief of Detectives Captain Luke P. Colleran, who was found guilty of neglect of duty and conduct unbecoming an officer while Scully and Ellis were on the run. Though their escapes from justice were not included in the evidence at trial, Colleran was accused in the press of submitting to the influence of a circus promoter, gambler, and confidence man named "Bunk" Allen, who encouraged Colleran to "square things" with the Boston police on behalf of the women.[38]

Tessie Ellis's luck ran out in November 1901 when she was picked up in Detroit, where authorities held her until the arresting officer in Boston, Inspector Alfred Douglass, arrived. He successfully transferred her into his custody, but the return trip was anything but ordinary. When Douglass and Ellis, accompanied by a Detroit detective named Brooks, changed trains in Toledo, Ohio, they were met by a local deputy sheriff with his own warrant for Ellis's arrest. In a scene that the creators of the Keystone Kops films might have found inspirational, the Toledo deputy pressed his case, provoking the Detroit detective to "feint to strike" him. As passengers, railway employees, and some of Ellis's nefarious friends looked on, the deputy, named Hurlbut, threatened to pull his revolver if the detective did not release Ellis to him. "Then Deputy Hurlbut's left arm encircled the woman's waist, and, with his clenched right hand waving for a passage through the crowd, the pair started

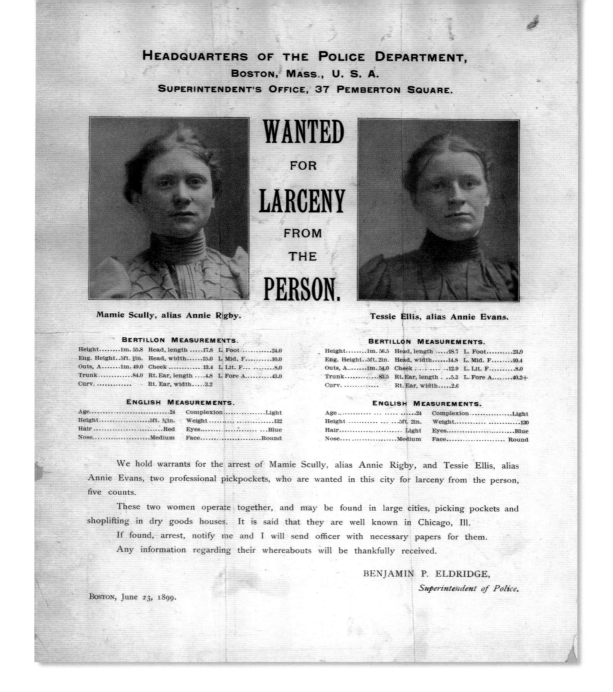

out of the Lake Shore yards. The detectives caught hold of the woman's free arm, and a pulling match followed . . . the controversy continued, both sides making dire threats until the eastbound train had come and gone, and then all parties to the dispute came down to the court house." It seems that the bondsman from Ellis's arrest in Milwaukee initiated the intervention in Toledo, perhaps at the request of Ellis's compatriots, in the hope of impeding Boston law enforcement and again delaying her trial.[39]

Douglass prevailed with the local judge and extradited Ellis to Boston immediately. A month later, she was convicted of larceny in the Suffolk County Superior Criminal Court and sentenced to one year in the Sherborn Reformatory, the first reform-minded facility for women designed to encourage inmates' personal growth through an incentivized program of disciplined work and education. Supporters hoped this model would more effectively convert prisoners into contributing members of society than would fear and hard labor.

Ellis might have been reformed by her time at Sherborn. She told the authorities she planned to return to Chicago, where her parents and siblings resided, upon her release on November 10, 1902. But because her trail ran cold the day she walked out the prison gates, it is unclear if she ever found a stable lifestyle.

Six years after the Boston incident, Mamie Scully remained at large. Her fate is unknown.

SAMUEL M. FINDLEY

Gene Rhea Tucker

Samuel Millian Findley, tax collector, said he was headed out to the eastern part of San Luis Obispo County, California, to collect license fees on November 18, 1898. He then disappeared. For several days after his disappearance, county officials believed that "some person or persons have done away with him." Someone then came forward and said he had seen Findley board a train for San Francisco on November 19. On November 29, the *San Luis Obispo Tribune* reported that around $11,000 was missing from the county's vaults. A warrant was soon issued for Findley's arrest on the charge of "unlawfully, fraudulently, feloniously and without authority of law [did] appropriate to his own use a portion of said public moneys." The Fidelity and Deposit Company of Maryland, who insured and bonded county workers, hired the Pinkerton National Detective Agency to track Findley and, they hoped, recover some of the stolen cash.[40]

The San Francisco office of Pinkerton's distributed a wanted poster on December 8, 1898. The circular included a recent photograph and a physical description, including the facts that he "chews tobacco . . . is a steady drinker; untidy in dress." Born on November 6, 1847, in Illinois, Findley had attended Monmouth College in that state and clerked for various federal government departments. Though married in Illinois, he lived in Washington, DC, and Virginia before making his way to California in the 1880s. A member of the Populist Party, he became the county tax collector in 1897.

Around the time the wanted poster was circulated, the absconding Findley mailed a package from Ciudad Juarez, Mexico, to Nellie E. Nesbitt, one of his coworkers. Though sent under a fake name, the label was in Findley's handwriting, and the package contained his official safe, desk, and drawer keys. With this clue in hand, Pinkerton's transferred the case to John C. Fraser of its Denver office. Fraser, a veteran detective with eighteen years of service, headed to El Paso on December 19, crossed the border, and followed Findley to Mexico City. Findley, who passed himself off as William Miller in Mexico City, had left for points south before Fraser arrived. Using a photograph and an offer of reward, Fraser pursued Findley, now posing as J. E. Miller, first to Coatzacoalcos on the Gulf of Mexico, then to Tehuantepec on the Pacific coast, then on to Panama, and finally to Lima, Peru.

Fraser reached Lima on March 6, 1899, finding Findley at the French and English Hotel registered under the name of John T. Millem. Fraser shadowed Findley's movements in Peru for about two months in order to trace the money and to negotiate with Peruvian authorities (Peru and the United States did not have an extradition treaty). On May 7, 1899, Fraser arrested Findley at the latter's new home in Barranco, a suburb of Lima. Findley had deposited about $8,000 in gold in Lima's Bank of London and Peru and had $149 in cash on his person. Findley did not seem to show any remorse for his crime, supposedly saying, "The county did not lose any money. My bondsmen paid it all back and I am not ashamed of it." He willingly chose to return to California for trial, believing that "such a course will bring more leniency" than if he contested extradition. On this point, a San Francisco newspaper remarked, "It is very kind of him, but he might have said something about a return of the money he stole." Fraser brought Findley to San Luis Obispo on June 17 and jailed him in the same courthouse building he had once worked in as tax collector.[41]

Findley pleaded not guilty by reason of insanity for his first trial, which began on October 30, 1899. The defense claimed that Findley's overindulgence in drink produced a temporary insanity. A deadlocked jury caused the case to end in a mistrial on November 21. Findley's second trial began the following March. Detective Fraser and several others testified for the prosecution, while the defense called Findley's wife, daughter, and a few more witnesses. The defense again maintained that drink had inspired his lunacy, along with a suicidal depression. This time, the jury convicted Findley. His wife and three daughters were in the courtroom and wept at the announcement. On March 31, Judge Edwin P. Unangast sentenced Findley to eight years in San Quentin State Prison. Findley told a reporter: "I was not surprised at the sentence. For my

Pinkerton's National Detective Agency

FOUNDED BY ALLAN PINKERTON, 1850

WM. A. PINKERTON, Chicago,
ROBT. A. PINKERTON, New York, } Principals

GEO. D. BANGS, Gen'l Sup't,
New York.

OFFICES.

SAN FRANCISCO, 14 CROCKER BUILDING.
C. E. VANNATTA, SUPERINTENDENT

NEW YORK, 57 BROADWAY.
BOSTON, 30 COURT STREET.
PHILADELPHIA, 441 CHESTNUT STREET.
CHICAGO, FIFTH AVENUE.
ST. PAUL, BANK BUILDING.
KANSAS CITY, MAIN STREET.
DENVER, OPERA HOUSE BLOCK.
PORTLAND, ORE., MARQUAM BLOCK.

D. ROBERTSON, Ass't Gen'l Sup't Middle Division, CHICAGO.
JAS. McPARLAND, Ass't Gen'l Sup't Western Division, DENVER.

ATTORNEYS,
SEWARD, GUTHRIE & STEELE,
New York.

CONNECTED BY TELEPHONE

SAMUEL M. FINDLEY

FACSIMILE OF HANDWRITING.

$500 REWARD

ARREST FOR EMBEZZLEMENT

SAMUEL M. FINDLEY

TAX COLLECTOR OF SAN LUIS OBISPO COUNTY, CALIFORNIA

LAST SEEN NOVEMBER 19th, 1898

DESCRIPTION.

Samuel M. Findley is 52 years of age; weight 183 lbs.; height 5 feet 10 inches; florid complexion; color of eyes, hazel; hair, dark; mustache, dark, mixed with gray; full, broad forehead; scar from burn on face below left ear; chews tobacco: carried mouth puckered up on account of this; is a steady drinker; untidy in dress; when walking carries head leaned over slightly on one side.

Had two new grips—one imitation alligator, light brown, 24-inch, price-mark Y. P. A. marked in ink on outside; the other a small, brown hand-grip, price-mark E. A. marked in ink on outside.

$500 REWARD will be paid by the Fidelity & Deposit Co., of Maryland, for the arrest and detention of Samuel M. Findley pending arrival of officer with necessary papers.

Send information (telegraphic or otherwise) to the undersigned at any of the above listed offices.

PINKERTON'S NATIONAL DETECTIVE AGENCY.

OR
C. E. VANNATTA, Resident Supt.,
Crocker Building, San Francisco, Cal.

December 8th, 1898.

family I am sorry, but for myself I do not care. I knew the judge was dead against me." He appealed his sentence on various grounds all the way to the Supreme Court of California, which ruled against him. On April 24, 1901, Findley, embezzler and absconder, was transferred and booked into San Quentin as prisoner 18996. Officials cut his hair, shaved his face, photographed him, and dressed the convict in prison stripes. Findley served his time until discharged on August 24, 1906. He lived afterward for about ten years in San Luis Obispo County, apparently quietly, until his death on July 15, 1917.[42]

CHARLES AND RACHEL FISHER

Jessica Webb

In early December 1878, a young man stood before the Jefferson Market Police Court in New York City to answer for breaking a glass window. Why, the presiding Judge Otterbourg wondered, did this nineteen-year-old boy, recently released from Sing Sing Prison for thieving, commit such an offense? The young man, Charles Fisher, said he was starving and unable to find work, so he broke the window to be arrested and sent back to jail. Judge Otterbourg responded by asking why, as a thief, he simply did not steal food for himself? "Because," Fisher said, "I promised my mother, who is dead, that when I got out of Sing Sing I would lead an honest life, and never steal again." The judge, struck by Fisher's honesty, helped him obtain employment, hoping to steer him onto an honest path. For the young ex-convict, this was an opportunity to reform his life and honor his late mother's wishes. Fisher, however, quickly squandered his chance and turned back to crime, becoming over the next forty years one of the most notorious forgers of the era.[43]

Charles Fisher was born in Germany in March 1859. His parents had high hopes for him, placing him in public school at the age of five, but Fisher did not share in their ambitions for him. Instead, he began his criminal career by taking money from his grandfather for over a year before graduating to stealing and cashing money orders. His father, tired of his son's antics, exiled him to America, where young Fisher continued to build a reputation as a good thief. On October 9, 1876, all his thieving caught up with him when he was arrested and charged with grand larceny. He pleaded guilty and went to Sing Sing Prison for two and a half years. During his prison sentence, Fisher swore to himself that he would lead an honest life, for his mother's sake. But not only did he stray from that path soon after his release, he also discovered a new crime he excelled at: forgery.

Charles Fisher quickly returned to his old network and was arrested with four other forgers for passing bad checks on almost all of the banks in Chicago. To avoid jail time, he testified against the other forgers. As part of the deal, they required him to leave the state of Illinois, so he went to New York City. Soon after arriving, police arrested him for larceny and sentenced him to Black-well's Island for six months. In 1883, free once again, he organized a plan to forge more checks. After obtaining over $1,000, the gang of forgers was arrested again, and again Fisher turned state's evidence to avoid jail.

Despite having been caught several times, Charles Fisher was undeterred. While free, he found both a wife and a partner-in-crime when he married a woman named Rachel. In October 1885, he devised a scheme with three other expert forgers to defraud New York City banks with checks seemingly signed by prominent merchants. They were arrested for attempting to cash a forged check for $460. About one month later, Fisher was found guilty and sentenced to another ten years at Sing Sing. He served seven years of his term, but he was hardly reformed when he was released on May 20, 1892. He immediately began planning an international crime spree.

While in prison, Charles Fisher met five professional thieves who helped him craft and execute a massive robbery and forgery scheme. Once they were all free in November 1893, the operation began. Essentially, they made keys so they could open letterboxes and steal letters containing money and checks that they could then use to forge more checks. The group of criminals began their exploits in New York City but quickly realized that their plan could be repeated throughout the country. Thus Fisher and company plundered letterboxes in St. Louis, New Orleans, Milwaukee, Cincinnati, Pittsburg, and Philadelphia.

In May 1894 the thieves and their wives sailed for England to attempt even more forgeries. They had to return to America, however, when one of the men was arrested in London. Authorities caught up to Charles and Rachel again in Baltimore, Maryland, on June 26, 1895, when they were arrested for stealing checks and changing the amounts indicated on them to larger sums. Baltimore police dropped the charges against them but extradited Charles back to Cincinnati to answer for his crime there. Instead, Fisher made a key from a knife and escaped the county jail.

Charles and Rachel Fisher fled to England to resume their illegal activities after the breakout, but he was arrested in July 1896 and May 1897 and sentenced to jail time in both instances. After the second arrest, the London authorities realized who Fisher was and arranged to extradite him when his time in the Holloway Jail in London concluded. On December 2, 1897, authorities placed Fisher on the steamer *Teutonic* and sent him back to the United States. Rachel, who was never arrested or jailed in England, accompanied her husband on the journey. Once in the US, authorities sent Fisher to Cincinnati, where he served his time. After

this release, he decided he and Rachel should return to England, but they did not find London a friendly place.

Charles Fisher resumed his letterbox thievery in the United Kingdom but was caught after only a few months. On September 27, 1902, an inspector from Scotland Yard caught Fisher in the act of making an impression of a letterbox key. He was sentenced to two years of hard labor. Rachel was also arrested and charged as an accomplice but was released for lack of evidence. After Fisher completed this two-year sentence, he tried his hand at burglary again, but that earned him ten more years in an English prison. During this long stretch, he lessened his sentence by testifying against four American forgers. And so, in December 1909, Charles Fisher returned to the United States. He sailed back alone, however, as Rachel had passed away during his incarceration.

Throughout Fisher's criminal career, Pinkerton detectives chased him across America. They went so far as to print and circulate wanted posters for both Charles and Rachel. Therefore, when he returned to New York City, Pinkerton's immediately put him under surveillance. They were soon rewarded. Predictably, Fisher began another scheme. He, along with two other well-known thieves, made nearly $15,000 from forged checks before they were caught. Eventually, Fisher did another two-year stint in Sing Sing Prison, but he remained unreformed. After his release he and another noted forger, John M. Doyle, teamed up to create and cash forged checks across the Northeast. They gathered over $300,000 within a few months. This crime earned Fisher eight more years in Sing Sing.

After Charles Fisher's release from his fourth term in that famous prison, one might hope he would lie low. He was aging, and many of his accomplices, including his wife, were either dead or jailed. Still, crime and forgery were all Fisher knew. In June 1920, at the age of sixty-one, he was arrested for the last time in New York City. He had been a part of the New Haven Band, a criminal group who defrauded banks in New York, Pennsylvania, Rhode Island, Connecticut, and Massachusetts of nearly $50,000. Fisher's extradition to New Haven to face trial is the last record of the infamous international criminal. It is likely he was jailed again and died in prison, but one can only guess. What is clear, though, is that Charles Fisher knew only one way to live—as a criminal. While he frequently claimed he was going to turn his life around, each time he was released from his many prison terms, Fisher always chose a life of forgery, thievery, and crime.

$500 REWARD!

(This photograph was taken in 1895 and gives him the appearance of being a little heavier than he now is.)

The above reward will be paid for the arrest and detention of **CHANNING B. BARNES,** *alias* **JOHN H. NELSON,** *alias* **"JACK" NELSON,** whose photograph appears above, until an officer from Kentucky can reach him with requisition papers, if arrested outside that State.

This man is wanted on the charge of holding up Illinois Central train No. 4 near Wickliffe, Ky., on the morning of July 11th, 1900, and robbing the safe of the American Express Company. His description is as follows:

Age about 32 years; about 6 feet tall; weight about 180 pounds; slim built; stoop-shouldered; light complexioned, red hair and mustache, might have had mustache cut off; blue eyes; wears 7⅛ hat; size foot, 7½; may have three front gold filled teeth. Have *information* that he has the following scars: A large depression or scar on back of head, covered by hair; large bullet scar on back near hips; several bullet scars on both legs and is an expert pistol shot. He is a good dresser, good talker and an educated man. Boards and lives among good society. Occupation as given, that of clerk. He is a free drinker and an inveterate smoker of cigarettes; also smokes cigars. Claims to be a mining irrigator, also claims to have a fruit ranch in California and live there. Served time in San Quentin Penitentiary, California, for robbing the State Bank of Ontario, San Bernardino County, California, January 4th, 1895. Was discharged from San Quentin Penitentiary on June 6th, 1899, where he was serving a six years sentence.

From the records of the Penitentiary the following additional description is obtained:

Scars: 2, left thumb; 3, left fore-finger; 1, back of head; 1, left eyebrow; 1, above left temple; vaccine mark, right upper arm.

Above photograph was taken in 1895 in State Prison, San Quentin, Cal. Makes him appear a little heavier than he now is. He is a dangerous man and a good shot.

This man was assisted in the above robbery by Charles W. Barnes and R. M. Doyle, now under arrest.

If arrested or located, communicate immediately with either of the undersigned.

ILLINOIS CENTRAL R. R. CO.,
By J. T. HARAHAN, Second Vice-President.

AMERICAN EXPRESS CO.,
By A. ANTISDEL, General Manager.

CHICAGO, ILL., JULY 16TH, 1900.

CHANNING B. BARNES

Brooke Wibracht

In December 1900, newspapers splashed headlines across their pages announcing that famed train robber Channing B. Barnes (alias John H. Nelson or Jack Nelson) was dead, his body discovered in a swamp outside New Orleans.

Barnes was born in 1868 to Charles and Lillie Barnes. The family lived in Ohio before moving to Texas in the 1870s. He grew up in Austin and graduated from the University of Texas. Not long after graduation, in the early 1890s, Barnes moved to California. By 1895 he had been arrested for robbing the Ontario State Bank in San Bernardino County. He was tried and sentenced to six years in the San Quentin Penitentiary. After completing less than five years of his sentence, he was released on June 6, 1899. Once he regained his freedom, he left California and moved to St. Louis, Missouri. He met Katherine Dowd shortly after arriving in the city, and they married on January 4, 1900.

That summer, Barnes traveled to Wickliffe, Kentucky, along with two accomplices. On the morning of July 11, the group robbed the Chicago Limited of the Illinois Central Railroad. They blew a hole in the express car with a stick of dynamite and raided the safe. After the robbery Barnes returned to St. Louis. When the police tried to arrest him at his apartment, Barnes climbed out a window. A detective caught him in the alley behind his apartment, and the two exchanged gunfire. Barnes received only flesh wounds, and again he gave the authorities the slip.

Barnes pulled his last caper in Louisiana. According to the police, on December 13, 1900, Barnes traveled to New Orleans, boarded an Illinois Central mail train, and robbed it. He took money and registered mail, along with the train conductor's watch. As Barnes was escaping, he ran into two watchmen. A gun fight ensued and Barnes was shot twice, once in his left forearm and once in his back. Authorities chased him into the swamp where he remained for several days. The police claimed that Barnes committed the crime alone; however, watchman W. H. Lucich (who shot Barnes) said that he and his partner got into a gun fight with two robbers, not one. The conductor, a Mr. Kinabrew, corroborated his coworker's story, saying that two men raided the train, not one.

Within a week of the robbery, a trapper found Barnes's body. The police identified him by his bullet wounds and the registered mail, money, sticks of dynamite, and the conductor's watch in his possession. Police found a note addressed to them from Barnes. It said, "Yes, you Curs, I am Jack Nelson, of St. Louis. I played you a merry old game and masqueraded under your noses . . . My devoted, undying love to my Kittie, My love, My sweetheart, My adored."[44]

Barnes had two slash wounds across his neck, indicating that he had slit his throat twice with a razor blade or a knife. According to the coroner, if Barnes slashed his own throat, he would not have been able to make the second incision by his own hand. The wound pattern indicated that a left-handed person made the cuts, but the police could not confirm whether or not Barnes was left handed. Even if he was, he had sustained a gunshot wound to his left arm, casting doubt on his ability to use it. The coroner did not rule the case a suicide, but stated noncommittally that Barnes's death resulted from hemorrhaging caused by two incised wounds on the throat.

To add to the mystery, a year later, a hunter found the skeletal remains of a man in the swamp near the location where Barnes's body was discovered. The skeleton was that of a white man, and in the pocket of the coat was a revolver with four discharged chambers. The body offered no other identifying clues. This find, however, called into question law enforcement claims that Barnes worked alone and supported the railroad employees' claims that they were attacked by two men.

The mystery surrounding the two bodies lingers. While his upbringing and education could have sent him down a less dangerous path, Barnes chose to be a thief. He spent most of his adult life living under aliases and evading the police, and met a violent death in the swamps of New Orleans.

PART III

MURDER

AND MORE

ANTONIO DI BLASI

Shirley Apley

One spring day in Boston, Massachusetts, a man died in an altercation over a pile of garbage. On May 23, 1898, James Ellis, a foreman in the street-cleaning division of the city, walked through the West End neighborhood on his appointed rounds. Many immigrants called this area of multi-story brick tenements home. As Ellis patrolled, he admonished residents and merchants alike to keep their sidewalks clean. One of the businessmen he confronted was Antonio Di Blasi, a native of Italy, who happened to be standing outside his fruit stand on Pitts-Street Place when Ellis passed by. When the foreman told him to remove the debris near his storefront, Di Blasi refused to comply and explained that the trash belonged to his upstairs neighbors, who had thrown it out of their window. Taking exception to the shopkeeper's insubordination, Ellis struck the man with his

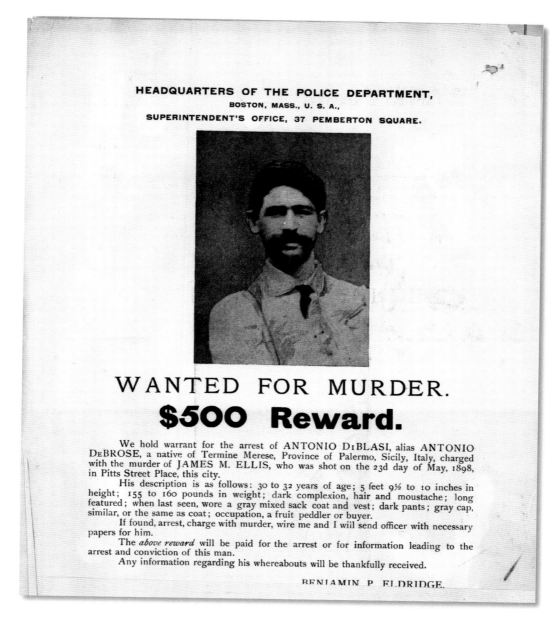

HEADQUARTERS OF THE POLICE DEPARTMENT,
BOSTON, MASS., U. S. A.,
SUPERINTENDENT'S OFFICE, 37 PEMBERTON SQUARE.

WANTED FOR MURDER.
$500 Reward.

We hold warrant for the arrest of ANTONIO DiBLASI, alias ANTONIO DeBROSE, a native of Termine Merese, Province of Palermo, Sicily, Italy, charged with the murder of JAMES M. ELLIS, who was shot on the 23d day of May, 1898, in Pitts Street Place, this city.

His description is as follows: 30 to 32 years of age; 5 feet 9½ to 10 inches in height; 155 to 160 pounds in weight; dark complexion, hair and moustache; long featured; when last seen, wore a gray mixed sack coat and vest; dark pants; gray cap, similar, or the same as coat; occupation, a fruit peddler or buyer.

If found, arrest, charge with murder, wire me and I will send officer with necessary papers for him.

The *above reward* will be paid for the arrest or for information leading to the arrest and conviction of this man.

Any information regarding his whereabouts will be thankfully received.

BENIAMIN P. ELDRIDGE,

club. In response, Di Blasi pulled a pistol from his hip pocket and shot the public works official in the eye. Surprisingly, Ellis managed to draw his own pistol and aim straight for Di Blasi's head. Di Blasi fired a second shot, which killed Ellis on the spot.

As part of the Street-Cleaning Division of the Boston Street Department, Ellis and his coworkers kept the public right-of-ways in the city clean. Though modern Americans often take public sanitation for granted, organized garbage pick-up in cities did not become an efficient process until the turn of the century. Residents of densely populated neighborhoods tended to throw all their waste into the streets, which created massive and putrid piles of trash on sidewalks and knee-deep muck in thoroughfares. Though everyone eventually agreed that health and cleanliness went hand in hand, it sometimes took persuasion that bordered on force for long-established habits to change.

Progressive-era Boston took sanitation seriously. The city increased its use of street-sweeping machines, the number of push-cart teams combing the streets, and strategically placed waste barrels. Departmental reports outline the likely source of animosity between Ellis and Di Blasi. In 1896 the Street-Cleaning Division stated in its annual report that if the populace obeyed the local statutes, its load would be greatly lightened. It argued that even with streets swept every night and patrolled during the day, "no condition of cleanliness can be preserved when the operations of the department are followed by a procession of the thoughtless, the indifferent, and the ignorant, casting [out] into the street refuse of fruit, torn scraps of letters, destroyed after perusal, the daily papers, and everything which ceases to have a use." The division specifically noted that "the tendency of fruit dealers and others selling goods . . . to throw refuse into the streets has been largely checked." Inspectors had the authority to report offenders to the police and require vendors to purchase trash barrels from the city if there were complaints about waste piles in front of their businesses. Failure to cooperate could result in the business permit being revoked.[45]

As a fruit vendor, Di Blasi undoubtedly attracted special attention from Foreman Ellis because of the governmental focus on his profession. Neither ethnicity nor geography were in his favor, either. In another report, the division head explained that conditions failed to improve in certain sections of the city such as in the West End, where there was a large foreign population of "entirely new and in many cases ignorant classes."[46] Official communications leave no doubt that the Ital-

ian owner of a fruit stand in Boston's West End would very likely run into problems with city inspectors over a trash pile. The fact that the matter escalated into a shoot-out indicates that the underlying social tension was palpable.

After Di Blasi killed Ellis, he hid out with friends and relatives in Boston until he could escape to New York City and board a ship back to Italy. He set sail on the SS *Fulda* on June 19, 1898, for the two-week trip. He travelled around the country for several months after his arrival, but eventually he renamed himself "Luigi," and settled into work as a fisherman in the vicinity of Messina, Sicily. In the interim, the City of Boston aggressively pursued Di Blasi on behalf of their murdered employee. They offered a reward of $500 (roughly equivalent to $14,000 today) for information leading to his arrest and conviction. The police department produced over one thousand circulars for distribution throughout the United States and Italy in hopes of solving the crime.

Antonio Cassette, an acquaintance of Di Blasi, had just returned to Italy himself. Not only did he know about the murder in America but he also knew about the substantial reward. Cassette arranged to meet Di Blasi, but first he advised the police in Palermo of his plan so that he might claim the money. Unfortunately for him, police chief Luigi Pastore already knew about the poster and Di Blasi's whereabouts.

When local authorities arrested him at the request of the Boston Police Department on February 4, 1899, he admitted to killing Ellis, but maintained that it was in self-defense. Though the department sent two officers overseas with a formal request from the United States for Di Blasi's extradition, the Italian government declined. They instead offered to prosecute him in their own courts. In Messina on the island of Sicily in January of 1900, Italian officials tried Antonio Di Blasi using testimony and documentation from the Boston policemen to make their case. To the great satisfaction of the City of Boston, he was convicted of the murder of James Ellis and sentenced to six years in prison.

Meanwhile, Cassette and Pastore quarreled over the $500 reward. Cassette felt that he was the first to inform the Italian police. We must assume that Pastore responded by reminding Mr. Cassette that they *were* the police or something to that effect, and they already had Di Blasi in their sights. The American consular agent in Italy sided with Pastore and recommended that he receive the award. The City of Boston agreed.

Escaped from the United States Penitentiary, F
Leavenworth, Kansas, July 12, 1899.

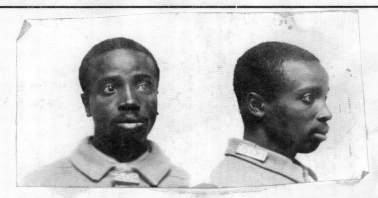

Sam Vaughn.

Age 25, 5 ft. 6 1-4 inches, Weight 131 lbs. Black hair, Black complexion, Dark brown eyes, Medium stout build, Small vertical scar 3-4 inch long 2 1-2 inch above inner left eyebrow near scalp, Small pit scar 1-2 inch above inner right eyebrow; Oblique scar 1-2 inch long on forehead 2 inches above center right eyebrow, Scar 1-2 inch long on left arm, outer 6 inches above elbow.

The reward of $60 will be paid for his arrest and detention until an Officer can reach him. Arrest and telegraph R. W. McClaughry, Warden, U. S. Penitentiary, Fort Leavenworth, Kansas.

SAM VAUGHN

Shirley Apley

In the wee hours of a cold Sunday morning in February 1898, two tenant farmers on the Ed Humdy farm awoke to flames. Their two places were about a quarter of a mile apart, but suffered similar damage. Barns and outbuildings containing tons of animal feed and tools were destroyed, and two lucky mules narrowly escaped when the rope that tied them burned in two. Conversation among neighbors revealed that the two fires began about the same time. In the daylight, clues suggested

that the culprit was a local named Sam Vaughn, so officers promptly arrested him for causing this major loss of property.

Since at least May of the previous year, several African American residents of the Humdy area north of Ardmore, Oklahoma, had been embroiled in personal conflict. One report in the *Daily Ardmoreite* concluded that "the idea of taking a quiet shot at each other is getting to be a daily business." One of the arson victims was

Bob Landers, who had once been arrested for attempted murder in a land dispute. The arrest of Sam Vaughn did little to resolve the unrest: late in 1898, while Vaughn sat in the federal jail in Oklahoma City, Ed Humdy's gin burned, and a murder occurred there a year later.[47]

In December of 1898, a jury convicted Sam Vaughn and sent him to Leavenworth Prison to do one year of hard labor. After several months, officials paroled him to drive a team back and forth to the rock quarries to retrieve materials for new buildings under construction at the prison. Apparently, this opportunity offered Vaughn a taste of the freedom he once enjoyed. After about a month on the new detail, he made a successful escape, and a wanted poster was issued that featured his prison mug shot and offered a $60 reward for his recapture. Interestingly, the circular that authorities distributed made no mention of what put him in Leavenworth in the first place.

The escapee, a native of Arkansas, headed for Texas. Vaughn settled into a comparatively quiet life in Fort Worth as Fred Brooks. He did odd jobs, apparently both legal and illegal, to support himself. One Sunday evening in March 1901, he attempted to liberate some items from the home of Claude Van Zandt, a grocery and grain broker who was the son of prominent Fort Worth physician Isaac Lycurgus Van Zandt. After the police apprehended him, he revealed his secret, and Fort Worth made it known to authorities in Kansas. "Dear Sir: The negro we have, Fred Brooks, insists that he is an escaped convict from your prison." Several letters passed between Fort Worth Police Chief William Rea and Leavenworth Prison Warden Robert McClaughry before they determined that Fred Brooks was indeed escapee Sam Vaughn. A deputy warden promptly took the train to Fort Worth to retrieve the wayward captive. While serving out the remainder of his sentence, Vaughn pleaded guilty in the burglary case in Texas and received a five-year hitch in the state penitentiary at Huntsville for that crime.[48]

Officials released Sam Vaughn from prison on March 19, 1906. He returned to Fort Worth, where some of his family resided, and attempted—unsuccessfully—to keep a low profile. He married in September 1907, but according to his new wife, Genie, there was little wedded bliss. Vaughn was arrested in August 1908 for aggravated assault upon his wife. Drawing upon past experience, he managed to escape again. This time, he found a broken bar in his cell and bent the adjoining one just far enough to squeeze out. If he intended to make amends to Genie, it was too late. He was recaptured, and she left him after he was convicted of the assault. When she filed for divorce in May 1909, Genie provided a long narrative of the abuse she had suffered at Vaughn's hand. She explained that throughout their short marriage he drank often and "treated her in a cruel and outrageous manner, beating her with chairs and anything he could lay his hands on." Furthermore, he "called her . . . indecent, obscene, and vulgar names and continually kept up a series of deliberate insults and studied vexations and provocations" that made it impossible for them to live together. The judge granted Genie her divorce in November 1910. Vaughn remained in the city until his death on October 30, 1944, the result of first and second degree burns he received in an accident. He was buried in the People's Burial Park by the Baker Funeral Home, a family-operated business which continues to serve the African American community of Fort Worth.[49]

$400 REWARD.

Wanted for murder of M. M. Bomar, Deputy Sheriff of Henry County, Tenn., Tom Tharpe, a negro, 30 years old, weight about 150 lbs., height about 5 ft. 10 in. Brown skin. Has asthmatic trouble. Pleasing manners. Holds head erect when addressing one. Smooth white teeth, light mustache thin in center.

Reward Good.

R. H. MILLS,
Chief of Police, Paris, Tenn.

TOM THARPE

Shirley Apley

On the evening of September 1, 1901, Tom Tharpe and Elzie Fields, two young black men in their late twenties, helped sponsor a fundraising picnic to support the efforts of a favorite minister. In a grove of trees by the railroad tracks near Mansfield, Tennessee, the men and their friends set up a Flying Jenny or homemade merry-go-round, a cake walk, an area for dancing, and several stands selling fried fish, watermelon, and lemonade for the African American residents of the area. Fields supervised the Flying Jenny while Tharpe operated the lemonade stand, using a galvanized tub he borrowed early that morning from Loge Tharpe, who lived roughly fifty yards from the grove.

Tom Tharpe brought two pistols to the picnic with the hope of selling one to his buddy Will Teague. He kept one in an outer coat pocket and the other on the inside. Throughout the day Tom participated in picnic activities, later reporting that he enjoyed the cake walk and dancing the most. When the picnic finally wound down, Tom intended to ride home with Willie Broach in a buggy; however, he had to decline when he remembered that he needed to return Loge Tharpe's tub.

As Tharpe walked the short distance to the house someone still in the grove of trees threw a rock at him. He hollered "mind what you're at" in the direction of the offender. He placed the tub on Loge's front porch and searched the timbers for the rock thrower. He saw only one person in the vicinity, and he was standing by the cattle guard near the railroad track. Suddenly, he heard someone shout, "look out," as a shot rang out in the night. He returned the fire. Confused and worried, he headed down the tracks toward the home of another neighbor seventy yards away.

As Tharpe approached the house, he saw two white men running toward him. Though he did not know it at the time, they were Deputy Sheriff Marshal Bomar and his friend, railroad section foreman W. M. McCabe, who intended to arrest him for disturbing the peace with his gunfire. When they were within a few feet of him, Bomar shouted "Halt!" and pointed a pistol at him. Tharpe stopped. As they stepped closer, McCabe asked why his companion did not just shoot the suspect who was now backing away. In response, Bomar opened fire. Tharpe shot back and fell into a gully by the railroad tracks, not realizing that he had wounded the deputy in the stomach.

Twenty-eight-year-old Marshal Bomar lived and labored on his parents' farm at the time of the incident. One brother served as a local constable and another worked in the dry goods store, so the entire family was well-known throughout the area. Bomar himself was popular in his social circle. As a result, it came as a sad shock to many in the community when they learned that despite the best efforts of local physicians, Bomar lived only a few hours after the shooting.

The death of the admired deputy at Tharpe's hands enraged his law enforcement colleagues and the public at large. The suspect's identity was no mystery. Tharpe's family were long-time Henry County residents and lived in close proximity to Bomar and McCabe, who must have recognized him immediately. Some reports even claimed Bomar had threatened to arrest Tharpe earlier in the day. Citizens began the search with bloodhounds, soon joined by Sheriff A. M. Wharton, a detective, and their own well-trained dogs, but the trail was cold. Undeterred, they spent days combing the county, but the only sign they found of Tharpe was one of his pistols dropped near his father's house. Meanwhile, no one doubted that should Tharpe be caught, mob violence was possible. With rumors flying and sightings reported near and far, the chief of police at the county seat of Paris issued a postcard. In addition to a brief description of Thomas Tharpe and a small photo, it advertised a $400 reward composed of $200 from the governor of Tennessee and $200 from county residents.

While McCabe attended to Bomar on the night of the shooting, Tharpe ran to his parents' farm through fields and back roads, pausing along the way because of his asthma. Soon he learned the severity of his crime, and surely understood this meant his life was in danger.

He fled into the bottoms of the nearby Big Sandy River. Having avoided the search parties, he hid out in the swamps, surviving with the help of friends who brought him supplies.

While law enforcement officers followed up on leads from Arkansas and Missouri on Tharpe's whereabouts, J. J. Lowry, a former Paris city marshal and Henry County sheriff, kept an eye out for him closer to home. He surveilled the black neighborhood near the picnic ground until he noticed two boys walking into the river bottoms carrying food. They led him straight to the fugitive. Lowry caught him off guard as he was eating and took him into custody without incident a little over a month after Bomar's death. The Circuit Court Judge William Swiggart ordered Tharpe to be taken directly to the jail in Union City, Tennessee, two counties away, to protect him from potential mob violence in Henry County.

Despite the court's concern for Tharpe's safety, he was charged with first-degree murder and brought to Paris for trial in January 1902. The State brought thirty-five witnesses. The defense? Only one. The weeklong trial ended in a conviction, but upon review Judge Swiggart determined that Tharpe had not received a fair trial, set the verdict aside, and ordered a new trial to be held elsewhere. As a result, a hundred or more enraged citizens finally organized the lynch mob everyone expected, but they were held back by special guards. When even larger numbers gathered with the same intent a few nights later, a deputy spirited Tharpe out of the jail just in time. The two men met the sheriff at a nearby railroad crossing and flagged down a train to transport the prisoner over sixty miles away to Clarksville, Tennessee, for safekeeping.

The second trial began in December 1902 in Dresden, where the jury pool would at least come from another county, albeit an adjoining one. Those jurors convicted Tharpe of second-degree murder and sentenced him to twenty years in the newly constructed Tennessee State Penitentiary at Nashville. Six months later the Tennessee Supreme Court confirmed the decision on appeal.

CHARLES B. HADLEY

O. K. Carter

The strangulation, sexual assault, and murder of fifteen-year-old Nora Fuller of San Francisco in 1902 still shows up on occasional media lists of the great unsolved mysteries in city history. Equally strange is the fact that the first identified suspect in the case, *San Francisco Chronicle* bookkeeper Charles B. Hadley, was never found. As the details of the investigation unwound, however, it became increasingly doubtful that Hadley was the culprit at all. Even so, his wanted poster was the only one ever issued for the crime.

Here is how it unfolded: On January 10, 1902, Eleanor "Nora" Fuller answered a job advertisement she found in the *San Francisco Chronicle* for a young girl to take care of a baby, offering a good home and good wages. The next day she received a postcard from a man who identified himself as John Bennett, who had posted the ad. He asked her to meet him at a local restaurant. That afternoon, Fuller left her home to meet her prospective new employer. She phoned home an hour later to say she was at Bennett's residence at 1500 Geary Street, and he wanted her to start work immediately. Mrs. Fuller told her to come home instead and begin the new job on Monday. The girl agreed.

But she did not return home. No one ever heard from the young woman again. It was later determined that 1500 Geary Street was a vacant lot. Inexplicably, her mother did not

ARREST FOR MURDER

DEPARTMENT OF POLICE.
San Francisco, California, U. S. A., May 2, 1902.

Handwriting of Charles B. Hadley

Photograph of Charles B. Hadley.

CHARLES B. HADLEY, whose photograph and handwriting appear hereon, is wanted by this department for the murder of Miss Eleanor Maude Fuller, a girl fifteen years of age. This girl, who was commonly known as Nora Fuller, left her home in this city on the afternoon of January 11, 1902, in response to a newspaper advertisement for a young white girl to take care of a baby in a good home and with a good family. She was to meet her employer at a restaurant in the business portion of the city. After leaving her home, the girl was not again seen alive. On February 8, 1902, the dead body of the girl was found in an unfurnished house at No. 2211 Sutter Street, this city. The house had, previous to January 11, 1902, been rented and supplied with a second-hand bed and second-hand bed clothing. The body of the girl was found on this bed. The girl had been strangled to death, and previous to death she had been sexually abused.

On the morning of January 16, 1902, the San Francisco newspapers published extended accounts of the mysterious disappearance of Eleanor Maude Fuller, together with portraits of the girl. On that day also Charles B. Hadley mysteriously disappeared from San Francisco, and has not since been seen. This department, acting upon evidence now in its possession, accuses Charles B. Hadley of the murder of Eleanor Maude Fuller, and demands his arrest and detention wherever he may be found.

PERSONAL DESCRIPTION OF CHARLES B. HADLEY: American; apparent age, 40 years; height about 5 feet 9 inches; weight about 180 pounds; hair dark and tinged with gray, parted on right side and combed flat, as per photograph; face square and full, and without beard or moustache; chin square and slightly dimpled; mouth large and straight; nose rather broad, bridge slightly humped, base slightly flattened, point of base hangs below line of nostrils; ears medium large and prominent; eyes gray, medium large and well open.

MARKS AND SCARS: Irregular oblique scar, right upper lip; thin scar, right eye-lid; slight droop to right eye-lid; concave irregularity, lower rim right ear; mole, center of throat.

DRESS: Generally wears plain business suit of good material, but has been known to assume garb which gave him the appearance of either a physician or a Protestant clergyman; wears diamond ring and diamond shirt-stud; generally wears collar and necktie as shown in photograph.

GENERAL APPEARANCE: Walks with body very erect, but with head tilted forward; one leg is slightly bowed, and it shows when he walks; is a man of pleasing address, good conversationalist, correct language as to grammar, fairly good education.

HABITS AND PECULIARITIES: Cohabited with a woman not his wife during one year prior to his disappearance; resided in lodging houses located in questionable portions of the city; his female companions were inmates of houses of prostitution, or other women of loose character; he drank heavily at times, often remaining drunk for a week; he spent his money freely, and was considered a good fellow by the men and women with whom he associated; he ate at restaurants, and always had his meals cooked to order, avoiding the regular bill of fare; he generally ate beefsteak, and would never eat the tenderloin portion of the steak; he was fond of salads, and of fried chicken and chicken prepared with mushrooms; he always carried a newspaper in his coat pocket; he sometimes wore false moustaches, and had them made to his order.

HISTORY: During the fourteen years prior to his disappearance, Hadley was employed as a bookkeeper by the San Francisco Examiner, a daily newspaper, and for some time prior to his disappearance he was subscription cashier for that paper. His mother's name is Mrs. John Start (widow) who now resides in Chicago, Illinois, U. S. A.

All officers who shall receive copies of this circular are requested to cause a diligent search of all hotels and lodging houses, steamship and railway ticket offices within their respective jurisdictions, for the purpose of ascertaining the present or prospective whereabouts of Charles B. Hadley. It is further requested that any positive information touching this matter be communicated without delay to this department. In the event of the arrest of any person suspected of being Charles B. Hadley, a photograph and full description of the suspected person should be at once taken and forwarded to this department.

GEORGE W. WITTMAN, Chief of Police.

report her daughter's disappearance for a week. One of Nora's girlfriends also told police that the teenager had a much older boyfriend, who she believed was called Bennett, and that she frequently met Bennett without her mother's knowledge. Newspapers described her as a missing person on January 16, coincidentally—or not—the same day Charles Hadley vanished.

A property inspector found Fuller's decomposing body on February 8, almost a month after she was last seen, on a bed in an otherwise unfurnished rent house on Sutter Street in San Francisco. She had been sexually abused and strangled. An autopsy determined that she had also been drinking alcohol. Her murder was prominently mentioned in local newspapers. It was possible she was killed the same day she answered the advertisement.

San Francisco police initially assigned a single detective to the case, though that number rose to a half dozen as time passed and no arrest was made despite some initial promising leads. They determined a man who said he was C. B. Hawkins leased the Sutter Street house two days before Fuller's disappearance. At a furniture store Hawkins bought just enough to temporarily furnish one room. He had an odd demand: his purchases had to be delivered that very night. He had the furniture arranged in a small room in the back of the second story of the new home, leaving the rest of the house empty.

The owner of a local eatery called the Popular Restaurant told detectives that at 5:30 p.m. on the afternoon Nora last spoke with her mother, a man who frequented the establishment many years—known to him only as "Tenderloin" because that was all the customer ate—told him a young girl was on her way there. He asked the proprietor to send her to his table when she arrived. He said "Tenderloin" waited impatiently, then went outside where he presumably met her. He was the not seen at the restaurant again.

Charles Hadley emerged as a suspect in the case when the police learned that the bookkeeper had stolen money from his firm and apparently fled. His former girlfriend, Ollie Blasier, told investigators that his handwriting resembled a facsimile of the signature of "C. B. Hawkins" that had appeared in newspapers. It was obvious that Blasier and Hadley had not departed on the best of terms. She appeared convinced Hadley was the murderer, but whether her claims were in earnest, in retribution, or both remained unclear. Police dug into the case and discovered Hadley was wanted for embezzlement in Minneapolis under another name. Blasier talked freely to both police and the press. She said that before he vanished, Hadley had intently read articles about Fuller's case, which "greatly disturbed" him. She said she had found some garments of his that had blood on them, and she too recalled his particular food preferences.

The wanted poster issued by the San Francisco authorities made note of Hadley's fondness for tenderloin and salads, but generally described him in unflattering terms. It reported that he was known to cohabitate with a woman not his wife, that he resided in lodging houses in questionable portions of the city, and that his female companions were inmates of houses of prostitution or other women of loose character. It noted that he drank heavily at times, spent money freely, always carried a newspaper in his coat pocket, sometimes wore a fake moustache, and for fourteen years had been employed as a bookkeeper at the *San Francisco Examiner*.

Ever optimistic, the *San Francisco Call* produced an article proclaiming "Police Nearing Solution of the Fuller Mystery" on March 24, after police warmed to the idea that Hadley was the culprit. Despite the publicity, the wanted poster offered no reward for Hadley, an oversight that might have helped draw out more information on his whereabouts.

Hadley, who was never found, may have spent the rest of his days living under yet another pseudonym. For that matter, he may not have had anything to do with the murder. With no arrest and nothing to build a case on but speculation, Nora Fuller's sad story quickly faded to smaller, often contradictory articles on the back pages of newspapers before it disappeared completely. Over the years, catastrophic earthquakes and fires in San Francisco destroyed detective case notes and other official documents related to the investigation. This is one cold case with little chance of ever being solved.

$600.00 Reward

Six Hundred Dollars Reward (which includes the three hundred dollars standing reward of Wells Fargo & Co.) will be paid by the Colorado and Southern Railway Co. and Wells Fargo & Co. for the arrest and delivery to the sheriff of Las Animas County, Colo., of Guy LeCroix, alias G. G. Gates, alias Guy Williams, alias Guy Endingscourt, wanted on the charge of attempted train robbery, near Beshoar Junction, on the line of the C. & S. Ry., the night of Nov. 18th, 1902.

DESCRIBED AS FOLLOWS:

Height, about 5 feet 10½ inches; Weight, about 165 pounds; Age, 23 to 25 years; Eyes, black, left one bulges slightly; Hair, black, parts in the middle; Complexion, dark; smooth face; rather short neck; stands erect; square shoulders; index finger on right hand crooked at first joint, index and second finger on left hand stiff, second finger not so stiff as index finger.

[The information in regard to the fingers may be wrong, but we think it is right.] Scar from gun-shot wound on left fore-arm. Wears No. 7 hat and about a No. 8 shoe; wears No. 15½ collar, slim hands, is neat in appearance. At times assumes Scotch or Irish brogue; has worked in coal mines at Sopris, Starkville and Gray Creek, Colo., but is not a practical coal miner; claims to have worked on range as cow-boy. We have positive evidence to convict this man. If arrested, hold and wire:

CHAS. DYER,
Gen. Supt. Colo. & So. Ry. Co.,
Denver, Colo.

December 5, 1902.

C. H. YOUNG,
Supt. Wells Fargo & Co.,
Denver, Colo.

GUY LECROIX (GEORGE GATES)

O. K. Carter

When the Pinkerton National Detective Agency president William Pinkerton delivered a speech titled "Train Robberies and Train Robbers" before the International Association of Chiefs of Police in 1907, he naturally included a list of now-infamous killers and gunmen—the Jessie James gang, Black Bart, the Dalton Brothers, Billy Miner, and the Younger brothers. He also noted an equally dangerous gang that is little known today—the Gates Boys, also known as the Copley Train Bandits. The group, led by George Gates with his younger brother Vernon as chief lieutenant, was among the final wave of post-1900 old West train and stagecoach robbers. They indiscriminately and routinely took loot from trains, stagecoaches, saloons, sheep camps, post offices, and any number of stores across Colorado, California, Oregon, and Washington before coming to an inglorious end in a shootout with a New Mexico posse in 1905.

Pinkerton noted a trend of brothers working together within many robbery gangs and ventured a guess as to the cause. "The hold-up robber originated among bad men of the gold mining camps," Pinkerton told the police chiefs. "Unsuccessful as a prospector, too lazy to work, and with enough bravado and criminal instinct to commit desperate crimes, he first robbed prospectors and miners en route on foot to stage stations, of their gold dust and nuggets, becoming bolder, looting stages and eventually after the railroads were built, he held-up railway trains and robbed express cars."[50]

Pinkerton's turn-of-the-century psychological profile seemed to fit the Gates siblings precisely. Because their exploits were so far flung and involved so many victims, a trail of wanted posters followed them across the western states. So many, in fact, that if all the rewards could be collectively claimed, they would amount to several thousand dollars.

Handsome, vain, well-spoken, and fancying himself a ladies' man, older brother George Gates initially studied to become a surveyor. He gave up that course to become a professional boxer, but that career was short lived, too. His opponent knocked him out in his first fight, giving him a slightly bulging eye for the rest of his life. After that, he drifted from job to job, mostly as a miner, but he also claimed to have done a little cowboy work. Because neither position paid well and both were physically difficult, Gates decided that a life of crime better suited his long-term goals.

George Gates endured some painful learning experiences early in his career. In his first attempt at armed robbery, a solo stickup of Piccardo's Saloon in Amador County, California, he left the saloon with an estimated twenty-five dollars and a double-barrel shotgun load of light birdshot. Nonetheless, he escaped capture. Thereafter, he used the name Guy LeCroix, one of the many aliases he lifted from the romance novels he read avidly.

In California, he persuaded his landlord, Abraham Hudson, that they could make more money robbing trains than by mining. On November 18, 1902, he and Hudson flagged down the Colorado and Southern Train No. 8 near Trindad with a red-light lantern rigged by Hudson's wife. This job was a bigger disaster than the first. When Wells Fargo messenger Hollis Schriber killed Hudson with a blast of buckshot to the stomach before they ever boarded the train, Gates fled without a dime.

Undeterred, he recruited his younger brother, twenty-year-old Edward "Vernon" Gates, a skilled sharpshooter, and James Arnett, described in wanted posters as "a half-breed Mexican," along with John Reid, a Swede, to collaborate with him. The gang began a series of robberies, moving from state to state and from legal jurisdiction to legal jurisdiction. Everywhere they went a different reward poster was issued, offering anything from a few hundred dollars to as much as $2,500.

The robbery that earned the gang its "Copley Train Bandits" name was a particularly ugly affair. In an attempt to rob the Oregon Express near Shasta, California, one of the group killed a messenger who dared open the door of his car to peer out during the commotion. Part of the recognition came because of the clerk's cold-blooded murder, but it also attracted attention because the men made such an explosive mistake this time. The conductor on board explained that because the robbers placed too much dynamite on the safe, "it broke the structure, but it blew all the contents of the safe to pieces and scattered it all over the surrounding country," along with parts of the express car. Witnesses felt certain that the Gates crew left with nothing. For that episode alone, however, they did gain an additional bounty of $850 on each man: $300 from the State of California, $300 from Wells Fargo, and $250 from the Southern Pacific Railroad.[51]

Before and after the holdup at Copley Station, the bandits had been staying at a boarding house in Dunsmuir, California, where George Gates used his legendary charms to seduce a married woman and persuade her to help feed and hide the gang. In a letter intercepted by the law, he wrote that she should "Give Tom Rough on Rats [poison] and get rid of him. Do it in a way that everyone will think it is a mistake." With her husband out of the way, Gates hoped she would join him on the road. The Copley bandits remained free, but the woman was charged as an accomplice to the lawbreakers.[52]

Eventually law enforcement put so much pressure on the group that two members decided to go their own way. Meanwhile, the Gateses lit off for Mexico via New Mexico, where they planned to steal some spending money for the trip. They held up a saloon in Lordsburg in the southwest part of the state on March 15, 1905, no doubt expecting an easy escape. Instead, the town sheriff quickly organized a posse which caught up to the brothers in a house near the town of Separ where they had stopped for the night. They resisted arrest, but their good luck had evaporated. They died at the hands of Grant County Deputy Sheriff Herb McGrath and were buried in unmarked graves—a swift end to the meteoric rise and fall of the Copley Train Bandits.

$3850.00 Reward!

JOHN P. DUNN,

Wanted for Murder at Clarksville, Ark., Feb. 5, 1902.

DESCRIPTION.

NAME: John P. Dunn, alias Dick Dines, alias Big Dick. Nationality, American; criminal occupation, bank burglar and gambler; age, 35; height, 6 feet; weight, 175 to 185 pounds; eyes, yellow gray; florid or sandy complexion; build, good; color of hair, dark, with a few gray hairs over each ear.

REMARKS: Wears a number eleven shoe; has large wrists; smoothe white hands; very positive talker; is known as a high-roller among gamblers. When he escaped from hospital at Wichita, Kansas, had smoothe face, but beard will be sandy or light brown. Teeth, fairly good, some gold in upper teeth on right side of jaw.

WOUNDED: Has gun shot wound in right hip, ball penetrated illium about one inch below crest. Abcess formed on inside of hip bone. The hole in hip bone made by the ball was enlarged by the surgeon in charge. Ball has never been found. When he escaped, April 3, wound was not healed. It may be healed at this time, but will leave a large deep scar on right hip. If not healed will have the appearance of a suppurating wound after a surgical operation. In this case Dunn will most likely be found in some private or public hospital for he will be compelled to have the care of a competent surgeon or nurse. It is the opinion of the physicans who examined Dunn that he will never recover unless the ball is located and taken out, as they think ball was infected from the fact that wound did not heal as fast as expected.

CRIME AND REWARD: At 2:30 on the morning of February 5, 1902, the Bank of Clarksville, Ark., was burglarized and John H. Powers, Sheriff of Johnson County, while trying to prevent the burglary, was murdered by the parties. The Governor of the State of Arkansas, the County of Johnson, the Banks of Clarksville, and reliable private subscriptions make the total reward for the arrest and conviction of the parties implicated $11,000.00, or $2750.00 for each one implicated. John P. Dunn and George Durham, alias Jersey Durham, alias Oklahoma George, were arrested in Wichita, Kan., February 16, 1902. Dunn was found in St. Francis hospital suffering from wound as above described, which he was supposed to have received at the hands of Sheriff Powers before his death. Durham was taken to Clarksville, Ark., where he waived preliminary examination and was bound over to the next term of Court. Dunn escaped from the hospital April 3. The pictures of Dunn are excellent and of recent date, but he will most likely have full beard at this time.

The Governor of the State of Kansas issued a proclamation offering $500 reward for the delivery of John P. Dunn to Sheriff King, at Clarksville, Ark., or for his body delivered to the Chief of Police at Wichita, Kansas.

Joe B. King, Sheriff Johnson County, Ark., offers a further reward of $600, for John P. Dunn, dead or alive delivered at Clarksville, Ark.

The above makes a reward of $1100 for John P. Dunn, dead or alive, delivered to either J. B. King or Chief of Police at Wichita, Kansas. In addition to the $1100 there is $2750 reward to be paid after the conviction of Dunn for the above crime.

ALL OFFICERS: The murder of Brother Officer Powers was a cold blooded one and occurred while in discharge of his duty. And this, outside of the fact of the large reward offered should be a sufficient inducement to put forth every effort to capture this man and to deliver him to the proper authorities. In case of capture or death of John P. Dunn notify J. B. King, Sheriff, Clarksville, Johnson County, Arkansas, or Chief of Police, Wichita, Kansas, and a man will be sent at once to identify him.

Clarksville, Johnson Co., Ark., April 29, 1902.

J. B. KING, Sheriff.

JOHN P. DUNN

O. K. Carter

Johnson County Sheriff John Hall Powers's peaceful sleep in Clarksville, Arkansas, ended abruptly the night of February 5, 1902, when he woke to a powerful explosion at the nearby bank. He realized right away that a robbery was in progress, so he grabbed his Colt revolver and shouted to his roommate, Chief Deputy Joe King, to bring a shotgun.

Only half dressed, Powers rushed to the nearby Bank of Clarksville, where he was greeted by gunfire. He followed a suspect from an alley into the street in front of the bank, where a second suspect began firing at the lawman. Deputy Joe King still had not appeared when another, more powerful explosion rocked the bank. When the sheriff tried to enter the building, he was shot by a man later identified as John P. "Big Dick" Dunn. Apparently, Dunn served as the lookout as a fourth member of the gang collected what he could from the demolished safe.

Powers stumbled back to the entrance of his nearby apartment. Deputy King was still there, trying to repair the shotgun, which wasn't working. A doctor was summoned, but Powers, who was in great pain, had been fatally injured. The doctor administered morphine, and the sheriff slipped into a coma and died. He was young, only thirty-eight-years old, and had joined the sheriff's office twelve years earlier.

The bank robbers—Dunn, joined by Fred Underwood, George Durham, and James "Smilie Joe" Wallace—escaped with an estimated $1,500 in silver—roughly $40,000 in 2016 dollars—but they had used so many explosives to open the bank vault that most of the currency and gold had been blown to bits.

The governor himself appointed Deputy King the new sheriff. King then made it his personal mission to track the gang down. As it happened, Sheriff Powers's efforts to stop the burglary had not been entirely in vain. His return fire struck Dunn, leaving him with a serious bullet wound in the hip that required extensive medical treatment. Indeed, law enforcement tracked him down to the hospital in Wichita, Kansas, where he was arrested.

An armed guard was posted at Dunn's hospital door, but Dunn once again escaped—inspiring talk of conspiracy and bribery. Some witnesses in Clarksville, however, said that five men were involved—not four, so it's possible that a fifth member of the gang helped Dunn escape.

Prosecutors tried Durham, Underwood, and Wallace together. Underwood and Durham were sentenced to hang in 1903, a year to the day after the robbery. Before their execution they both read speeches to the people of Clarksville. They apologized for their misdeeds and thanked the people of the city for the kindnesses they showed the criminals during their confinement. Their bank-robbing careers ended on the gallows that day: the last men ever to be executed in Clarksville, Arkansas. "Smilie Joe" Wallace was sentenced to life in prison but somehow managed to escape. He was never recaptured.

That left newly anointed Sheriff King still looking for Dunn, the thirty-five-year-old killer of King's good friend Sheriff Powers. The prospects for Dunn's capture seemed good. Doctors predicted he would die without medical treatment, not only because the bullet had never been removed, but it had knocked a chunk out of his hip bone. His wanted poster featured two excellent photos and a description so complete it included the position of his gold teeth (upper right), his florid complexion, his "yellow gray eyes," and even his shoe size: eleven. The advertisement described his occupation as "bank burglar and high-roller gambler."

The financial incentives offered on the poster were considerable. For killing a lawman, they offered a combined reward—dead or alive—of $3,850. The average American workman at the time earned $400 annually, so the substantial sum must have been appealing, even to one of Dunn's criminal acquaintances.

King was confident the reward would lead him to Dunn soon enough. The public reported many sightings, but no arrest came. Clues to his whereabouts steadily dried up. Newspaper coverage, particularly after the 1903 hanging of Underwood and Durham, slowed to a trickle and then stopped.

No one appeared to claim the reward. Dunn, who was known to use several aliases, simply disappeared for twenty-eight years. King was no longer sheriff in 1930 when authorities received a tip that a man calling himself John Brown, a Las Vegas gambler, was in fact the notorious "Big Dick" Dunn. John Brown may or may not have been Dunn, but despite suspicions that he was, and had a murder charge pending against him, a Nevada judge released him on a fairly stiff $5,000 bail bond—a bond equivalent to about $70,000 in 2016 dollars. Clearly "John Brown" had financial resources. Dunn—if John Brown was, indeed, Dunn—disappeared again. In the end, John P. Dunn was never brought to justice.

The people of Clarksville did not forget John Hall Powers. A ten-foot-tall granite and marble monument to the slain lawman still stands at historic Oakland Memorial Cemetery on the outskirts of the city. Citizen donations funded the monument, which was constructed a year after Powers's death, and for years the bullet-riddled walls of downtown buildings outside the bank reminded the citizenry of that fateful night. In 2013, 111 years after the robbery and murder, Sheriff Jimmy Dorsey represented Powers in a touching way. Dorsey watched as Sheriff John Hall Powers's name was finally placed on the National Law Enforcement Officers Memorial in Washington, DC, during the annual candlelight vigil honoring slain lawmen.

JOHN B. (STOKES) SHAW

Kevin Foster

$700 REWARD!

Escaped from the Cleburne, Johnson County, Jail, on Tuesday, August 9th, 1898.

JOHN B. (STOKES) SHAW.

Age 43, but don't look to be over 40; 5 feet, 7 inches tall; weight about 115 pounds; has large blue eyes, sunk in his head; very prominent roman nose, crooked to the right side. Escaped jail last night, August 8th. Sentenced to hang for the murder of Tom Crain last November.

The governor has offered $500.00 reward for him and I will pay $200.00 reward for him in any jail in the United States.

The above picture is a good one and he will be easily recognized from it.

W. A. STEWART,
Sheriff Johnson County.
Cleburne, Texas.

Tom Crane, a farmer in Johnson County, Texas, reportedly had a very attractive wife. Unfortunately for him, one of his farm hands, John B. Shaw, fell in love with her. Shaw wanted to marry her and believed that killing Crane was a logical step toward his goal. On November 3, 1897, Shaw enlisted the help of his coworker, Lee Wilson, and together they lured the farmer away from a cotton patch he was working. Pulling a gun, Shaw marched Crane at gunpoint to the base of a hill, where he shot him three times and bashed in his skull. Shaw then returned to the farmhouse, where he sat down to have dinner with his victim's family. When Crane did not return by the next morning, a search was organized. Searchers found his body two days later.

Suspicion fell on the two farm hands, so Sheriff Tom Stewart brought them in for questioning. Shaw initially denied involvement and blamed Wilson for the murder, but later he admitted his crime. Johnson County quickly organized a trial, and Wilson, the coconspirator, testified against him. The jury convicted Shaw of the murder and sentenced him to death by hanging. In exchange for his testimony, Wilson was given a life sentence.

On August 8, 1898, just days before his execution, Shaw escaped from the Johnson County Jail. Jail guard Tom Morgan lived in the building and was asleep on a cot just outside of Shaw's cell door. He locked his prisoner in and shackled him to the floor of the cell, so Morgan relaxed to the extent that he took his pants off to be cooler, leaving them beside the cot. With a file he had acquired, Shaw somehow broke the lock on the chain so he could move around his cell. He then used a piece of wire he found to fashion a hook, which he attached to a rolled-up issue of the *Dallas Morning News*. With that he snagged the jailer's pants and dragged them across the room. Shaw got the keys from the pocket and unlocked his cell door. He bound and gagged the sleeping guard, removed the shackles from his legs, and slipped out the jail's front door.

A furor arose over the escape. Johnson and adjoining counties formed posses. Sheriff W. A. Stewart and Texas Governor Charles Culberson offered rewards totaling $1,000. Sheriff Stewart also issued a wanted poster offering a $700 reward from Johnson County alone. Circulars went out to law enforcement agencies across Texas. Clues suggested that Shaw hid for awhile in the Brazos River bottoms of Johnson County, a largely impenetrable brushy area. Then Sheriff Tom Bell of Hill County, Texas, received his first real lead: three days after his escape, Shaw had visited the home of an old friend named Frank Knight. Shaw stayed around the house for a day and a night, then disappeared. Bloodhounds followed Shaw's trail from Hill County through Navarro County, southeast of Dallas. Shaw eluded his pursuers by sticking to the Trinity River bottoms, where, according to news reports, "it [was] as hard to catch a man as to find a particular pebble on a beach."[53]

Shaw travelled by night and slept by day as searchers from four separate counties combed the area. Authorities watched railroad bridges, guarded ferries, closed roads, and took every possible precaution to prevent Shaw's escape. Finally, on the summer evening of August 20, 1898, news came from the city of Malakoff in Henderson County, Texas, that Shaw was captured while trying to cross the Cotton Belt Railroad Bridge over the Trinity River, five miles south of town. Thanks in large part to the wanted poster issued by Sheriff Stewart, Henderson County Constable Walter Anthony recognized Shaw as he was crossing the bridge and drew his gun, ordering Shaw to "throw up his hands." Shaw walked to Constable Anthony and surrendered. His flight through rugged terrain had taken a toll on the fugitive, leaving him "ragged, hungry, and footsore."

Anthony transported him to Malakoff, where Shaw admitted his identity. Henderson County sent telegrams all over the state announcing the capture of the convicted killer. The following day, Shaw was returned to his jail cell in Johnson County. Incarcerated again, Shaw told his story to the local lawmen and newspapers. He said he knew there would be a large manhunt, but he thought he could remain hidden in Cleburne. He thought he could get a head start by heading to Knight's house in Hill County. Once there, Shaw decided to head for the swamps—an experience that left his body torn, scratched, swollen, bloody, and covered with insect bites. His plan had been to hop a freight train and make his way to Mississippi, where he had family. Although he feared he might be captured when he decided to cross the bridge, even prison, he said, was preferable to the swamp.

After his capture, Shaw made one last attempt to appeal his sentence by claiming insanity. Shaw reported that his father, a Confederate soldier, had died during the war and that his family moved frequently, leaving him with no attachment to a home or a sense of security. Even his mother testified that when young, Shaw had a very cruel disposition and had participated in much violence in his life. His mother informed the court that he would kill chickens and turkeys, and one time even a horse, just to watch the animals die. Shaw admitted that when he was around fourteen or fifteen years old, he spent a year in jail for cattle theft in Lee County, Texas. He later served time in the penitentiary for a murder in Hill County, which he said he committed in defense of a friend. Shaw went so far as to suggest that being incarcerated had blunted his moral sense. His attorneys argued that under these circumstances, Shaw was not responsible for his crimes and that he should be confined in an asylum instead of being hanged. The appellate court disagreed, and on November 21, 1898, they rejected his appeal. His execution was immediately rescheduled for the following Friday, November 25. Tom Morgan guarded him yet again, but this time there were no mistakes.

On that fateful Friday morning, Sheriff Stewart led John B. Shaw from his cell to the gallows at the Johnson County Jail. Shaw stood calmly as the executioners made their preparations and slipped the noose around his neck. Though he proclaimed his innocence to that very day, hardly a soul in Texas believed him. When he dropped to his death, his chin hit the trap door as he fell; then the body was still. Sheriff Stewart cut the rope at 11:46 a.m. In Fort Worth, someone wrote a brief note on Shaw's wanted poster: "Executed in Cleburne, Johnson County Nov 2 / 98."

enhance their surveillance and to sift out any information that would lead to the capture of the dynamitards. The *St. Louis Republic* blamed European immigrant agitators with socialistic and anarchistic leanings.

A break in the case came when the St. Louis Transit Company surgeon, A. V. L. Brokaw, learned from a patient that an explosion was planned for midnight that evening. His informant gave him the names of the dynamitards, who were former company employees, and the location of the stored explosives. Dr. Brokaw immediately relayed the news to the transit company Division Superintendent James F. Davidson and the Night Chief of Police John N. Pickel. Officer Pickel deployed men but hesitated going after the stored dynamite without a warrant. Dr. Brokaw retorted, "Damn the search warrants. I tell you the stuff is where I say it is. If it is not, I will be responsible for any damage that may be claimed."[57]

The police, including Davidson and Dr. Brokaw, rushed to the scenes of the possible sabotages. On their way, they heard an explosion and realized they were too late. They encountered private watchman Patrick J. Higgins, who told them he had stopped two men in the vicinity. They claimed they were going fishing—one of them carried a bucket—and he allowed them to leave. When he mentioned Fred E. Northway, Officer Pickel looked on his sleeve cuff to confirm the the name matched one of the suspects. The party rushed to Northway's home and roused him from his sleep around 12:30 a.m. He first denied any involvement with dynamiting, but after further questioning he confessed that Morris Brennan had stored the dynamite in his home. The party dashed to Brennan's residence, located around the corner, and found explosives. After Brennan and Northway implicated James Swartz, Officer Pickel and his men tracked him down also. All three were jailed around 4:00 a.m. on Sunday, August 12.

Under "sweating" by police, Brennan and Northway admitted that they sought to dynamite the tracks, but not the cars. Swartz denied any involvement with the explosions and claimed he had seen the other suspects before

and after the sabotage. The police charged Brennan, Northway, and Swartz with obstructing street car tracks with explosives, a felony punishable with a maximum prison sentence of twenty years.

On November 22, 1900, a jury found Brennan guilty. After a dramatic plea for his release by his family, jurors sentenced him to ten years in prison instead of twenty. Brennan appealed the decision to the state supreme court and was freed on a $3,500 bond. When the justices affirmed the decision of the lower court on November 12, 1901, he fled. Law enforcement advertised a reward of $650 for his capture and return to the warden of the Missouri Penitentiary, but he remained a fugitive as late as 1905.

Fred Northway, who could not afford his bond, was found guilty on January 5, 1901, and sentenced to eight years in prison. After his release, he returned to St. Louis, married, and worked as a printer's assistant. On April 30, 1937, at the age of sixty-eight, Northway died of chronic emphysema.

James Swartz forfeited his $1,000 bond after he failed to appear in court on January 21, 1901. The chief of police posted a $250 reward for his capture. Swartz escaped to San Francisco, California, where he worked as a trolley car conductor. He was killed on April 9, 1902, when a train hit the vehicle he was operating. His body was returned to St. Louis a few days later.

Brennan, Swartz, and Northway represented the explosive disaffection of union members with the St. Louis Transit Company. Underlying class tension roiled the dispute that resulted in street fighting, property damage, injuries, and deaths. Despite repeated efforts of union leaders to seek mediation, the transit company hired scabs, called on the police to punish the strikers, and enlisted a posse of shotgun-toting guards. Ultimately, Local Union 131 voted on September 11, 1900, to stop the boycott. They acknowledged that they had failed to pressure the company into an acceptable agreement.

In 1918, the transit union went on strike again. This time they won most of the concessions they sought in 1900.

OTTO MATTHES

Peter R. Hacker

On August 16, 1898, Hampton W. Wall and two companions set out from Wall's home in Staunton, Illinois, to work on one of his farms. The sixty-six-year-old banker and former state senator owned thousands of acres in Macoupin and adjoining counties. As the wealthiest man in the region, Wall was well-respected, powerful, and feared. As events unfolded that day, it was also clear that he could be obstinate. That characteristic would cost him his life.

As Wall approached his farm, his temper flared when he spotted two stray horses, a mare and a colt, grazing in his clover field. He knew they belonged to the Schaedlichs, his German neighbors across the road, because their animals had trespassed before. He decided to impound them this time to teach the family a lesson. Dismounting from his buggy, he pursued the mare and caught it directly in front of the Schaedlich home. An irate Ernestina Schaedlich, described in the press as "a poor, wretched, ignorant German woman," and her fifteen-year-old daughter, Martha, emerged from their home to confront him. August, Ernestina's husband, was away working in the coal mines. Horse thieves were shot dead with impunity in nineteenth-century America, and Mrs. Schaedlich did not appreciate these men nabbing her animals.[58]

As Martha interpreted, her German-speaking mother conveyed clearly to Wall that she would pay any damages, but the horses would remain with her. He insisted on impounding them regardless, and told her to follow proper legal procedure to obtain their return. Seeing that Wall fully intended to take the horses, Mrs. Schaedlich attempted to shoot him with an ancient muzzle-loading shotgun. She was unsure how to fire the relic, however, and it failed to discharge. Wall then grabbed the gun barrel and a shoving match ensued. At some point, Otto Matthes, a German immigrant who worked as the Schaedlich's hired hand, joined the fray. At six feet tall and one hundred and seventy pounds, the young man cut an imposing figure. Somehow, he gained control of the old shotgun, and he knew how to fire it. As a hysterical Mrs. Schaedlich implored him to shoot, he calmly complied. At point blank range he pulled the trigger, spattering Wall's blood and brain matter onto the nearby horse. He then reentered the house, grabbed a few necessities, and disappeared. Wall's companions raced to town to sound the alarm.

Thus began one of the most extensive and fruitless manhunts in Illinois history. Over one hundred searchers beat the brush looking for Matthes. A pack of bloodhounds shipped in on a special train from Litchfield joined the party. There was little doubt as to Matthes's fate if he was apprehended. Headlines proclaimed, "Lynching Probable if the Murderer is Captured." Wall had been a pillar of Staunton society, a kingpin. His bank was one of the largest in Illinois, and his roots ran deep in the community. Born to Macoupin County pioneers, he rose from humble beginnings to an estimated worth of over $350,000 (well over $10,000,000 in today's dollars). His upper-class status seemed to garner more respect than envy, as evidenced by the fifteen hundred residents who attended his funeral. The citizens lamented his tragic death and vowed to make the seemingly cold and thuggish German immigrant who had killed him pay—if only they could catch him.

Most locals assumed Matthes would be apprehended after only a few hours, especially with the aid of the bloodhounds. But much of Southern Illinois was covered by wilderness, and the perpetrator had a head start. The eager citizens thoroughly probed miles of wild undergrowth for days, but came up empty. The bloodhounds picked up his trail occasionally, but his back-tracking completely befuddled them. Rumor spread that residents of the coal-mining community of Glen Carbon, where he'd been employed previously, were sheltering him. A somewhat hesitant sheriff's posse visited the mining area, the site of recent violent labor strife. Searching for the fugitive in the serenity of the woods had been one thing, but poking through a community of agitated coal miners was another. During the 1890s Illinois coal boom, incessant striking and strike breaking tore the area apart. It was a hotbed of trouble. Matthes, a member of the American Miners Association, and Wall, a major stockholder of the Consolidated Coal Company, took opposing sides in this polarized environment.

When Glen Carbon officials refused to allow the bloodhounds to stay in their calaboose, the posse's efforts in that town proved short-lived.

Wall's sons increased their initial reward from $500 to $2000, encouraging "every man who could get away from home to get his gun and go out on the scent for the murderer of our father." At a time when the average annual income was $380 for American families, and only $190 for local miners, $2000 seemed an inconceivable sum. The family also hired the Thiel Detective Service, a private agency based in nearby St. Louis that specialized in breaking labor unions, Pinkerton-style. Motivated by the $2000 reward, Thiel agents poured themselves into the hunt with frenzied dedication. The reward "has had the effect of stirring up dormant police officials all over the Middle West," stated one report. Newspapers and police departments circulated a simple image of Matthes sporting a boater's hat cocked to one side of his head. Later, the *Seattle Post-Intelligencer* ran a nearly identical portrait with the addition of a beer mug and a pool cue, opining that "everything about his pose indicates a reckless character."[59]

Accompanying descriptions placed his age at between twenty and twenty-four years and pointed out his prominent Adam's apple and Roman nose. They also highlighted his German origins and broken English. The wanted poster created by the Thiel Detective Service included an extra identifier: anarchist. The use of such an inflammatory word could ignite more interest in the case among mainstream Americans. Strikes, bombs, and assassinations were routinely attributed to anarchist immigrants, whether the accusation was valid or not. The allegations of anarchism combined with the huge reward succeeded beyond all expectations in lighting a fire under the Matthes case.

Between 1898 and 1902 newspapers nationwide reported no fewer than thirteen false arrests for the crime. The $2000 reward effectively kept the case from dropping out of sight. In a particularly embarrassing incident, the sheriff of Poplar Bluff, Missouri, arrested a highly suspicious man who fit the Matthes description perfectly. Further investigation revealed that the suspect was actually a Thiel operative. The most tragic case of mistaken identity occurred in Henry County, Tennessee, when Farmer Cole shot a German who appeared to be Matthes.

When the deputy sheriff arrived at the scene where the wounded man lay bleeding, Cole's wife held him off at gunpoint to prevent him from taking custody of the prisoner and claiming the reward. As Mrs. Cole held the deputy at bay, the German bled out. When Wall's son later viewed the corpse, he stated definitively that it was not Matthes. Public opinion turned against Cole as "it [was] feared he has unwittingly murdered an innocent man."[60]

In 1918 a man named Otto Matthes was arrested in New York City for attempting to blow up a flour mill. He was convicted of treasonous behavior and sent to Ellis Island for deportation. There is no hard evidence, however, that this was the same Otto Matthes. Mrs. Schaedlich was tried as an accessory to the murder, but the jury acquitted her in one of the "hardest fought legal contests ever held" in Macoupin County.

At the widow Martha Wall's funeral in 1928, thirty years after her husband's murder, a man named Hugh E. Menk came forward with a story he'd heard about Matthes. Menk once worked as an electrician in the mines and had often conversed with an old miner about the case. He claimed the elderly man told him that Matthes hid in a mine airshaft for months after the murder, and that every midnight he would take him food. Matthes eventually made his way back to Germany, according to the miner, but he would give no further details.[61]

FRANKLIN WILLIAMS

Gayle Hansen

On Thanksgiving Day, 1901, Franklin Williams, age twenty-five, clubbed his employer to death over a twenty-five-dollar debt the man owed him. A newcomer to Trenton, New Jersey, Williams claimed to be a former Catholic theology student. Though that was probably a lie, Williams did work on a variety of religious projects of different denominations. He also took a position with a small-time cigarmaker named John Kraus to support himself and his new bride.

Problems arose when Kraus, who owed Williams back wages, refused to pay. Each time Williams approached the cigarmaker about the money, he said the only way he would get it would be through the civil court because the business was not doing well. Two days before the murder, Williams made another effort to resolve the situation. Kraus offered Williams cigars in lieu of money, but Williams did not take kindly to this proposition and made it clear that he preferred cash. He went so far as to speak to the Justice of the Peace Manfred Naar about the issue, hoping that he might issue a warrant for Kraus, but he could not. Later, when he and Naar crossed paths again, the justice politely inquired about the matter. An angry Williams made a fateful mistake by telling Naar, "If that man don't pay me what he owes me, I'll fix him for good."[62]

Williams confronted Kraus for the last time with a wooden tool used in cigar making. He bashed in the man's head while his wife, eighteen-year-old Letitia "Lottie" Williams, looked on through a window in disbelief. She later told police that after Kraus was dead, her husband commanded her to help him scrub the floor to remove the traces of blood, and to help tie up the body, which Williams wrapped into a tight ball covered in newspaper and oilcloth for disposal. She was afraid to disobey, she said. She went along with his plan until she found herself waiting alone outside the livery stable as he hired a wagon to haul the body to the town incinerator. Overcome with the horror of the entire affair, she ran away. She ran frantically up and down the street looking for help, which she found in the arms of a fireman. Despite the fact he thought she was an escaped lunatic screaming about a fictional murderous husband,

he did take her into the kitchen of Anton Jaeger's saloon. There, they allowed her to tell her story and acted as though they knew what she was talking about in an attempt to calm her down. Discovering his wife missing when he exited the stable, Williams too ran frantically up and down the street trying to find her. Upon discovering her in the saloon kitchen, he put on a good show, coaxing her to rejoin him, calling her by endearing terms. When she refused to accompany him, he decided to leave the wagon where it stood and make for the nearest train station. Because the present company all thought they were merely dealing with a hysterical woman, no one bothered to stop him.

The authorities took Lottie Williams into custody to question her about her claims. Then they found Kraus's body wrapped in an oilcloth bundle, just as she had described. Immediately they mounted a search for the killer. They held Mrs. Williams as a witness for the State until the murderer was apprehended, although their concern was with finding the fugitive, not implicating his wife. She could not be compelled to testify against her husband, in any event.

Investigators tracked Williams as far as Bound Brook, New Jersey. Witnesses who saw a man there matching Williams's description told Trenton detective Charles Pilger that he seemed to be headed for Albany, New York. Although there was no corroboration of this idea, police hoped to apprehend the fugitive there.

Trenton Mayor Briggs meanwhile met with the Trenton Common Council Finance Committee and authorized a reward of $200. The city distributed five hundred circulars to law enforcement agencies in cities and towns across the East. Knowing that Williams could speak six languages fluently and would not hesitate to disguise himself, everyone feared he would be difficult to catch.

In the meantime, the Wilmington, Delaware, police notified their compatriots in Trenton that they knew the whereabouts of Franklin Williams's wife and two children. It seemed Williams was a bigamist and then some. Young as he was, he had married four, perhaps five women without bothering to divorce any of them. That being the case, his most recent bride was not his legal wife, and should the need arise, she could testify against him.

On December 19, 1901, William O'Brien, the deputy chief of police of Syracuse, New York, apprehended Franklin Williams in a saloon. Williams admitted his guilt and said not only was he not sorry for the crime, but he would do it again. He also confessed that he was not Franklin Williams but was actually George Hettrick, a native of Buffalo, New York.

Once they put the captured Hettrick on trial, his lawyers attempted an insanity defense. Several members of his Buffalo family testified that he was previously confined in an insane asylum. They claimed he had episodes not unlike epileptic fits, during which he knew not what he did. Apparently their testimony didn't help much, and insanity was ruled out. In fact, in the face of overwhelming evidence, including his own confession, the prosecution did not feel they needed Lottie Williams's testimony.

The Jury convicted George Hettrick of murder in only fifteen minutes. He promptly received a death sentence. The *Philadelphia Inquirer* reported that Hettrick lost his nerve and seemed in a state of collapse when the death sentence was announced, but his jailors reported that he was back in good spirits by the next morning. John Backes, counselor for the prisoner, was asked if there would be an appeal, but he stated that in this case he would appeal the verdict only if the court ordered it.

On April 4, 1902, George Hettrick, alias Franklin Williams, was hanged at the Mercer County Jail for the murder of John Kraus. The local news noted that though he seemed to lose his bravado in the days leading up to the execution, Hettrick regained his composure and calmly walked to the gallows between two Catholic priests on his last day. The trap door was sprung at 10:56 a.m. They pronounced him dead ten minutes later. His brother escorted his body back to Buffalo, to be buried by his grieving parents.

$200---Reward for Arrest and Conviction---$200

WANTED FOR MURDER!

Committed on November 28th, 1901, at Trenton, N. J.

FRANKLIN WILLIAMS, age 25; height, 5 feet 6 or 7 inches; stout build; weighs 160 pounds; dark complexion; long black hair; dark eyes; smooth face; good teeth; wore black suit, sack coat; long, dark blue cadet overcoat, with large collar; low black shoes; black Derby hat; had a scar on forehead and on right side of nose.

WILLIAMS formerly wore eye-glasses, but wore none when he left Trenton. Williams studied for the Roman Catholic Priesthood, and photograph taken dressed in that garb. He is a cigar maker by trade, and is a member of the Cigar Makers' Union.

Had in his possession an 18 size, 14-karat hunting-case, engraved, 15 jewel, Elgin movement gold watch.

The above reward will be paid for the arrest and conviction of the above person.

If located, arrest, hold and wire

JUDSON HINER,

TRENTON, N. J., Nov. 29th, 1901.   CHIEF OF POLICE.

CHARLES GREEN AND JOHN DOYLE

Harry Max Hill

Buffalo, New York, June 28, 1902: less than a year after the fatal shooting of President William McKinley at the Pan-American Exposition on September 6, 1901, a less momentous murder occurred. The victim was thirty-eight-year old Austin Joseph Crowe, who left behind five brothers and four sisters to mourn him. Known as a kind man with an excellent reputation among the citizens of Buffalo, he was a prominent member of St. Bridget's Catholic Church and the Catholic Mutual Benefit Association. Crowe operated a saloon and grocery at the intersection of Chicago and Fulton Streets, a business that had been in the family for almost forty years. He had taken over for his uncle, Austin Hanrahan, eight years before.

The police traced the movements of four well-dressed young men on the night of the murder. Witnesses observed them walking along the streets around 11:00 p.m. and going into a saloon. They bought a round of drinks and moved on to another saloon, where they bought another four beers and tobacco before they departed at around 11:30 p.m. When they entered Crowe's establishment it was almost closing time. No one saw the four go in. It is unclear whether what ensued was a planned robbery or a dispute over payment. Mrs. Julia Sexton, who lived above the saloon, claimed to have heard the conversation. She stated that the men paid five cents for the beers, but that Crowe demanded an extra fifteen cents. Apparently, he moved out from behind the bar and confronted the patrons while trying to evict them from the premises. She said a struggle ensued, and four shots were fired. Two of the shots hit Crowe, one in the breast and one in the mouth. Three of the culprits left the saloon through the door, and the other jumped out through a window. They headed toward East Buffalo and the train station.

The Buffalo police began an extensive search of the city and region for the killers. They arrested several suspects, but the witnesses could not identify any of them. In a canvas of the railyards, Detective Conover of the Pennsylvania Railroad reported that he saw four men who fit the right description at around 1:30 or 2:00 a.m. Sunday, but he did not know their current whereabouts.

Eventually, the police identified two of the suspects. The first was Charles Green, an eighteen-year-old from Buffalo. He had been released from the State Industrial School in Rochester, New York, on June 28, the day of the murder. The second was John Doyle, alias Fred Mercer, alias Timmy, a twenty-year old from Toronto, Ontario, Canada. He had been on parole from the New York State Reformatory since February 20. Their previous crimes had been committed in Buffalo. Mayor Erastus C. Knight, authorized by the Common Council of Buffalo, offered a reward of $1000 for the identification, arrest, and conviction of Charles Green and John Doyle.

The suspects turned up about a month later in Colorado. On the night of July 29, Denver police received a tip that the suspects were in the city. They first arrested John Richards, who had been seen in the company of John Doyle and Charles Green. Richards led them to the boarding house where he was sharing a room with the other suspects. The police caught Green there, but Doyle escaped. After learning that Doyle and an associate, Fred Chilton, were heading for Cheyenne, Wyoming, Denver detectives headed out in pursuit. Meanwhile local police searched rooming houses and staked out railroad tracks, hoping to find any sign of the other two fugitives.

Authorities learned that since leaving Buffalo, the group had been on a grand tour of sorts. Either together or in pairs they had visited Chicago and Omaha. At least two of them had made a side trip into Toronto, where they blabbed to other criminals about their exploits in New York. The police kept the two suspects they had in custody in widely separated jail cells and used the third degree to sweat confessions out of them. As part of their interrogation, the police woke them up during the night and told each that the other had confessed. Charles Green stuck to his story that he had been in Buffalo during the night of the murder, but never visited Crowe's saloon. Green identified a man he encountered on the road to Denver, Jimmy Gunnion, as the fourth man and the actual killer, but the police doubted his story. Eventually, John Richards fingered Chilton as the fourth man in the saloon. Buffalo Police Department Sergeant Cain O'Connor went to Denver to transport the prisoners back to Buffalo, where they were again placed in separate cells.

The court appointed Philip V. Fennelly to represent John Richards and Charles Green soon after their arrest in Denver. He recommended they waive extradition and demand separate trials. Fennelly appeared before Justice Daniel Kenefick seeking a writ of habeas corpus, but it was denied by another judge while Kenefick was away. Jury selection for Green's trial started October 9, 1902. At that time, at the age of seventeen, Green was the youngest person ever to be tried for capital murder in Erie County, New York. Assistant District Attorney Willard Ticknor prosecuted the case before a full courtroom that included the boy's father. Witnesses identified Charles Green as one of the four young men who entered the two saloons earlier in the evening on the night of the murder. Julia Sexton—the woman who lived above Crowe's—could not positively identify Green, however. The young man took the stand in his own defense and carefully detailed all his movements the day he left the State Industrial School. Defense witnesses corroborated his story. He repeated for the jury his encounter with Jimmy Gunnion and Gunnion's confession to the murder. Ticknor could not break the young man's testimony. Green made a good impression, and many court observers predicted an acquittal.

After deliberating for less than five hours and calling for three ballots, the jury found him not guilty of the murder. Before adjourning the court, Judge Kenefick took the opportunity to lecture Charles Green for looking up his old cronies and roaming about the country begging rather than becoming a contributing member of society. He reminded him that a suspended burglary charge lingered on his record, then gave the firm instruction that "if word comes to me . . . that you are loafing about the city I shall have you brought in and will sentence you to imprisonment." In light of Green's acquittal, Ticknor dismissed the indictment against John Richards, but in November Richards was convicted of stealing a bicycle in Erie, Pennsylvania, and received a sentence of two years and eight months. Despite the efforts of determined local detectives, John Doyle and Fred Chilton could not be found to stand

trial. Police never believed Green's tale about Jimmy Gunnion and did not investigate his whereabouts seriously. [63]

WANTED FOR MURDER.
$500.00 REWARD.

CHARLES GREEN.
Photograph taken Jan. 30, 1901.

Bertillon Measurement.

Height	58.5	Head, length	18.1	L. Foot	25.8
Outer Arms	59.5	Head, width	15.1	Mid. F.	11.0
Trunk	84.0	R. Ear, length	6.1	Lit. F.	8.7
				Fore Arm	43.0

General Description.
18 years; 5 feet 4; 110 pounds; hair light blonde; eyes blue; complexion fair; faint scar on left third finger; 1 upper front tooth gold.

JOHN DOYLE alias FRED MERCER alias TIMMY.
Photograph taken Oct. 24, 1900.

Bertillon Measurement.

Height	66.3	Head, length	19.0	L. Foot	24.6
Outer Arms	65.0	Head, width	15.1	Mid. F.	11.0
Trunk	88.0	R. Ear, length	15.5	Lit. F.	8.1
				Fore Arm	42.5

General Description.
20 years; 5 feet 5½; 123 pounds; build slim; hair dark; eyes blue; complexion medium; woman's bust on left arm; clasped hands, American flag and heart on right arm.

Charles Green and John Doyle, alias Fred. Mercer, are wanted for the murder of Austin J. Crowe, in this city, on the night of June 28th, 1902; the two other men connected with them in the murder are still unidentified, but will probably be found in their company, as the gang left the city together shortly after the murder.

Austin J. Crowe conducted a grocery and a saloon at the corner of Chicago and Fulton Streets, this city; on the evening of June 28th had closed his grocery and gone into his saloon for the purpose of closing his day's business; four men (two of them identified as Green and Doyle) entered the saloon and ordered drinks, which were furnished by Crowe. From a tenant occupying rooms over Crowe's, it is learned a dispute occurred as to the payment for the drinks. Crowe who was a courageous and athletic man, and never known to have had trouble in his saloon ordered the men to leave his place, and undoubtedly endeavored to eject the men from the saloon, several shots were fired; three of the men escaped from the saloon through the door, the fourth man by jumping through the window carrying glass and sash with him.

See Circular dated July 7th, mailed you.

Green and Doyle, alias Mercer, are both professional thieves, sneaks and pickpockets. Green belongs in this city, and was released from the State Industrial School, Rochester, June 28th, the day of the murder; he was sentenced to the Reformatory for sneaking a jewelry store in this city with four others, all being arrested in Toronto and brought back.

Doyle, alias Mercer, belongs in Toronto, Ont., where he has a bad record; he was paroled from the New York State Reformatory, Elmira, N. Y., February 26th, 1902, and was still under parol; he was committed there for larceny committed in this city.

It was either Green or Doyle that jumped through the window, and the one that did is supposed to be cut by the broken glass, either on the hand or leg or both, as we learn since they left the city that a person connected with the gang called on a doctor here and asked for bandages and instructions in binding a wound, but would not inform the doctor what the patient was or the nature of the injury.

They hang out at newsboys' and bootblacks' homes, working boys' homes and cheap lodging houses.

The Common Council of the City of Buffalo at their regular sessions June 30th and July 3d, 1902, adopted a resolution requesting the Mayor to offer a reward of $1,000 for the arrest and conviction of the murderers. In compliance with the resolution of the Common Council of the City of Buffalo, I hereby offer a reward of $1,000 for the identification, arrest and conviction of the murderers of Austin J. Crowe, under the following conditions:

$500 REWARD for information that will lead to the arrest and conviction of the murderers.

$500 REWARD for the arrest and conviction of the murderers upon information furnished through the Department of Police of the City of Buffalo, or

$1,000 for the arrest and conviction of the murderers independent of information furnished through the Department of Police of the City of Buffalo.

ERASTUS C. KNIGHT,
Mayor.

Address all communications to
WILLIAM S. BULL,
Superintendent of Police.
BUFFALO, N. Y., July 12th, 1902.

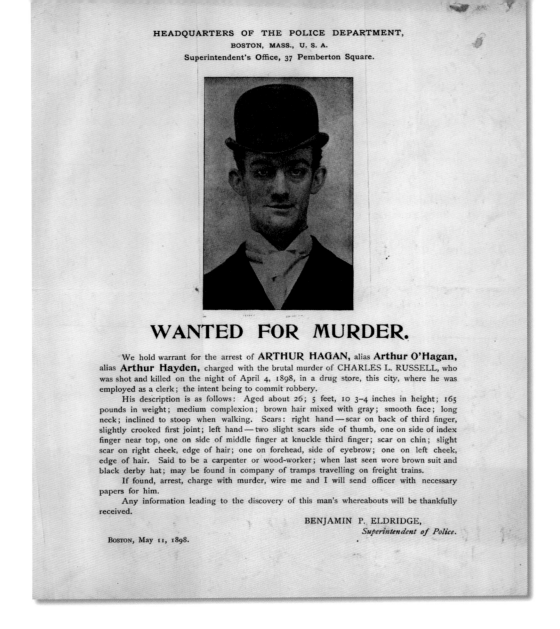

HEADQUARTERS OF THE POLICE DEPARTMENT,
BOSTON, MASS., U. S. A.
Superintendent's Office, 37 Pemberton Square.

WANTED FOR MURDER.

We hold warrant for the arrest of **ARTHUR HAGAN**, alias **Arthur O'Hagan,** alias **Arthur Hayden,** charged with the brutal murder of CHARLES L. RUSSELL, who was shot and killed on the night of April 4, 1898, in a drug store, this city, where he was employed as a clerk; the intent being to commit robbery.

His description is as follows: Aged about 26; 5 feet, 10 3–4 inches in height; 165 pounds in weight; medium complexion; brown hair mixed with gray; smooth face; long neck; inclined to stoop when walking. Scars: right hand — scar on back of third finger, slightly crooked first joint; left hand — two slight scars side of thumb, one on side of index finger near top, one on side of middle finger at knuckle third finger; scar on chin; slight scar on right cheek, edge of hair; one on forehead, side of eyebrow; one on left cheek, edge of hair. Said to be a carpenter or wood-worker; when last seen wore brown suit and black derby hat; may be found in company of tramps travelling on freight trains.

If found, arrest, charge with murder, wire me and I will send officer with necessary papers for him.

Any information leading to the discovery of this man's whereabouts will be thankfully received.

BENJAMIN P. ELDRIDGE,
Superintendent of Police.

BOSTON, May 11, 1898.

ARTHUR HAGAN

Jody Hokes

It was a spring evening in Boston, April 1898. Clerk Charles L. Russell waited on customers at Chapin's Drug Store on the street level of the United States Hotel, corner of Lincoln and Beach Streets. The store was only a few blocks from the Boston and Albany Railroad Station, and situated in a well-lit, high-traffic area filled with pedestrians and streetcars. Russell, who had worked at the drug store for thirteen years, was forty-four years old, married, and had two children. Sometime between 8:00 p.m. and 8:30 p.m., a police officer walking his route noticed a man described as, "about 24 years old, weight 160 pounds, height 5 feet 10 inches, smooth shaven, clear cut face and was dressed in a light spring overcoat strapped seams and box pockets, dark pants and black derby, and [wearing] shoes either of patent leather or highly polished" pacing in front of Chapin's, but he assumed the gentleman was waiting for a car. Not long after the officer passed by, shots rang out, and Charles Russell, bleeding from two bullet wounds, staggered out of the store and onto the street, where he lost consciousness. Two bystanders carried him back inside and laid him on the floor. He died just as police arrived.[64]

The assailant, later identified as Arthur Hagan, ran out of the store and into the nearby rail station. Several witnesses started to pursue the shooter but withdrew after he threatened to kill them. He dashed through a crowd of at least sixty people, gun in hand, and left the station through the baggage room. Attempting to head him off, police used a different exit and followed Hagan into a blind alleyway, but Hagan had disappeared. Apparently, he entered the basement of a house, ran up the stairs and out to the street.

Police had no leads on the case until the family whose house Hagan entered discovered an overcoat in their basement several days later. Investigators visited the tailor, who identified the owner as John H. Chance. Police immediately arrested Chance, who claimed he had lent the coat to Arthur Hagan on the night of the robbery. He informed police that on the day after the murder Hagan showed Chance the story in the newspaper and said he was leaving town. Chance repeatedly denied any involvement in the murder, but as he was the primary witness against Hagan, he remained in jail.

Boston police put a warrant out for Hagan (aliases O'Hagan and Hayden) and began a massive search, scouring army and navy records and distributing over ten thousand wanted posters to all major cities. After receiving information that their suspect traveled to Chicago to visit his father, Boston officials gave their Chicago counterparts Hagan's parents' address and asked them to be on the lookout. Their diligence was rewarded. Chicago police arrested Arthur Hagan at his parents' home on September 30, 1898, almost six months after the murder. Two Boston police officers went to Chicago to escort Hagan, now described as "pale and thin" with long hair and "several days' growth of beard," back to the east coast. He remained calm and collected throughout the trip and his subsequent questioning. Except for a "somewhat restless shifting of the eyes," he refused to provide any information that would incriminate him.[65]

Due to the confusion over possession of the coat, and the fact that some witnesses reported seeing two men the night of the robbery, prosecutors tried both Hagan and Chance for murder in 1899. Hagan did not testify at the trial, but his lawyer called witnesses who presented a solid alibi for him over the days leading up to the murder and the night in question. Furthermore, his defense appeared to be an attempt to discredit Chance. As Hagan's story went, Chance and a mutual friend stole some revolvers and razors from a cutlery store a couple nights before Chapin's was robbed. The day before the murder, Chance lent Hagan his coat to wear on a date. Hagan claimed to have returned the coat to an inebriated Chance later that same evening, so that it was back in Chance's possession at the time of the murder. When he stopped by Chance's house the next morning, he found Chance reading newspaper articles about the death. Hagan further claimed that witness Liz Nagle, a woman Hagan lived with for a few weeks before the crime, told him she believed Chance had committed the drugstore murder, as she had seen him with a revolver a few days before.

Chance testified on his own behalf, but his inconsistent statements about his whereabouts the night of the murder cast doubt on his innocence. At first he admitted to wearing the overcoat the evening of the murder; later he stated that he was in bed at the time of the crime. Meanwhile, a woman he lived with, possibly his wife, reported that he was out until after 8:00 p.m. Liz Nagle, who had been one of a group of people in Chance's room that evening, stated Chance did not return until an hour after the shooting. Possibly in an attempt to protect Hagan while extricating himself, Chance suggested that a third party, a Mr. O'Brien, committed the crime. At one point he even testified that he had a disability which prevented him from running from police. The contrast between Hagan's level-headed testimony and Chance's inconsistencies on the witness stand was not lost on the jury. They acquitted Hagan but convicted Chance of murder in the second degree and sentenced him to life in prison.

After the trial, Arthur Hagan returned to Chicago, where he had been working as a barber until his arrest. He became a respected citizen and eventually married. John Chance continued to maintain his innocence. In 1905, he wrote a letter to the governor of Massachusetts stating that Hagan had confessed to the murder. Unfortunately, the court delayed an investigation into his claims for six years. When confronted, Hagan admitted that he murdered Charles Russell. Knowing that under the double jeopardy rule he could not be tried again, he signed a sworn statement that he had acted alone and was wearing Chance's coat during the crime. He recalled that he saw Chance immediately after the shooting and explained what happened. Assuming Hagan now told the truth, Chance knew of Hagan's guilt at the time of the trial but tried to protect his friend with his testimony. John Chance was pardoned and released on June 7, 1911, twelve long years after his arrest.

Pinkerton's National Detective Agency.

FOUNDED BY ALLAN PINKERTON, 1850.

OFFICES.

ROBT. A. PINKERTON, New York, }
WM. A. PINKERTON, Chicago. } Principals.

GEO. D. BANGS, Gen'l Manager, New York.
J. H. SCHUMACHER, Sup't.
ALLAN PINKERTON, Asst. General Manager, New York.

JOHN CORNISH, Gen'l Sup't., Eastern Division, New York.
EDWARD S. GAYLOR, Gen'l Sup't., Middle Division, Chicago.
JAMES McPARLAND, Gen'l Sup't., Western Division, Denver.

CHICAGO, 201 FIFTH AVENUE.
NEW YORK, 57 BROADWAY.
BOSTON, 30 COURT STREET.
PHILADELPHIA, 441 CHESTNUT STREET.
MONTREAL, MERCHANTS BANK BUILDING.
ST. PAUL, GERMANIA BANK BUILDING.
ST. LOUIS, WAINWRIGHT BUILDING.
KANSAS CITY, 622 MAIN STREET.
DENVER, OPERA HOUSE BLOCK.
PORTLAND, ORE. MARQUAM BLOCK.
SEATTLE, WASH. BAILEY BLOCK.
SAN FRANCISCO, CROCKER BUILDING.

Attorneys.—GUTHRIE, CRAVATH & HENDERSON, New York.

TELEPHONE CONNECTION.

REPRESENTATIVES OF THE AMERICAN BANKERS ASSOCIATION.

INFORMATION CIRCULAR No. 3.

$5,000 REWARD.

PHOTOGRAPH OF HARVEY LOGAN.

The above is the aggregate amount of reward offered by the GREAT NORTHERN EXPRESS CO. for the arrest and identification of the four men implicated in the robbery of the Great Northern Railway Express train No. 3 near Wagner, Mont., July 3, 1901. A proportionate amount will be paid for one, two or more, and $500 Additional for each Conviction.

Under date of Aug. 5th, 1901, we issued a circular bearing a picture of HARVEY LOGAN showing him with a full beard, making it difficult to identify. We herewith present a later and better picture of him which has been identified in Nashville, Tenn., as a good likeness of the companion of a woman arrested there for attempting to exchange some of the stolen currency.

DESCRIPTION.

Name, HARVEY LOGAN.

Alias Harvey Curry, "Kid" Curry, Bob Jones, Tom Jones, Bob Nevilles, Robert Nelson and R. T. Whalen.

Residence, last known, Landusky and Harlem, Montana.

Nativity, Dodson, Mo.
Color, white.
Occupation, cowboy, rustler.
Age, 36 years (1901).
Eyes, dark.
Height, 5 feet, 7½ inches.
Weight, 145 to 160 lbs.
Complexion, dark, swarthy.
Nose, prominent, large, long and straight.

Criminal Occupation, Bank robber, train robber, horse and cattle thief, rustler, "hold up" and murderer.
Build, medium.

Color of Hair, dark brown, darker than mustache.
Style of Beard, can raise heavy beard and mustache, color somewhat lighter than hair.
Marks, has gun-shot wound on wrist, talks slowly, is of quiet reserved manner.

On Oct. 27th, 1901, a man believed to be GEORGE PARKER, alias Butch Cassidy, whose photograph and description appeared in our circular of Aug. 5th, 1901, attempted to pass one of the $20 bills of the stolen currency at a Nashville store. He escaped from officers after a severe struggle.

On the night of Nov. 5th, 1901, the St. Louis Police arrested Harry Longbaugh, alias Harry Alonzo, one of the train robbers, after he had passed four of the stolen bills at a PAWNSHOP. A female companion was also arrested. They had in their possession about $7,000 of the stolen notes.

Officers attempting to arrest these men are warned that they are desperadoes, always carry firearms and do not hesitate to use them when their liberty is endangered.

Send all information promptly to the undersigned to the nearest office listed at the head of circular, using telegraph if necessary.

PINKERTON'S NATIONAL DETECTIVE AGENCY.

OR WM. A. PINKERTON, 199-201 Fifth Avenue, Chicago, Ills.

CHICAGO, ILL., NOVEMBER 8, 1901.

Below appear the photographs, descriptions and histories of GEORGE PARKER, alias "BUTCH" CASSIDY, alias GEORGE CASSIDY, alias INGERFIELD and HARRY LONGBAUGH alias HARRY ALONZO.

Name..George Parker, alias "Butch" Cassidy, alias George Cassidy, alias Ingerfield.
Nationality...............American
Occupation...........Cowboy; rustler
Criminal Occupation...Bank robber and highwayman, cattle and horse thief
Age..36 yrs. (1901). Height....5 feet 9 in
Weight..165 lbs. Build......Medium
Complexion - Light . Color of Hair..Flaxen
Eyes....Blue........Complexion
Remarks:—Two cut scars back of head, small scar under left eye, small brown mole calf of leg. "Butch" Cassidy is known as a criminal principally in Wyoming, Utah, Idaho, Colorado and Nevada and has served time in Wyoming State penitentiary at Laramie for grand larceny, but was pardoned January 19th, 1896.

GEORGE PARKER.
First photograph taken July 15, 1894.

GEORGE PARKER.
Last photograph taken Nov. 21, 1900.

Name...Harry Longbaugh, alias "Kid" Longbaugh, alias Harry Alonzo, alias Frank Jones, alias Frank Boyd, alias the "Sundance Kid"
Nationality......Swedish-American. Occupation....Cowboy; rustler
Criminal Occupation...Highwayman, bank burglar, cattle and horse thief
Age....35 years. Height................5 feet 10 in
Weight...165 to 175 lbs. Build...............Good
Eyes....Blue or gray......Complexion......Medium
Mustache or Beard..........(if any), natural color brown, reddish tinge
Features......Grecian type......Nose........Rather long
Color of Hair.....Natural color brown, may be dyed; combs it pompadour.
IS BOW-LEGGED AND HIS FEET FAR APART.

Remarks:—Harry Longbaugh served 18 months in jail at Sundance, Cook Co., Wyoming, when a boy, for horse stealing. In December, 1892, Harry Longbaugh, Bill Madden and Henry Bass "held up" a Great Northern train at Malta, Montana. Bass and Madden were tried for this crime, convicted and sentenced to 10 and 14 years respectively; Longbaugh escaped and since has been a fugitive. June 28, 1897, under the name of Frank Jones, Longbaugh participated with James Curry, Tom Day and Walter Putney, in the Belle Fourche, South Dakota, bank robbery. All were arrested, but Longbaugh and Harvey Logan escaped from jail at Deadwood, October 31, 1899. Longbaugh has not since been arrested.

HARRY LONGBAUGH.
Photograph taken 1890.

We also publish below a photograph, history and description of CAMILLA HANKS, alias O. C. HANKS, alias CHARLEY JONES, alias "DEAF" CHARLEY, who may be found in company of either PARKER, alias CASSIDY or LONGBAUGH, alias ALONZO, and for whom a proportionate amount of a $5,000.00 reward is offered by the GREAT NORTHERN EXPRESS COMPANY upon arrest and conviction for participation in the Great Northern (Railway) Express robbery near Wagner, Mont., July 3rd, 1901.

Name...O. C. Hanks, alias Camilla Hanks, alias Charley Jones, alias Deaf Charley
Nationality......American......Occupation................Cowboy
Criminal Occupation.....................Train robber; an ex-convict
Age.........38 years (1901)......Height................5 feet 10 in
Weight....136 lbs......Build................Good
Complexion...Sandy......Color of Hair......Auburn
Eyes.......Blue......Mustache or Beard......(if any), natural color sandy

Remarks:—Scar from burn, size 25c piece, on right forearm. Small scar right leg, above ankle. Mole near right nipple. Leans his head slightly to the left. Somewhat deaf. Raised at Yorktown, Texas, fugitive from there charged with rape; also wanted in New Mexico on charge of murder. Arrested in Teton County, Montana, 1892, and sentenced to 10 years in the penitentiary at Deer Lodge, for holding up Northern Pacific train near Big Timber, Montana. Released April 30th, 1901.

CAMILLA HANKS.
Photograph taken 1892.

HARVEY LOGAN, alias "KID CURRY," referred to in our first circular issued from Denver on May 15, 1901, is now under arrest at Knoxville, Tenn., charged with shooting two police officers who were attempting his arrest.
BEN KILPATRICK, alias JOE ARNOLD, alias "THE TALL TEXAN" of Concho County, Texas, another member of the "Harvey Logan band" of outlaws, was arrested at St. Louis, Mo., on November 5th, 1901, tried, convicted and sentenced to 15 years imprisonment for participation in the robbery of the GREAT NORTHERN EXPRESS COMPANY, near Wagner, Mont.
WILLIAM CARVER, alias "BILL" CARVER, of Sonora, Sutton County, Texas, another member of this band, was killed at Sonora, Texas, April 2nd, 1901, by Sheriff Eli Briant, while resisting arrest on charge of murder.

IN CASE OF AN ARREST immediately notify PINKERTON'S NATIONAL DETECTIVE AGENCY at the nearest of the above listed offices.

Or

JOHN C. FRASER, Resident Sup't., DENVER, COLO.

Pinkerton's National Detective Agency,
Opera House Block, Denver, Colo.

requested to give this circular to the police of their city or district.
Police official, Marshal, Constable, Sheriff or Deputy, or a Peace officer.

BUTCH CASSIDY, THE SUNDANCE KID, AND THE WILD BUNCH

Tom Kellam

Three men walked into the First National Bank of Winnemucca, Nevada, at noon on September 19, 1900, and made off with $32,640—a tidy sum in that year. On Circular No. 2 issued eighteen months later, the Pinkerton National Detective Agency attributed the robbery to George Parker, alias "Butch" Cassidy; Harry Longbaugh, alias "the Sundance Kid;" and Harvey Logan, alias "Kid Curry." The poster named other members of the so-called Wild Bunch, including Will Carver, who probably participated in the Winnemucca robbery rather than Harvey Logan. The Pinkertons believed two more criminals, Camilla Hanks and Ben "the Tall Texan" Kilpatrick, "may be in the company of either Cassidy or Longbaugh," so they too were pictured. The authorities wanted both Hanks and Kilpatrick in connection with the Great Northern Railway Express robbery near Wagner, Montana, on July 3, 1901. While they suspected that Cassidy and Longbaugh also participated in the Great Northern job, historians of the crime later decided that was unlikely. Questions linger about the identities of the Winnemucca bank robbers too, but modern researchers credit Butch Cassidy, the Sundance Kid, and Will Carver with the crime.

About ten days before the bank was hit, three cowboys—Butch, Sundance, and Carver—set up camp about fifteen miles from Winnemucca on George C. Bliss's CS Ranch. Since it was roundup time, a busy season for the farmers and ranchers of northern Nevada, they did not seem out of place. The cowboys were a friendly bunch. Ten-year-old Vic Button, the ranch foreman's son, recalled that he chatted pleasantly with the group when he passed the encampment on his way to school every morning. Also, an especially fine white horse belonging to the cowboys attracted his attention. Button was so taken with the animal he repeatedly offered to trade his for it, but each time the men politely declined. In spite of the failed deal, he and his friends often listened to the cowboys' stories about life on the trail and answered questions from the strangers about their town and the immediate area. "What's the shortest route to Southern Idaho?" they wondered. And "What is the fastest way out of town?"

The outlaws spent their days planning. They studied the First National Bank building in Winnemucca and the surrounding streets carefully. With the unwitting help of their young local friends, they charted the quickest getaway route. To facilitate their escape, they organized a series of relays with fresh horses stationed every few miles. By the morning of September 19, they were ready. The three broke camp, rode into town, and tethered their horses in an alley behind the bank. At the appointed hour Butch and Sundance entered the bank while Carver, disguised as a hobo, guarded the door. Sundance covered the cashiers and the bookkeeper while Butch held a knife to the throat of George Nixon, the bank president, and forced him to open the safe. Nixon handed over three heavy bags of gold coins amounting to $31,000. The contents of the cash drawers and the president's desk brought the total haul to $32,640.

They led Nixon and his four colleagues out the back entrance to the alley where the horses waited. After they galloped away down the alley with their loot, the president ran back into the bank. Grabbing a pistol, he ran out the front doors firing into the air to raise the alarm. As an impromptu posse formed behind the robbers, a bag fell from the horse of one of the outlaws, scattering coins over the ground. Butch and Sundance desperately gathered up what they could while Will Carver kept the posse at bay with his rifle. They resumed their race out of town but left several thousand dollars behind in the dust.

Deputy Sheriff George Rose climbed a windmill and managed to get off a few shots at the gang as they fled east out of town. He spotted a switch engine on the railroad track running parallel to the road and commandeered it for the pursuit. Once the engine gained steam, the pursuers closed in on the outlaws. In the exchange of gunfire, they winged Butch's horse, but a bullet to the engine's steam pipe disabled it as well. The outlaws stopped at the Sloan Ranch, eight miles outside of Winnemucca, to secure fresh horses and coincidentally took one belonging to George Nixon. "This was the unkindest cut of all," he reportedly complained later. "They robbed my bank and then stole my horse on which to escape." They left the ranch along a route they learned from Vic Button and his schoolmates.[66]

Their first planned relay stop was the Silve Ranch, where they had friends among the cowboys. Four horses—three for the riders and one for loot and provisions—were ready to go. As they prepared to leave, one of the ranch hands noticed the posse approaching in the distance. When questioned, they admitted they had just robbed the bank in Winnemucca. The trio suggested that the ranch hand tell the group following them that further pursuit would be "unhealthy." Before they rode out, Butch asked Silvian Siard, the ranch foreman, to "give the white horse to the kid at the CS Ranch." So Vic Button finally got his beloved horse, which he rode proudly for many years.[67]

Sundance, Butch, and Carver eventually escaped after days of evading their pursuers. Once they divided the money, Butch and Sundance made their way to Fort Worth, Texas. There they met up with Will Carver, Ben Kilpatrick, and Harvey Logan and posed for the now-famous photograph by John Swartz. Law enforcement cropped faces from that image for the Pinkerton wanted poster. After their stay in Texas, Butch and Sundance traveled to New York with Etta Place and boarded a ship for South America.

FRANK DUNCAN

Tom Kellam

In January 1899, when Southern Illinois Penitentiary paroled Frank Duncan, alias Frank Edwards, Frank Winters, or Dayton Slim, he was eager to get back to work in the larceny trade. Duncan was a career criminal gifted with an enterprising spirit and a talent for organization. By the spring of 1900, he was leading a band of burglars and safe crackers that operated across southern Illinois, Ohio, Kentucky, Tennessee, northern Alabama, and parts of Georgia. He liked to take risks, but in Duncan's world poorly calculated risks had deadly outcomes for both victims and crooks.

The Standard Oil Company offices in Birmingham, Alabama, must have seemed like an attractive target with a safe possibly full of payroll cash and other valuable loot. Duncan and his partner in crime, Frank Miller, a German immigrant variously known as John Hendricks, Frank Manning, or "Dutch Henry," led a band of thieves to Birmingham. The crew consisted of "New York Harry" O'Dowd, John D. West, Tom Fay, and Frank Duncan.

The bandits arrived in Birmingham on March 27. That afternoon Duncan and Miller went out to case the Standard Oil property. Between nine and ten that evening, three of the bandits broke into the Standard Oil building—Duncan, Miller, and probably New York Harry. When they encountered night watchman J. A. Clayton, they knocked him in the head, shot him in the foot, stole his gun, and locked him in a closet. Afterward, they blew the safe, but found only three hundred dollars and some change—disappointing, to say the least. Their fortunes would not improve.

Around midnight, officers George Kirkley and J. H. Adams patrolled the streets near the scene of the crime on the lookout for likely suspects. They spotted Frank Miller and probably Frank Duncan, who fit the descriptions of the bandits, but when they attempted to arrest them they pulled out their guns and started shooting. Both officers were hit immediately, at close range, but they were still able to open fire on the fleeing suspects. Witnesses to the shootout reported a curious sight. One of the suspects carefully removed his coat, laid it gently on sidewalk, and continued to flee. Officials later found a small bottle of liquid in one of the coat pockets, which was later determined to be nitroglycerin. A bullet had passed through the coat, barely missing the explosive bottle.

The men fled to a prearranged hideout in Chattanooga, Tennessee, but they were quickly captured along with the other members of the gang and returned to Birmingham. New York Harry O'Dowd escaped. On his deathbed, Adams identified Miller and Duncan as the men who had shot him and his partner, who had died the previous day.

Miller started talking shortly after his arrest. He admitted to participating in the robbery and to being involved in the shoot-out with Adams and Kirkley. He denied having shot either lawman, however, because he was certain that he had fired over their heads. He also insisted that the man arrested with him was O'Dowd and that he fired the fatal shots, rather than Duncan. This claim would be repeated by both Duncan and Miller throughout the twists and turns of this affair. O'Dowd's absence had become a presence.

The State of Alabama tried Duncan and Miller for first degree murder. Both admitted to the robbery, but they denied killing Adams and Kirkley. During the trial, the defense raised questions about who fired the fatal shots and whether the man arrested with Miller was really Duncan or New York Harry O'Dowd. Both Duncan and Miller maintained to the bitter end that New York Harry fired the fatal shots. Miller always argued that he shot in the air. Both men were found guilty. Miller was condemned death. Duncan received a life sentence.

Duncan still faced trial for the murder of Kirkley, and he knew that the prosecution would certainly seek the death penalty. Meanwhile, every passing day brought Miller closer to the gallows. Out of desperation, Duncan, Miller, and two other criminals attempted a jailbreak using improvised tools and hacksaws smuggled in by Duncan's wife. The *Birmingham Age-Herald* described it as "the most daring jail delivery ever attempted in the state of Alabama." Daring or not, the attempt failed.[68]

The State executed Miller by hanging on the June 28, 1901. On the scaffold, Miller told those present "I am an innocent man, and Duncan is innocent too. If you hang Duncan, you will hang an innocent man." In September of that year, Duncan's trial for the murder of Officer George W. Kirkley began. Duncan also invoked the presence of the elusive Harry O'Dowd. He gave interviews to the press, hoping that O'Dowd would step forward and provide an alibi. He even sent his wife to track the man down, but to no avail. On September 21, the jury found Duncan guilty of Kirkley's murder and soon sentenced him to death. Innocent or not, Duncan did not want to share Miller's fate. On January 20, 1902, he and two other prisoners successfully broke out of the Birmingham jail.[69]

Almost three years later, on August 23, 1904, police captured a gang of safe crackers in St. Augustine, Florida. They were run to ground by intrepid St. Augustine Detective Jim Ahn, who had been hot on their trail for weeks. Fred "Kid" Stafford and Jim Ward led the group. Ward turned out to be none other than the notorious Frank Duncan. Undeterred, Duncan tried one last time to escape, but his efforts were quickly squelched. While he awaited his date with the noose, Duncan's wife and lawyers worked feverishly to get his sentence changed to life. There was a flurry of appeals that went all the way to the Alabama Supreme Court. Supporters circulated petitions to the governor.

Late in October Duncan experienced a moment of hope when New York Harry finally turned up. O'Dowd had been having his own adventures in St. Louis. Police captured him after a bloody shoot-out in the aftermath of a failed train robbery. Duncan dispatched his wife to St. Louis, telling reporters she "knows New York Harry quite well." The trip was futile. Harry did not seem interested in adding a murder charge to his current difficulties. Authorities eventually returned O'Dowd to Birmingham to stand trial for his role in the Standard Oil theft, but not for the murder of the policemen.[70]

Time finally ran out for Frank Duncan on November 25, 1904. Duncan marched to the gallows stoically, "with a firm step." He made a lengthy speech to the roughly one hundred spectators attending his execution.

☞ Hand to some Officer.

$600.00 REWARD !

FOR TWO WHITE MEN WHO ESCAPED FROM JEFFERSON COUNTY JAIL, JANUARY 20, 1902.

FRANK DUNCAN.   **FRANK DUNCAN.**

FRANK DUNCAN, alias Frank Edwards, alias Frank Winters, alias Dayton Slim; condemned murderer of Policemen Kirkley and Adams; age 35 years; height, 5 feet 8⅜ inches in bare feet; weight, 168 pounds; fair complexion; light brown hair, said to have a small patch of gray hair on left side of head, ¼ inch in diameter; small moustache; beard lighter than hair; medium blue eyes; chin rather pointed and protruding; nose rather long and slightly turned to right; medium-sized vaccination scar on outside of left arm above elbow; oblique cut scar on inside left thumb on second joint; oblique cut scar on inside right thumb on second joint; irregular cut scar just above second joint of right thumb on inside; small oblique cut scar just above edge right eyebrow, near inside point of brow; several scars on neck under right ear, have appearance of scrofulous scars. Has been in jail two years and is bleached from confinement. Bertillon measurements: 73.7; 77.0; 89.9; 19.9; 15.6; 13.9; 7.4; 26.702; 11.8; 8.9; 47.1.

I will Pay $500.00 for him delivered in Jefferson County Jail.

He is well known in Illinois, Chattanooga, Atlanta and Augusta, Portsmouth, Cincinnati, Scioto County Ohio, and North-Eastern Kentucky. Married Myrtle Haas, of Chattanooga, whose people came there from Cincinnati and Covington. He was paroled from southern Illinois penitentiary January 2nd, 1899, after serving sentence for burglary, from Adams County, Ill. Criminal occupation, professional burglar and safe cracker; former occupation, stoker on river steamer. Operated in this County in spring of 1900, blowing safes. On March 27th, 1900, he, with several others, blew the safe of the Standard Oil Company, and nearly killed their watchman. On the same night, the policemen mentioned attempted to arrest them, when Duncan and his companion shot and killed both of them. On June 28th, 1901, his companion, Frank Miller, alias Jim Ferguson, alias John Manning, alias John Hendricks, alias "Dutch Henry," was hanged. On Sept. 12th, 1901, Duncan was sentenced to hang, but an appeal was taken and was pending, when he escaped.

Three companions of Duncan in the Standard Oil robbery were given long terms in the penitentiary. Their names were Frank Randolph, alias Frank Edwards, alias Frank Hahn; John D. West, alias R. T. Isaacs, of Richmond, Va.; and Tom Fay, alias J. W. Rogan.

At the same time and place of Duncan's escape, one **GEORGE BULLARD** escaped, charged with robbery. Age 25 years; height, 5 feet 7 inches; weight, 155 pounds; dark complexion; black eyes; black hair, with possibly a few gray hairs; small black moustache.

I will Pay $100.00 for him delivered in Jefferson County Jail.

PLEASE POST. Please examine all Tramps passing your way.
ANDREW W. BURGIN, Sheriff,
March 14th, 1902.   Birmingham, Alabama.

In it he repeated his claim that he was innocent of murder and that he was the victim of persecution by public officials and the police. He ended his speech and his life with "sarcastic flings" at the police. The rope was placed about his neck, and the drop fell at 11:36 am. Twelve minutes later, he was pronounced dead of a broken neck.[71]

SAMUEL H. MARSHALL

Tom Kellam

In 1898, Portland, Indiana, the seat of Jay County, was a small town of about five thousand souls. It is not much larger than that today. It was a quiet place that seemed an unlikely setting for a grisly murder.

On the morning of Saturday, February 12, Portland City Marshal Montgomery Mahan received an anonymous postcard asking him to "go to the old lady's house who lives next to the north end of the heading factory she's been robbed please go." The correspondent referred to the small cluster of houses near a manufacturing plant which made staves and rings for wooden barrels. Mahan knew that the "old lady" was most likely Louisa "Grandma" Stoltz, a seventy-five-year-old widow who was a well-known figure in Portland. She was likable, but eccentric. Locals considered her to be moderately wealthy, but were likewise aware of her reputation for miserliness and a mistrust of banks. Rumors circulated about large sums of money she kept hidden in her house.[72]

Marshal Mahan visited the widow's home, but no one responded to his knock. He proceeded across the street to the home of Stoltz's nearest neighbor, Loretta Bose, and showed her the card he had received. Though Bose was alarmed by the news, Mahan decided not to pursue the matter further and returned to his office. Bose, however, took action. She enlisted the help of two men from the heading factory and entered the Stoltz residence through the back door, which they found standing open. The house had been ransacked. Among the debris of overturned furniture and the contents of drawers scattered across floors, they noticed several empty money sacks. The body of Mrs. Stoltz lay bound and gagged on her living room floor. After being called back to the scene, law enforcement officials assumed that the murder has occurred the night before, perhaps because witnesses claimed to have seen the deceased around town the previous day. The condition of the body, already bloated with the first stages of decay, suggested that the crime had occurred earlier. The lingering confusion over Stoltz's time of death had serious consequences when the time came to try the suspected murders.

Wanted for Robbery and Murder.

SAMUEL H. MARSHALL.

The above is a good photo of Marshall, who is wanted for robbery and murder. Height, near six feet; weight about one hundred and sixty; dark complexioned, dark hair, long and wavy; short cropped sandy moustache; eyes brown; talks with a Kentucky accent; wore brown clothes, brown crush hat, bottom of rim black; tan shoes; Red Man's button in lapel of coat; occupation beater engineer in straw board mill, also has worked in flouring mills. Supposed to be in your state. A suitable reward will be paid for his arrest and conviction.

Also, Wanted for Robbery and Murder,

ALBERT MUSSER, alias WATSON; age about 24 years; height five feet, ten inches; weight about one hundred and fifty pounds; complexion, medium dark; hair, dark; wore. when last seen, brown tailor-made clothes, brown hat, tan shoes; small scar on left hand across knuckle of little finger; square shoulders; smooth face; walks with head slightly stooped forward. When last seen on May 16th, had fresh sores on one hand. Supposed to be in the Indiana Gas Belt. A suitable reward will be paid for his arrest and conviction.

Address all communications to

GEO. W. BERGMAN, Mayor,

May 23, 1898.

PORTLAND, INDIANA.

A few days before neighbors discovered Stoltz's body, a small-time crook and itinerate factory worker named Samuel H. Marshall jumped off a freight train in Anderson, Indiana. Marshall sought out Albert Musser, an old friend who had been recently released from jail after a vagrancy charge. Marshall convinced Musser that he should join him on a trip to Portland. En route the men stopped in Muncie, where they spent the night in the boiler room of a paper mill where Frank Markle, a buddy of Musser's, worked.

Over the course of the evening, Marshall informed Mr. Markle of his and Musser's plan to enrich themselves at the expense of a wealthy widow. He explained that he had a knowledgeable contact in Portland who would guide them to her isolated house on the edge of town. This enlightening conversation eventually made Markle an ideal witness for the prosecution.

Early on Thursday, February 10, Musser and Marshall road the rails to Portland to connect with their man on the ground, Herschel LaFollette. Another small-time crook, LaFollette had permanently injured one of his arms in a botched attempt to blow a safe. Around seven o'clock that same evening, a witness saw the men near Louisa Stoltz's home.

From the moment they encountered their victim, things went awry. Stoltz weighed about ninety pounds and stood only five feet tall, but she apparently put up a vigorous struggle. The police report stated that she had dried mud in her hair and on one of the shoulders of her dress. Investigators noticed at least two sets of male footprints in the mud at the foot of her back steps along with smaller impressions that matched Stoltz's soaked slippers. Her assailants dragged her inside, where she was killed. They absconded with several thousand dollars in cash and gold coins. Marshall and Musser caught a freight train headed west out of town, while LaFollette remained in Portland.

When Marshall and Musser returned to Anderson the next day, witnesses observed that the men had suddenly come into money. None too discreetly, Marshall asked if anyone had heard about an elderly woman who had been robbed in Portland, but Stoltz's neighbors had not yet uncovered the crime. Though they parted company after a few days, the men seemed incapable of being inconspicuous. They bought new clothes, went on drinking sprees, and flashed impressive wads of cash publicly. Before leaving Anderson, Marshall impulsively married a Miss Glaisser, but left her a few days later. He was next seen on February 25 in Terre Haute, where he was arrested for public intoxication. Musser lived in various boarding houses between February and April, and though he had no visible means of support, he spent freely.

By May authorities had identified both men as suspects and issued a wanted notice late in the month. Within days both men were in custody. Marshall was caught hiding in a boxcar in Monmouth, a village just southeast of Indianapolis. Meanwhile, Musser must have run through his share of the loot. He burglarized a laundry and assaulted the Chinese man who owned it. On the night of his arrest in St. Louis, Missouri, he attempted to hang himself in his cell, but was cut down in time.

Back in Portland, Hershel LaFollette raised the suspicion of authorities early on. Someone identified him as one of the men seen in the vicinity of the Stoltz house around the time of the murder. Investigators brought LaFollette and another thief named Frank Collum in for questioning, but both vigorously denied any knowledge of the crime. When they showed the anonymous postcard around town, however, someone recognized LaFollette's handwriting. Police found him holed up in his mother's house on the morning of March 11. When he spotted the officers, LaFollette went upstairs to his room, locked the door, and cut his throat with a straight razor. Of all those involved in the Stoltz murder, only the hapless LaFollette had some vestige of conscience. He must have been tormented by the thought of her bound and gagged on the floor of that dark, cold house. The postcard was possibly a feeble attempt to save her life, though she was probably dead when they left the premises.

By July 11, the grand jury had indicted both Marshall and Musser. Marshall was tried first and was acquitted, to the astonishment of all. The verdict came as a direct result of the error about the time of death. The attack most likely occurred on Thursday, February 10, but authorities argued that it happened the next day because a handful of people claimed to have seen Mrs. Stoltz around town on Friday. Because Marshall's attorneys provided statements from these witnesses and Marshall could prove he was in Anderson on Friday, the architect of the whole tragic fiasco walked away a free man. Musser's lawyers received a change of venue to nearby Hartford City for his trial, set for December. In the intervening months, the prosecution had recognized the problem in their timeline and built a solid case against Musser. He was sentenced to life in prison on December 22, 1898. His appeals were denied.

HOWARD CLARK,
Alias
W. K. ADAMS.

Doth Kieed at Owensboro Ky, while resting arrest 1894-98~

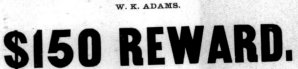

$150 REWARD.

WANTED FOR MURDER!

HOWARD CLARK, alias W. K. Adams, age 35 years, height 5 feet 8 inches, weight 175 pounds, black hair, brown eyes, dark complexion, teeth full and regular, black mustache—may have cut it off; has been reported to have been seen since murder with full beard; mark on bridge of nose. Burglar, fiend for robbing saloons, always entering from the rear; is a good safeman. Has been arrested at Covington, Ky., Cincinnati, Ohio, Bowling Green, Ky., and Indianapolis, Ind. Shot and killed policeman Jos. Heffernan, of this city, Friday night, August 12, 1898. Is a sneaking coward; have information that he fainted the following day, when notified of the death of the officer, then immediately fled the city. Is a fiend for gambling. Machinist and railroader by occupation. Cannot look you in the face. Has Mattie Mahoney with him and represents her as his wife.

BERTILLON MEASUREMENTS.

Height	1 M. 69.5	Head Length	19.2
Eng. Height	5.7½	Head Width	15.5
Outs. A	1 M. 77	Right Ear	6.4
Trunk	87.6	L. Foot	26.9
L. Mid. F	11.9	L. Fore A	48.1
L. Little F	9	Brown Eyes.	
Black Hair.		Sullen Look.	
Weight, 175 pounds.			

Send any information to **J. H.**

MATTIE MAHONEY.

Description: Age 17 years, height 4 feet 9½ inches, weight 100 pounds, build short and stocky; grey eyes, dark chestnut hair, small scar above right eyebrow, three burnt scars on back of right hand, one vaccination scar on left arm, small scar on first joint of left index finger; three upper front teeth filled with gold.

The above cut is a good likeness of little Mattie Mahoney, the paramour of Howard Clark, both of whom are madly in love with each other. I have positive evidence that the above pair are traveling and living together as husband and wife. Her condition is such that in course of four or five months time she will need the services of a physician or midwife, as she was four months gone in pregnancy at the time she left here. Mattie Mahoney is not wanted in this city for any offense. The reasons for adding her picture and description to this circular is that it might be the means of more readily locating Clark.

Height	M. 49.7
Eng. Height	4.9½
Outs. A	1 M. 46
Trunk	82
L. Mid. F	9.9
L. Little F	7.8
Head Length	17.3
Head Width	14.0
Right Ear	5.7
L. Foot	21.6
L. Fore A	39.1
Dark Chestnut	
Grey Eyes.	
Very small, midium	

BOTH KILLED.

Howard Clark, Wanted in Louisville for Murder, and His Girl Shot While Resisting Arrest.

Cincinnati, O., Oct. 9.—The Enquirer's special from Owensboro, Ky., says:

Howard Clark, who was wanted in Louisville for murder and burglary, and his girl, Hattie Mahoney, were both killed while resisting arrest on the Indiana side of the river near here to-day. Clark was wanted for the murder of Officer Hefferman at Louisville last August and was attempting to escape in a skiff by rowing down the Ohio river.

Word had been sent along the river by telegraph to arrest him. Officers from Owensboro went in pursuit when Clark tied up his skiff on the Indiana side and took to the woods. When detected at burglary in Louisville he killed the officer that caught him.

When the officers came upon him to-day Clark and his girl both opened fire in the most desperate resistance. Clark was well armed and the girl also. Both Clark and Hattie Mahoney were shot dead, riddled with bullets, in the fight that ensued and the escape of the officers was most miraculous.

HOWARD CLARK AND MATTIE BELLE MAHONEY

Keven McQueen*

During the Great Depression, Bonnie Parker and Clyde Barrow shared a passion for robbery and each other that made them criminal legends. Slightly more than a generation before Parker and Barrow shot their way across the Midwest, another pair of felonious lovers emerged out of Louisville, Kentucky. Mattie and Howard were never as notorious as Bonnie and Clyde, but their stories have remarkable parallels.

Although her mother was still alive, Mattie Belle "Maymie" Mahoney, a young, emotionally disturbed teenager, roomed at the Morton Home for Orphans. Howard Clark, a house painter by profession, seduced the underage Mahoney in 1897 while he completed a job at the home. In his spare time he was a safecracker and burglar whose lawbreaking had "driven the whole police force of Louisville to drink," according to the *Louisville Courier-Journal*. Newspapers described Clark with dramatic flair as a villain, and his sweetheart as his innocent victim, although she was apparently only too willing to be led astray. The duo first moved in together, then ran away to Indianapolis, Indiana, where they were apprehended and returned to Louisville. Police released the wayward Mahoney into the custody of her outraged mother who had a warrant sworn out on Maymie's thirty-five-year-old boyfriend, charging him with abduction. He was deemed the worst kind of bad influence and went straight to jail.

Clark returned to his old thieving tricks after a short incarceration. On August 12, 1898, while he and a cohort burglarized a store, he shot Louisville Patrolman Joseph Heffernan. Clark fled, and Heffernan died two days later. Like fellow cop-killer Clyde Barrow, Howard Clark had a reputation as a hard man to catch. Police almost nabbed him a day after the crime when they staked out the boardinghouse where Mattie Mahoney now lived. She alerted her paramour, however, and Clark escaped through a rear window. Shortly thereafter, the fugitive visited Louisville barber David Cotner, who shaved off Clark's distinctive mustache. Cotner, a former policeman, told authorities that his customer was in a rush,

seemed inexplicably nervous, and held a .44 caliber revolver in each hand while being shaved. This close encounter proved that Clark might be less recognizable, but he had not left the city.

The Louisville police did not wait around for Clark to decide to surrender. They circulated a wanted poster that included unflattering comments about him, such as "Is a sneaking coward; have information that he fainted . . . when notified of the death of the officer, then immediately fled the city. . . . Can not look you in the face. . . . Sullen look." Like similar posters created in the days before fingerprinting and DNA testing were common, Clark's sheet also included laborious measurements of anatomical parts. Thus investigators knew his height and weight, as well as such minutiae as the exact dimensions of his head, feet, and fingers. One might assume that the well-equipped policeman of 1898 carried calipers and a tape measure.

When they learned Clark might be in the vicinity, police chief Jake Haager and Corporal Lapaille went undercover to Belleville, Illinois. Haager dressed as an effete summer vacationer, complete with a golf cap and bowtie, while Lapaille wore the duds of a railroad switchman. Upon their return, the *Louisville Courier-Journal* ran a story describing the detectives' search—complete with illustrations of them in their disguises—which would seem to reveal too much about their techniques, since criminals read newspapers, too.

In mid-September Mattie Mahoney vanished. Rumors soon confirmed what the authorities had already guessed, that she had joined Howard Clark in hiding, so her likeness appeared next to his on the next run of wanted posters.

On the night of October 7, a reliable informant told law enforcement in Owensboro, Kentucky, that Clark, accompanied by a young woman, had been seen rowing a skiff on the Ohio River. Chief of Police Lyman Pierce and two officers hurried to the river and cast off in their own boat, hoping to beat Clark to the opposite shore and surprise him. Instead, Clark's boat overtook them.

He and Mahoney aimed guns at the lawmen and ordered them to drop their pistols in the river and leave. Unwilling to possibly harm a woman, the officers followed his command and slunk back to shore.

Clark and Mahoney abandoned the skiff and took off across country, remaining at large for the next twenty-four hours. They spent the night in a cornfield in Spencer County, Indiana, just across the state line. At eleven the next morning, three officers from Owensboro accidentally encountered the fugitives, who sat by the roadside under a tree. Clark was dressed in rags, while Mahoney poorly disguised herself in men's clothing.

Howard Clark was armed to the teeth with a .44 caliber Colt revolver, a breech-loading shotgun, a short-barreled .32 caliber revolver, bullets, and a dirk or long dagger. He shot at the officers three times with the .44 caliber pistol, then handed the weapon to Mattie as he scrambled for the shotgun. She managed to shoot once. None of the shots fired by Clark and Mahoney had any effect, but when the policemen opened fire with two shotguns and a rifle, they struck both fugitives several times. Before she received her fatal wound, Mahoney leaped in front of Clark to protect him from the volley. She died with bullets lodged in her brain, heart, hand, and arm. A reporter noticed that she managed to retain her looks even in death, writing that "a slight trace of blood on the cheek was the only mark which was plainly in evidence." Howard did not fare as well. He lingered more than three hours despite having parted company with the top of his head. The journalist graphically described his less than pristine condition for his readers: "Clark's hair was clotted with blood and earth, and blood gushed from his lips and nostrils and gurgled in his throat as he lay in his death agony."[73]

The bodies lay where they fell for hours. Before the coroner came to collect the remains, hundreds of people gathered to ogle the outlaw lovers, dead under the tree. The *Courier-Journal* included a drawing of the death site, but the artist chose to depict Mattie in a proper dress rather than in boy's clothing.

A hearing was held in Rockport, Indiana, on October 10, which ruled that the Kentucky officers had acted justifiably. Officials expressed regret that the young woman had been killed, but she left the police no choice. The *Courier-Journal*'s editorialists disagreed. They called Mattie's death "a shocking incident" and disclosed that she was pregnant at the time of her death. Clark deserved his fate, thundered the writer, "but by no stretch of imagination could this child of sixteen be regarded as an enemy to be engaged in a duel to the death." Noting that her pistol was nothing compared to the policemen's shotguns, the sentimental journalist proclaimed that Mattie "was practically as defenseless as a sheep." A sheep that was shooting at us, the officers might have countered.[74]

Much later Hiram Young, a farmer who had been an eyewitness to the shooting, claimed that Mattie was unarmed. He had said just the opposite under oath during the original inquest, however, and it was remembered that Mattie aimed a gun at a policeman's belly during the adventure on the river. Few people believed Young, but the *Courier-Journal* used the occasion to run another editorial decrying "the reckless use of firearms" by officers.[75]

The Clark and Mahoney families dealt with the aftermath in their own ways. Mattie's mother refused to be responsible for her estranged daughter's burial, while Howard's mother denied it was her son who died.

---

* Adapted by Keven McQueen from his book, *Louisville Murder and Mayhem: Historic Crimes of Derby City* (Charleston, SC: The History Press, 2012).

CHARLEY ELLIS

Bob Oliver

The deceptively boyish, fresh-faced appearance of Charley Ellis concealed the enigmatic and sly cunning of a young man with the heart of a murderer. Historians know little about Ellis, alternately known as "the Kid," "Burrows," W. L. Burris, Lucius Burris, or Charley Ellis. Whether any of these was his real name remains unknown, as are his origins and what ultimately happened to him. All that is known for certain is that he committed two murders and never faced justice for his acts.

Around 10:00 p.m. on the night of July 21, 1898, Charley Ellis and his partner, Jim Darlington, slipped aboard the southbound train to Fort Worth when it slowed to a near-stop in Saginaw, Texas, a small town just north of the city. Their plan was to commandeer the train and drive it to a predetermined "cut" in the grade about four miles north of Fort Worth, where they would be joined by the rest of their gang, W. R. (Will) Petty, Dave Evans, and Darlington's cousin George Moore.

Unbeknownst to the rest of the gang, Will Petty had betrayed the gang and informed the police of their plans.

Well-armed, the would-be robbers brought dynamite to blow open the express car and steal the valuable goods and cash secured there. While seizing control of the train, the men shot two railroad workers and threw them from the moving cars. Fireman Watson Whitaker was shot in the stomach, and he died immediately. Seriously wounded, engineer Joe Williams lingered for two days before he succumbed. Charley Ellis and James Darlington, two young men in their mid-twenties, had transitioned from small-time petty thieves into murderers.

As the train neared the gang's predetermined rendezvous point, Darlington slipped and his pistol discharged, prematurely giving the signal for the others to join Ellis and him on the train. Darlington's shot also alerted Hardin D. Gunnels, the assistant chief of the Fort Worth Police, and the three deputies who were lying in wait for the lawbreakers. A shootout ensued between the criminals and police. By the end of the chaos, the police had averted the robbery, but one man was dead, another was dying, and all of the thieves had escaped.

The posse quickly caught most of the conspirators. Petty turned himself in the next day. Although he had

Confidential. Do Not Post.

Arrest and hold on charge of Double Murder and attempted Train Robbery, Lucius Burris, alias Charley Ellis. Height, about 5 feet 8 or 9 inches; age, about 25 years; weight, about 160 pounds; eyes, light blue; complexion, light; hair, light brown, with auburn cast, inclined to be curly and generally worn tolerably long and bushy. Generally smooth shaved; quick spoken and quick action; nervous temperament; carriage erect.

Wells Fargo & Co. will pay Three Hundred Dollars ($300.00) reward for the arrest and delivery to the Sheriff of Tarrant County, Texas, in any jail in the United States, of the above named and described man.

The Gulf, Colorado and Santa Fe Railroad offer a reward of One Hundred and Twenty five ($125.00) Dollars for the arrest and conviction of this man.

The Governor of the State of Texas offers a reward of One Hundred and Fifty Dollars ($150.00) for the arrest and conviction of this man. The evidence is conclusive and will warrant a conviction.

Write or telegraph any information to

STERLING P. CLARK,   or to   F. J. DODGE,
Sheriff Tarrant Co.,   Special Officer,
Fort Worth, Tex.   Wells Fargo & Co.,
                    Kansas City. Mo.

acted as an informant, he went to jail on July 30, and spent the next fifteen months incarcerated. Why had Petty not received more lenience? Perhaps because his law enforcement contact, Hardin Gunnels, had his own criminal scheme. Gunnels reportedly convinced the thieves to rob a train instead of a diamond merchant, so that he could collect the reward for thwarting a train robbery. His speedy "resignation" from the police force on August 9, 1898, and his subsequent indictment support allegations that Gunnels had conspired with the robbers. The police quietly dropped the matter of his involvement, however, perhaps because they did not want to showcase the wrongdoing of one of their own.

Not long after charges against Petty were dropped, he attempted suicide by taking a large dose of morphine, purportedly because of family issues. Within days of his suicide attempt, Petty penned a letter to the *Fort Worth Register* to explain his role in the robbery. He explained that he had cooperated with the police from the beginning and did not turn state's evidence, as the newspapers reported. Petty declared that it was the police who had broken faith with him. They had promised to notify the railroad company of the plan and to arrest the gang as they reentered Fort Worth following the crime. Instead, the police gave the railroad company no warning and confronted the gang at the site of the robbery. Petty also asserted that the reason the police kept him in custody for over one year was to protect him from the allies of gang members who might harm him.

Authorities captured George Moore on August 12, 1898, in Ardmore, which was then Indian Territory, now Oklahoma. Two weeks later, on August 27, police arrested James Darlington near Corsicana, Texas. The last arrest in the case occurred on September 26 with the apprehension of Dave Evans. Criminal proceedings moved quickly for all three of the men. Dave Evans pleaded guilty and received two two-year prison terms but died within weeks of sentencing. George Moore received two successive ninety-nine-year sentences for murder and robbery, but went free after serving fifteen years. James Darlington received the ultimate punishment when a Fort Worth jury convicted and sentenced him to death.

Historians know by far the most about Darlington due to his confession and openness to speaking about his life. He had spent the two previous years studying to become a licensed Baptist minister in El Paso, performing missionary work in Louisiana, and attending school in Lampasas, Texas. The summer before the train robbery, the authorities arrested and indicted Darlington and Ellis for fraud in an embezzlement scheme. That crime occurred in Kaufman County, just east of Dallas. Although the men escaped punishment when the State of Texas's judiciary bureaucracy became confused over the proper court jurisdiction, Darlington and Ellis failed to take advantage of their good fortune and turn from a life of crime. Instead, the pair decided to "double down" and get rich quick by robbing a train.

Why did authorities take a harder line on Darlington than his accomplices? The 1898 Saginaw raid was the first train robbery in Texas, and both local citizens and authorities were hell-bent on quashing any motivation for other ne'er-do-wells to follow suit. Further, the Texas Court of Criminal Appeals supported local officials by interpreting the law in the most punitive terms possible and upheld the prosecution's decision to withhold from the jury the option to convict Darlington of a lesser charge than first-degree murder. The appeals court also "bundled" the two crimes, robbery and murder, together and ruled in Darlington's appeal that the confessed robber either committed both of the crimes (robbery and murder) or none of them. Since Darlington had confessed to the robbery, by the appeals court's definition, he was guilty of both crimes. The court ruled that "the evidence in this case discloses a case of murder in the first degree, or else no offense at all." [76]

Executioners hung Darlington on July 28, 1899, a little over one year after the failed robbery. Although he confessed to his role in the robbery, he maintained even on the gallows that Charley Ellis was the one who had shot and killed both men.

As to the fate of the clean-cut young man who appears on the wanted poster? Charley Ellis narrowly escaped capture in early 1902 when he was discovered living and working as a cowboy in Indian Territory. Officials optimistically speculated that Ellis would soon be captured, but he remained free. Unconfirmed press reports suggested Ellis, under a different name, was imprisoned elsewhere on other charges. As time passed, however, the press forgot about Charley Ellis, and he never paid for his crimes.

VINCENT BRISCOE

Michael H. Price

Chicago Police Detective Patrick Duffy spent his lunch hour at home on May 1, 1902. After he ate, the father of four young children helped his five-year-old son repair a swing in the yard and then headed back to the Stockyards Station house. En route, Duffy noticed a man lingering furtively near a street corner and engaged him in conversation. Soon another man joined the first. He, too, looked uneasy. Neighbors took notice of the interaction but thought little of it. When Duffy reached out as if to put a hand on the shoulder of one of the men, a shot rang out. Duffy had taken a bullet to the head and fell where he stood. Onlookers rushed to his aid, but Duffy was dead. In the commotion, the killers ran.

The police force quickly rallied to exact justice for the death of one of their own. Two hundred Chicago lawmen combed the streets for the murderers. Their rapid dragnet brought in more than fifty suspects, but eventually all were cleared and released. They had descriptions of the guilty parties from local witnesses, but no one had recognized the two.

The first break in the case came about a week later when police arrested "Red" Nell McCarthy, a well-known character in the Chicago stockyards area, for fencing stolen property. Anxious to get out of a larceny charge, she declared, "You have got me with the goods," but she could "put you wise to something big if you can fix me." McCarthy knew that her live-in sweetheart, Frank O'Reilly, was about to dump her, so she had few qualms about telling police what they wanted to hear. She explained that O'Reilly and a friend named Vincent Briscoe, alias Vincent Brittan, were the men wanted for the murder of Detective Duffy. As McCarthy understood it, O'Reilly had killed or wounded a member of his own crew because he feared the man would surrender and incriminate him in a robbery. He shot Duffy because he feared he knew him to be the murderer in that earlier case. McCarthy gave specific details of where they could be found, no doubt hoping that this would all work out in her favor. After some fits and starts, another dragnet, and a shootout with the wrong suspects, the police found O'Reilly and, after a brief struggle, captured him. Vincent Briscoe, however, had left the scene before they arrived.[77]

For O'Reilly, judgement came quickly, even though his version of events varied significantly from Nell McCarthy's. He claimed that he and Briscoe were casing a house for a break-in when they encountered the policeman, but that it was Briscoe who pulled the trigger. That September, a jury found him guilty of Duffy's murder anyway. O'Reilly reportedly declined to pursue a new trial after his conviction, saying, "I guess the sentence will be all right." He was given fourteen years in the penitentiary.[78]

After Vincent Briscoe had been named as the second man involved in the incident, police began digging into his past. Any detail of his life might help them narrow down his possible whereabouts and ultimately identify the twenty-nine-year old fugitive. Word of Briscoe's crime resonated in his native state of Maryland, where the *Baltimore Sun* reported on May 11, 1902, "Vincent Briscoe, alias Brittain, alias Harry Blake, a former inmate of the Maryland Penitentiary and well known to the Baltimore Police, is wanted by the Chicago Police

on a charge of murder." They went on to remind their readers that "Briscoe was sentenced to three years in the Maryland Penitentiary for burglary in August of 1889. Shortly after completing his term, he was again arrested for burglary and served five years. There is . . . a warrant out here for his arrest on a similar charge. . . . He is regarded by the police of Baltimore and Chicago as a most desperate criminal."

The hunt for Briscoe resulted in a number of false alarms. The most embarrassing for the Chicago Police came when they announced that "Police Inspector Shippy, who was said to have gone to Boston to watch for [serial killer] Johann Hoch as a possible passenger on a vessel bound for Hamburg, did not go to Boston at all. Instead, he went to Mobile, Alabama, where he . . . arrested Vincent Briscoe, who is wanted for the murder of Policeman Duffy, in May of 1902." Shippy escorted the man to New Orleans, where the *Times–Picayune* picked up the narrative on January 31, 1905: "Vincent Briscoe seems to be William Lewis, who was brought to the Parish Prison last night by Inspector George Shippy, of the Chicago Police, and the fellow will be hurried back to Chicago and made to stand trial." Unfortunately for Shippy, in the rush to claim success he failed to accurately identify the prisoner, who was in fact William Lewis, a working man from Mobile, who was quietly released and allowed to return to his job a few days later. The search continued.[79]

Briscoe, who rechristened himself Frank Bennett, retreated to the West Coast, where he resumed his larcenous career. He eluded the law until he picked the wrong San Francisco store to rob. He attacked the Japanese merchant with a gas pipe, but the man fought back long enough for the police to arrive. While he served his sentence for that crime, "Frank Bennett" was recognized by prison staff as the long-missing cop killer, Vincent Briscoe.

Unwilling to make any more mistakes in this case, George Shippy, now Chief of Police, sent Captain Patrick Harding, who had known Briscoe since he was a boy, to verify the identification. Once certain they had their man, the authorities requested that he be extradited to Illinois, but he preferred to serve out his California sentence first—and it was apparently his choice to make. The day he completed his stay at San Quentin, however, police scooped him up and shipped him back to Chicago. Three months later he was convicted of Detective Duffy's slaying and sentenced to fourteen years like his pal O'Reilly. By all known accounts he died a jailbird.

BENJAMIN BABBITT JOHNSON

Michael H. Price

No one can say for certain whether James C. Johnston, a newcomer to Orange City, Florida, knew he would be harboring fugitive train robbers, not to mention homicidal louts, when his twin brothers-in-law barged in on his household toward the close of 1898. Certainly Johnston found the Johnson boys, Ben and George (alias Dudley), aged twenty-six, disagreeable and ungrateful for his hospitality. He may have wondered about a satchel of wrecking-and-prying tools they brought with them, ones like burglars might carry, but it seems he did not understand its significance. Whatever his suspicions might have been, he no doubt recognized that his wife's protective attitude toward her brothers could only cause tension between him and his bride.

The anxieties building at home came to a reckoning on a Saturday, December 10, when Johnston had enjoyed all the family togetherness he could tolerate and confronted the unwelcome Johnson brothers with an order to scram. Ida Johnson Johnston, who seems to have been no dainty creature herself, erred in favor of her blood kin. She and her brothers caught Johnston off guard and "only partially clothed," according to a police report. They locked him out of the house that had been ceded to the couple by his mother, adding insult to injury to indignation, and back again.

Furious, Johnston sought out the town marshal, a man named Sperry. He lent Johnston a suit of clothes and carried him by buckboard to the Volusia County seat, DeLand, Florida. Sheriff John R. Turner secured warrants for the arrest of the brothers on grounds of provoking a ruckus.

Sheriff Turner sent Chief Deputy William Parks Edwards, fifty-nine, and the spontaneously deputized William Kurtz Kremer, twenty-two, to accompany Marshal Sperry to Orange City with orders to rout or arrest the Johnson twins. Kremer, who had recently returned to

WANTED, For Train Robbery and Murder: BENJAMIN BABBITT JOHNSON.

BEN JOHNSON.

Attached is a photograph of him. He, with his twin brother, Dudley, while resisting arrest at Orange City, Florida, December 10th, killed Deputy Sheriff Wm. Kreamer. At the same time Dudley Johnson was killed by Deputy Sheriff Edwards, Ben making his escape. The Sheriff of Voulsia County, Florida, offers a reward of $100 for the arrest of Ben Johnson.

On the night of the 22d of March, 1898, train No. 18 of the Southern Pacific was held up by masked robbers, the express car and safe were demolished and contents taken. The Southern Pacific Railroad Company and Wells, Fargo Express Company jointly offered $1000 reward, the same to include a standing reward of $300 offered by Wells, Fargo & Co. for the arrest and conviction of each of the train robbers. The Officers of the Railroad Company and the Express Company consider that they have sufficient proof to warrant the conviction of Ben Johnson for the robbery of said train. The following is a description of him.

5 feet 7 inches in height; weight, 150 to 160 pounds; age, 26 years; complexion, light; hair, light; stands erect and square-shouldered. The attached photograph was taken in 1895. He is able to grow a scattering light beard. He beats his way on trains, and is noted as a burglar, possessing considerable mechanical genius; is a native of Amsterdam, New York State, having been raised there. He has traveled pretty thoroughly throughout the Middle and Western States, and might be looked for in the southwest. After the killing of the Officer at Orange City he made his way north on a freight train either to Alabama or Georgia. He is determined and will make a resistance with arms if about to be captured. Look for him in Syracuse, Amsterdam, Ann Harbor or about St. Paul.

Address any communication in reference to the matter to

C. C. CROWLEY,
Chief Special Agent Southern Pacific Railroad Company,
San Francisco, Cal.

(12-27-98—1,500.)

town after a hitch with the army in the Spanish-American War, got the nod only because his father, a night watchman, was unavailable. The job of administering a warrant in an outlying region required deputy status.

When the officers and the wronged Mr. Johnston reached the house on West French Avenue around 7:00 p.m., Johnston balked at alighting from the buggy lest his in-laws besiege him. Deputy Kremer approached the rear of the house, and Marshal Sperry staked out the front yard. Deputy Edwards stepped onto the porch and gave a knock. Mrs. Johnston answered, but realized that his visit was no neighborly social call and slammed the door in his face. She ordered him to vamoose or else there might be trouble. He braced as if to force his way inside.

Sperry saw two figures cautiously emerge from a side door and shouted a warning to Kremer and Edwards. Kremer ran to one corner and found himself confronted by the Johnson brothers. The twins stood shorter than average at five-foot-seven, but stocky at around 160 pounds each. Both were armed, and neither meant to withdraw.

They opened fire on the rookie. The first blast to the left side of Kremer's forehead proved instantly fatal, but they kept firing in a response that seemed like overkill for a couple of house guests who had overstayed their welcome. Deputy Edwards vaulted a porch railing and landed a few feet from the Johnsons. When his first shot missed, the brothers' return fire caught Edwards in the right side of the chest. He rallied sufficiently to keep firing, and one volley to the chest killed George "Dudley" Johnson outright.

Ben Johnson exchanged gunfire with Edwards and Sperry until the lawmen ran short of ammunition. He declined to press the advantage, however, and ran through the neighborhood to find a doctor, presumably in the hope that his brother might be saved. He then headed for the outskirts of town in search of a train bound northward for Alabama or Georgia. "He beats his way on trains," the wanted poster later advised. Though there was no hope for Johnson or Kremer, Deputy Edwards recovered sufficiently to return to duty until another set-to with an armed hoodlum proved fatal in 1907.

Marshal Sperry summoned Sheriff Turner from DeLand to take Mrs. Johnston into custody on grounds of harboring killers and inciting mayhem. On December 17, 1898, the *Volusia County Record* reported that Turner was "keeping the wires hot" in search of any trace of the surviving twin. The trail grew cold in short order, although there were rumors that Johnson had landed in Cuba, or maybe in California, or just at large in the Southwest. A nationwide felony *dodger*, or man-wanted bulletin, surfaced on Ben Johnson only after the Orange City debacle had proved fatal to his brother and a newly sworn lawman, tested in time of war but a rookie at police work. Ben Johnson remained at large—never to be taken into custody, at least not under his legal name.

The authorities in Florida determined a little too late that these no-account Johnson brothers were hardly run-of-the-mill homewrecking parasitic in-laws. After the deadly encounter at the Johnston home, they found the abandoned kit of burglary tools and learned that authorities in California wanted the Johnson boys for express-coach banditry and general destruction of corporate property. The Southern Pacific Line and Wells, Fargo & Co. had posted a reward offer of $1,000 in connection with a nighttime raid on March 22, 1898, augmented by a standing $300 bounty from Wells Fargo for any such conviction. From the killers' hometown of Amsterdam, New York, the chief of police informed Sheriff Turner that the Johnsons had come from an upstanding family but had gone bad while on the Western frontier.

J.C. Johnston went unaccused in connection with the matter. Neither a pillar nor a pariah of the community, Johnston had arrived several months earlier in Orange City. The *Florida Times–Union* in Jacksonville declared that the husband knew little about his wife's family since they had been married only a few months. Johnston had learned more than he might have wanted to know in short order.

Ida Johnson Johnston was a different matter. Police records showed that she had shouted encouragement to her brothers during the fracas. They charged her accordingly and held her without bail as an accessory to murder. A subsequent hearing freed her on a bond of $10,000. James C. Johnston must not have been too disturbed by the whole affair, however. He reconciled with his wife, and they skipped town together. She was never recaptured to stand trial.

JOHN LEGG

Michael H. Price

Cruel Willie, a recurring character in Southern folklore by way of Scots-Welsh-Irish balladry, is a man of murderous impulses. In a twentieth-century version by the balladeer Burl Ives, Cruel Willie winds up owing a debt to the devil. In another, preserved in 1985 by the East Texas songster Louis "Buddy" Hale, Cruel Willie is a remorseless seducer who imposes himself upon the sister of a prior victim, who "stab[s] him in the belly with a knife."

That restless spirit sometimes entwines itself with another backwoods tradition, the chronic blood feud. Another standard of folklore, the desperate flight through trackless swamplands, intersects with these images in the case of John M. Legg.

A citizen of Northwestern Alabama, Legg apparently had a good reputation, according to a newspaper account of 1900, until he went all Cruel Willie on two upstanding citizens, a father and son. Then got away without a trace. For a good many years, too.

Provincial journalism being as much a matter of folklore and gossip as of empirical fact, newspaper accounts from January of 1900 merge and sometimes clash, but all accounts agree on the essential facts of the case. Legg had for some years been at odds with the Bedingfields, a prominent local family, and held a particular animosity toward John Bedingfield and his son, Jerome. Late in the afternoon of January 24, 1900, following a dispute at a lumber yard over Legg's share in the profits of a business deal,

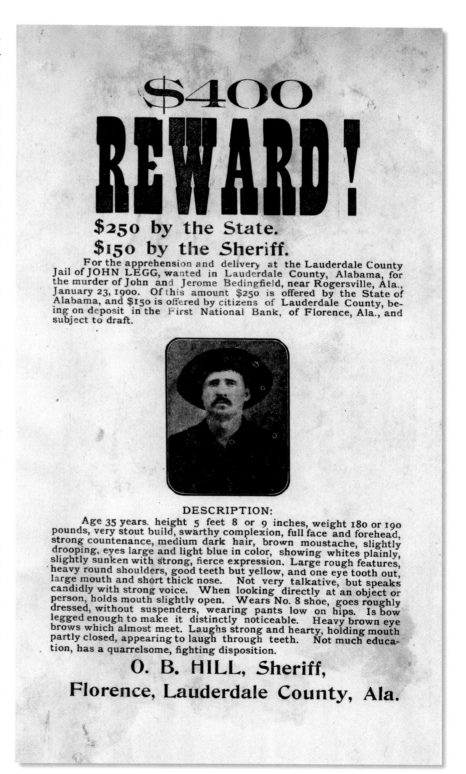

$400 REWARD!

$250 by the State.
$150 by the Sheriff.

For the apprehension and delivery at the Lauderdale County Jail of JOHN LEGG, wanted in Lauderdale County, Alabama, for the murder of John and Jerome Bedingfield, near Rogersville, Ala., January 23, 1900. Of this amount $250 is offered by the State of Alabama, and $150 is offered by citizens of Lauderdale County, being on deposit in the First National Bank, of Florence, Ala., and subject to draft.

DESCRIPTION:

Age 35 years, height 5 feet 8 or 9 inches, weight 180 or 190 pounds, very stout build, swarthy complexion, full face and forehead, strong countenance, medium dark hair, brown moustache, slightly drooping, eyes large and light blue in color, showing whites plainly, slightly sunken with strong, fierce expression. Large rough features, heavy round shoulders, good teeth but yellow, and one eye tooth out, large mouth and short thick nose. Not very talkative, but speaks candidly with strong voice. When looking directly at an object or person, holds mouth slightly open. Wears No. 8 shoe, goes roughly dressed, without suspenders, wearing pants low on hips. Is bow legged enough to make it distinctly noticeable. Heavy brown eye brows which almost meet. Laughs strong and hearty, holding mouth partly closed, appearing to laugh through teeth. Not much education, has a quarrelsome, fighting disposition.

O. B. HILL, Sheriff,
Florence, Lauderdale County, Ala.

Legg brutally murdered John and Jerome. The Columbia (Tennessee) *Herald* gave this version of the attack, based upon a statement given by Jerome Bedingfield as he lay dying:

> Buck Bedingfield, a younger brother, aged about 21, was engaged in hauling lumber from the saw-mill to the river . . . John Legg drove up and called to him to get out of the way . . . Young Bedingfield replied he would not give way . . . and could not get his wagon out of the way if he wanted to as there was no way for him to turn, [so] Legg unhitched his wagon and started home for his shotgun. Securing this he started back to the saw-mill.
>
> [He] met Jerome Bedingfield walking along the road. . . . Legg asking Bedingfield if he had anything against him. Bedingfield said that he had not. Legg then said, "Well, I have nothing against you, either, but I'm going to kill you, just the same." . . . Eighteen buckshot struck Bedingfield in the hip going through and tearing an immense hole . . . Legg asked his victim, "Must I finish you?" Bedingfield replied, "No Cousin John, you've done enough, you've killed me." Legg turned on his heel, saying, "I'm going to kill your damned old daddy, too."
>
> Overtaking the old man in the road . . . he opened fire on John Bedingfield. Several women . . . witnessed the cold-blooded killing.
>
> "I told Cousin John that he had done me wrong for he killed me without giving me a show, and after telling me that he had nothing against me." These are the words of young Jerome Bedingfield on his death-bed.
>
> The two families had been on bad terms for ten years, on account of a quarrel which occurred between a sister of John Legg and some of the Bedingfield children who were school children at that time. There was some suspicion that Legg or some of his people had set fire to the schoolhouse at Rogersville and the feud started in this way.[81]

A much younger son, Charles Bedingfield, who was roughly thirteen, also witnessed the slaying of John Bedingfield. Legg reportedly walked to his brother's house, situated in between the two crime scenes; there he procured a horse and disappeared. Though a posse conducted a systematic search of the area, Legg was not found. After the initial shock of the murder subsided, the community went on about its business, although two large families had been left fatherless. John and Frances Bedingfield had nine offspring. Legg had vanished, leaving his wife and four children to fend for themselves.

Twelve years later, Legg was captured in Jasper, Arkansas. It was said he had spent eight years on the dodge in the swamps of Mississippi. Toughened, but broken in spirit, Legg lived under an alias, James McLemore, for another four years in the Ozark Mountains. Locals said he was regarded as an honest man working in a blacksmith shop. Well, perhaps not by all who knew him. Though seeming immune to alligators and altitudes, the fugitive finally proved vulnerable to disagreeable dealings with a gossip-prone youth to whom he had confided too much. Legg had entrusted this supposed friend to retrieve his family, or at least news of them, from Alabama, but he had gone to the authorities instead. After his arrest, Legg, who had not been in contact with his loved ones in the intervening years, was visited in jail by, among others, a twelve-year-old daughter whom he had never met.

Legg received a life sentence. The *Florence Gazette* commented that Legg was apparently relieved to have avoided the death penalty. The paper also noted that three of the surviving Bedingfield men and a brother of the prisoner attended the trial. John Legg died in prison during the early 1920s.

CHARLES F. COOLEY

Brennan Gardner Rivas

Lowell, Massachusetts, was home to the nation's first textile mills, all of which were originally powered by water. The mills sat on the banks of the Merrimack River. Canals radiating from the river crisscrossed the heart of the industrial center. The abundance of water channels in Lowell meant that the city had quite a few bridges, and in 1901 one man seemed especially fond of them. During that summer Charles F. Cooley stood on the Merrimack Canal Bridge and stared blankly into the water below. Overcome with despair at his misadventures in love, Cooley contemplated ending his life and might have jumped off the bridge had not a friend spotted him and intervened. Over the next several weeks, Cooley visited other bridges near the Tremont and Suffolk Mills, but he no longer seemed to have suicide on his mind. He took with him opera glasses to spy into the apartment of his former lover, Elizabeth Casey—the woman who had spurned him and broken his heart. That fall he came to believe that Casey was seeing another man. At noon on October 5, an enraged Cooley burst into Casey's apartment and beat her over the head with a blunt object. She died in the hospital that night. Casey's roommate in the apartment, Josephine Wills, saw Cooley as he left the building and was struck by the "wild look in his eyes." Shortly after the brutal assault, Wills told the Lowell police about Cooley, and a multi-state manhunt ensued. [82]

As long as the Casey murder was fresh on the minds of Lowell residents, details of the former lovers' history covered the front page of the newspapers. Cooley was a widower, but he had been an abusive husband who abandoned his infant daughter to his former in-laws. He failed to contribute to the support of his daughter, attempted tax evasion, and even shirked payment of his wife's funeral expenses. Casey, who claimed to be a widow, had in fact abandoned

THIS IS A GOOD PHOTO.

Charles F. Cooley,

C. F. Cooley.

Lowell, Mass., Police Headquarters,
Superintendent's Office, Market Street.

WANTED FOR MURDER
of ELIZABETH CAISSE, October 5, 1901.

CHARLES F. COOLEY (American) described as follows: Age 41 years, height 5 feet, 8 or 9 inches, about 155 lbs. weight, medium complexion, dark hair, cut short, sprinkled with gray, mustache light brown, long and straight at the ends (may cut mustache off), straight nose, chin somewhat pointed, thin features, upper and lower sets of false teeth. When talking has a stern look and inclines his head slightly to the right, walks slow and erect with a swing of the shoulders. When last seen was dressed in a brownish suit of clothes, sack coat, black soft hat, and carried a small valise. He has worked in hotels and summer resorts in Maine and New Hampshire, also on railroads; has done canvassing in New York, New Hampshire and Massachusetts; his last occupation was that of a corporation night watchman; receives considerable mail as a result of answering advertisements when only postage is required for full particulars.

Please cause every search and enquiry to be made for the above described. Should he be found, arrest and notify, or should any trace of him be obtained, communicate with the undersigned and steps will be taken to procure his arrest and bring him back with necessary papers for trial.

LOWELL, OCT. 15, 1901.
WM. B. MOFFATT, *Supt. of Police.*

her husband, Joseph Caisse, in the 1880s and altered the spelling of her name to hide her whereabouts. Though she had a teenaged son, Peter Casey, she did not provide a stable home for him, often leaving him to fend for himself. Prior to her relationship with Cooley, she had spent a year in the Massachusetts Reformatory for Women in Sherborn for the crime of adultery, under yet another alias. During the spring of 1901, Casey and Cooley lived together as husband and wife until they were arrested on morality charges. The pair would have gone undetected had they not gotten into an argument that resulted in the police arresting Cooley for threatening Casey. Once the policemen found out that the couple was unmarried, they held them both for "lewd and lascivious cohabitation." Though the charges were ultimately dropped, Casey rebuffed Cooley's offer to resume living together—a refusal that probably pushed him over the edge. [83]

The Lowell police searched for Cooley in town, at streetcar stops and train stations nearby, and sent over one thousand circulars to policemen and postmasters throughout New England. Heading the case was Superintendent William B. Moffatt, a man who, according to one report, picked up his first murder case the night Elizabeth Casey died at St. Joseph's Hospital. When Lowell police failed to locate Cooley, Massachusetts State Police helped create a joint task force based in Lowell to collect clues. The investigators relied heavily upon tips and information from local residents and former acquaintances of the killer and his victim. One man reported that he saw Cooley shortly after the assault, and upon informing him that Casey was expected to die, watched the fugitive disappear into the woods. The man assumed that his despondent friend was finally going to kill himself, as he had threatened to do many times before. There were other theories: Cooley ran away to a Southern New Hampshire lumber camp where an acquaintance worked; Cooley rode the streetcar from Lowell to Nashua, New Hampshire, but jumped off near a "tramp's retreat" along the way; Cooley rode the streetcar to Boston and blended into the crowd there before the local police knew to look for him; Cooley escaped to nearby Pelham, New Hampshire; Cooley sought refuge at a Shaker commune in Enfield, Massachusetts. Detectives pursued all of these tips, and many more, as they searched for Cooley in the fall and winter of 1901.

As the search for Cooley dragged on, he joined the ranks of notorious criminals of the greater Boston area. One outlaw that commentators often associated with Cooley was Joseph Wilfred Blondin, a man from Chelmsford, Massachusetts, who strangled and decapitated his wife around the same time that Cooley and Casey were arrested for lewd and lascivious cohabitation. Blondin quickly achieved infamy in Eastern Massachusetts, and the *Lowell Sun* claimed that the Cooley case had become "as exciting as Blondin." Cooley's trail went cold by the end of October 1901, but police continued to find clues about Blondin's whereabouts through the end of the year, and his capture in February 1902 made headlines even in New York City. During the previous fall, a couple of bank robbers stole headlines from both of these "wife-killers." Albert Smith and Lewis Swift worked for Merchants National Bank of Lowell, and they stole all of the bank's assets as part of an elaborate effort to cover up their years-long embezzling scheme. That robbery was the largest recorded against a national bank up to that time. These big four of Boston crime—Cooley, Blondin, Smith, and Swift—garnered much attention in 1901 and enjoyed prominent display in many a rogues' gallery throughout New England. The fact that all avoided arrest for a time created a public relations problem for police—residents wondered how so many criminals could simply disappear into the woods. [84]

Cooley was last seen on the afternoon of the murder, October 5, 1901, and police never captured him. In his absence a local judge declared him guilty of the murder, though the decision had little impact. Elizabeth Casey's family never claimed her body, and she was buried in the potter's field of Lowell. Her son, the lone mourner at her funeral, moved to Adams, Massachusetts, with his long-lost father, Joseph Caisse. The two claimed that they had never met, but Peter was surely born prior to the time that Caisse claimed his wife had abandoned him. Reporters questioned the situation, but local officials conducted no investigation, ostensibly relieved to have anyone claim guardianship of the young man. Records indicate that Joseph Caisse remarried in 1902, and that his son eventually raised a family in Norwich, Connecticut.

JOHN E. GALLAGHER

Esther Rivera

In the twilight hours of November 21, 1899, John E. Gallagher climbed through a window into the home of his in-laws and shot his wife's brother in the stomach. Joseph McMahon died from his wound two days later. Rumors and theories about the crime swirled in the media and among neighbors in Taunton, Massachusetts. It was said that after Gallagher shot McMahon, he fired wildly at his estranged wife before he escaped. Some people, including Gallagher's own nephew, believed that he intended to shoot his wife all along.

Elizabeth McMahon, who became Gallagher's second wife on September 3, 1896, had recently thrown her husband out of the house where they lived with her parents, her brother, her daughter, and his sons from a previous marriage. Joseph McMahon often mediated encounters between the couple, which probably put him in a precarious position with his brother-in-law. As they investigated the crime, police discovered that McMahon had quarreled with Gallagher over his treatment of his sister in the days leading up to the shooting. Elizabeth had evicted her spouse when she learned that Gallagher had visited a brothel in another city.

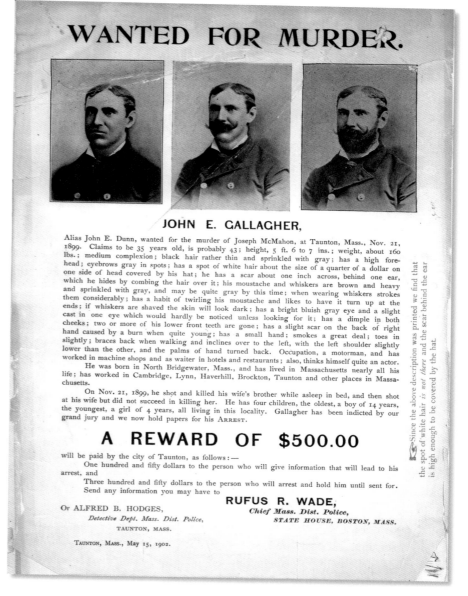

WANTED FOR MURDER.

JOHN E. GALLAGHER,

Alias John E. Dunn, wanted for the murder of Joseph McMahon, at Taunton, Mass., Nov. 21, 1899. Claims to be 35 years old, is probably 43; height, 5 ft. 6 to 7 ins.; weight, about 160 lbs.; medium complexion; black hair rather thin and sprinkled with gray; has a high forehead; eyebrows gray in spots; has a spot of white hair about the size of a quarter of a dollar on one side of head covered by his hat; he has a scar about one inch across, behind one ear, which he hides by combing the hair over it; his moustache and whiskers are brown and heavy and sprinkled with gray, and may be quite gray by this time; when wearing whiskers strokes them considerably; has a habit of twirling his moustache and likes to have it turn up at the ends; if whiskers are shaved the skin will look dark; has a bright bluish gray eye and a slight cast in one eye which would hardly be noticed unless looking for it; has a dimple in both cheeks; two or more of his lower front teeth are gone; has a slight scar on the back of right hand caused by a burn when quite young; has a small hand; smokes a great deal; toes in slightly; braces back when walking and inclines over to the left, with the left shoulder slightly lower than the other, and the palms of hand turned back. Occupation, a motorman, and has worked in machine shops and as waiter in hotels and restaurants; also, thinks himself quite an actor.

He was born in North Bridgewater, Mass., and has lived in Massachusetts nearly all his life; has worked in Cambridge, Lynn, Haverhill, Brockton, Taunton and other places in Massachusetts.

On Nov. 21, 1899, he shot and killed his wife's brother while asleep in bed, and then shot at his wife but did not succeed in killing her. He has four children, the oldest, a boy of 14 years, the youngest, a girl of 4 years, all living in this locality. Gallagher has been indicted by our grand jury and we now hold papers for his ARREST.

A REWARD OF $500.00

will be paid by the city of Taunton, as follows:—

One hundred and fifty dollars to the person who will give information that will lead to his arrest, and

Three hundred and fifty dollars to the person who will arrest and hold him until sent for.

Send any information you may have to

Or ALFRED B. HODGES, *Detective Dept. Mass. Dist. Police,* TAUNTON, MASS.

RUFUS R. WADE, *Chief Mass. Dist. Police,* STATE HOUSE, BOSTON, MASS.

TAUNTON, MASS., May 15, 1902.

Since the above description was printed we find that the spot of white hair *is not there* and the scar behind the ear is high enough to be covered by the hat.

If that were not insult enough, he had contracted a sexually transmitted disease at the establishment which he then passed to his wife her during her pregnancy. As a result of the disease, their daughter was born blind in one eye. Gallagher attempted to make amends, but to no avail.

Newspapers did not hesitate to publish negative personal details about Gallagher. Acquaintances reported that he had a peaceful temperament until he drank alcohol. Witnesses at a saloon in the area testified that he drank heavily in the days leading up to the event. Some accounts noted that proprietors of one bar ejected him for an altercation the very night of the shooting. Others noted that Gallagher, a motorman on the local streetcar line by trade, was not steadily employed during the fall of 1899. Ironically, he held an unpaid constable position, but the suspects he attempted to arrest often bested him and escaped.

Immediately following the shooting, Gallagher fled the scene and hid at the home of his sister in nearby Brockton, Massachusetts, but he departed about the time McMahon died. A few months later, police indicted Gallagher for murder. Although they hoped to capture him quickly, their confidence soon waned. Massachusetts State Police Detective Alfred Hodges gathered photographs of Gallagher to create circulars for distribution to newspapers and law enforcement agencies. Tens of thousands of posters went into rogue's galleries in police stations across the United States, Canada, Europe, Africa, and South America. The *Boston Morning Journal* later stated that the images were crucial to the capture of Gallagher because they made him one of the most recognizable criminals in the country. The poster, advertising a five-hundred-dollar reward, contained height and weight measurements for Gallagher, as well as descriptions of his complexion and gait. It explained that he smoked and twirled his moustache so that it curled up at the ends.

Despite the widespread publicity, Gallagher evaded the police. Erroneous reports resulted in several false arrests, and some sources speculated that he committed suicide or fled the country. In reality, he enlisted in the army during this time under the alias George Holmes, and later moved to Washington State. Over time, he also used the names John E. Dunn and John Rund to hide his true identity.

During the spring of 1903, "George Holmes" tended bar at the Ruby Saloon. He attracted the attention of the Seattle police when he appeared as a witness to an altercation. Officers noticed the remarkable similarities between Holmes and the man described in Gallagher's circulars, right down to his scars and his mannerisms. Upon questioning, Holmes denied being Gallagher or having ever murdered anyone, but local law enforcement officers were highly suspicious of his story. To confirm their theory, they sent Holmes's photos and measurements to their colleagues in Taunton for verification. Without delay, Detective Hodges and a local patrolman went to Seattle to investigate. They recognized Gallagher immediately. Though he fielded a few of their questions deftly, he became emotional at the mention of his mother, whom he had not communicated with in

the four years he had been on the run. Unable to contain himself, he admitted he was John E. Gallagher, agreed to return to Taunton, and then burst into tears.

Eleven months after he pleaded not guilty to the crime, Gallagher's wife testified against him in court in the murder of her brother. The *Boston Post* dramatized the scene of Elizabeth Gallagher and her sister crying during the reading of the crimes and described Gallagher as visibly nervous during the proceedings. Gallagher's lawyers insisted that he had acted in self-defense. Milton Reed and Harold F. Hathaway, his assigned counsel, maintained that Gallagher visited the McMahon home to see his wife and children, and that McMahon attacked him. They insisted that Gallagher shot his brother-in-law by accident when his wife threw herself onto him during the incident.

The trial concluded nearly five years after McMahon's death. On February 16, 1904, the jury found John E. Gallagher guilty of second-degree murder and handed down a life sentence in the state prison. Massachusetts state officials cited the successful conclusion of the case as one of the most significant accomplishments of the year. Gallagher managed to elude capture for over three years despite the circulation of thousands of posters with his picture, and yet with perseverance, they finally got their man.

In May 1914, Gallagher petitioned the state for a pardon, an effort which several key players in the crime supported. His son William from his first marriage wrote to officials saying that if his father was released, he would allow him to live with him. Representatives from the Massachusetts State Prison added that Gallagher was an exemplary prisoner and thus a good candidate for absolution. In his interview with the advisory board of pardons, he appeared apologetic and vowed to maintain sobriety. Even Elizabeth Gallagher agreed to his release. She hoped he would support their partially blind daughter and insisted that he would not have committed the crime if he had been sober. Though it was to her advantage and that of her daughter for him to become a wage earner again, Elizabeth Gallagher made it clear that she did not seek any contact with him following his release. Upon consideration of the case, the parole board reduced John E. Gallagher's sentence to sixteen years and released him from custody on March 26, 1915.

JAMES REDMOND

Richard Selcer

On the night of December 8, 1897, James Redmond and John Kennedy tried to rob the Kansas City grocery store of Miss Emma Schumacher. Kennedy preferred robbing trains but needed some quick cash. Redmond was a small-time crook who fancied himself an accomplished "yegg" (burglar). The pair probably thought robbing this woman would be like taking candy from a baby, but they were wrong. As soon as they walked in, things started going south. Emma recognized Redmond and called him by name, then pulled a revolver from under the counter and opened fire. In the exchange that followed she was killed, but not before one of her shots hit Redmond full in the face, entering at the center of his lower lip and ripping through the left cheek. The safe forgotten, the pair of would-be robbers fled to a waiting buggy and drove off into the night.

Redmond and Kennedy had met while cellmates in the Jackson County, Missouri, jail, where Kennedy was awaiting trial for train robbery and Redmond for burglary. Both were small fry in the criminal underworld. Kennedy claimed to have been pals with the James-Younger gang once upon a time, which gave him bragging rights over Redmond. When Redmond was released, Kennedy steered him to the boarding house of Kit Carson Rose, a friend of his whose wife Henrietta was a sister of the Youngers.

The night of the botched robbery, Kennedy and the badly wounded Redmond went to the Roses. Henrietta dressed Redmond's wound, and the pair lay low for a night and a day. They warned the Roses' old black servant, Uncle Billy Handy, that they would kill him and his wife if he ratted them out.

The second night Redmond felt well enough to travel so they decided to leave, each man going his own way. Kennedy figured Redmond would only slow him down, and he wanted to get back to what he knew

Wanted
for Murder !

$200 REWARD

JAMES REDMOND is wanted for the murder of Miss Schumacker in this city on the night of December 8th, 1897 while in the act of robbing her.

Redmond is 30 years old, 5 feet 8 1-2 inches in height, weight 165 pounds, Large Ears, Blue Eyes, Sandy Hair, Dark Complexion; under skin on forehead are some buck shot which you can feel but not see; Tattooed on left fore-arm is Ballet Girl with sword in her hand; on right fore-arm is a Tombstone, Weeping Willow Sailor and Anchor; Wart on left side of neck.

At the time of the murder he was shot in the mouth, and I am informed the bullet entered in center of lower lip and came out in the left cheek—this may have left an ugly wound.

He is a burglar and would steal lead pipe or blow a safe. His talk is of Bowery order, and uses an oath with most every word. May have a Sandy Mustache. Is a dope fiend and is fond of women.

If found arrest and wire

JNO. HAYES, Chief of Police.

KANSAS CITY, MO., February 7th, 1898.

PICTURE TAKEN IN 1897

best—train robbing. Redmond somehow managed to get out of town unseen and began a long criminal odyssey using half a dozen aliases.

Kansas City, Missouri, police got their first break in the case when they arrested Kennedy on January 28, 1898. He was on his way out of town to hit another train when his horse fell, leaving him senseless and bloody. Police were still holding him about a month later when Uncle Billy came in and identified Kennedy as one of the men who killed Emma Schumacher. With no other evidence in the case, Police Chief John Hayes hid Uncle Billy, hoping to protect him from possible retaliation before the trial by friends of Cole and Jim Younger. The two Youngers were serving life sentences in the Minnesota State Penitentiary for the 1876 Northfield, Minnesota, bank job and angling for paroles. Chief Hayes launched a full-scale manhunt for Redmond, which included a wanted circular issued on February 7 based on information provided by Uncle Billy.

The picture on the notice tells us that Kansas City police already had a mug shot of Redmond in their rogues' gallery. The circular advised law enforcement agencies that the subject was "Wanted for Murder!" and that there was a $200 reward on his head. Hayes used the US mails and newspapers (sans photo) to spread the word, as opposed to telegrams or notices in trade papers like the *National Police Gazette*. At the time he was unaware that Redmond was also wanted in Chicago under the name John Healy for murdering Ferdinand Pommeranz during an argument in 1886.

Redmond proved elusive. Unbeknownst to Kansas City police, he changed his name to Seville and enlisted in the US Army in the spring of 1898. Uncle Sam was looking for volunteers to fight the Spanish, and Redmond enlisted in Jay Torrey's Wyoming Volunteer Cavalry, one of three regiments of Rough Riders authorized by Congress, the best-known being Teddy Roosevelt's. Volunteers had to be no older than 45, between 5'4" and 5'10" tall, and weigh no more than 165 pounds, all of which fit Redmond. Naturally, he was also an excellent horseman to get into an outfit like the Rough Riders. The regiment never left the country. (Contrary to some newspaper reports, Redmond was not part of Roosevelt's Rough Riders and never distinguished himself in combat.) In August the troops were ordered to Camp Wikoff on Long Island to demobilize. It was there that someone from Kansas City recognized Redmond and informed the New York police. Theodore Roosevelt, former Rough-Rider-turned-police-commissioner, wired Chief Hayes to confirm the fugitive warrant, but refused to arrest Redmond without the proper army requisition papers. He did agree to keep him under surveillance until Kansas City detectives arrived with the paperwork. Unfortunately, Redmond figured out he was being watched and fled. He was now a deserter on top of being an accused murderer, but the only people really interested in tracking him down were the Kansas City police.

When old Uncle Billy, the state's only witness, passed away in January 1899, it became practically impossible to make a case against either Kennedy or Redmond. Kennedy was already out on bail on the train-robbery charges, and authorities dropped the murder charge against him altogether. He was finally tried and convicted in the former case in June 1899 and sent to the penitentiary. Paroled in 1912, he wasted no time returning to his old ways. In the meantime, the hunt continued for James Redmond. Chief Hayes may have thought if he could ever get both men in custody at the same time, he could turn them against each other.

Redmond continued to drift west, picking up work as a cowboy and calling himself William A. O'Neill. He turned up in Seattle in 1900, signed on with the army as a horse wrangler, and shipped out to the Philippines. In Manila he promoted himself to artillery sergeant but didn't fool the army. While he was in the guardhouse for impersonating a noncommissioned officer, a lieutenant with the Thirty-Ninth Infantry who had been a reporter for the *Kansas City Times* in civilian life recognized Redmond, and another former Rough Rider confirmed the identification. The army put him on a transport back to the States, and San Francisco police took him into custody on April 13.

They sent word to the Kansas City police to come and pick him up, and on April 24 he was booked into the Jackson County Jail. John Hayes finally had his man, but little good it did him. In November, the county attorney dismissed murder charges against Redmond for lack of evidence; specifically, no Uncle Billy. It looked like Emma was never going to get justice in what the newspapers were now calling "one of the most cold-blooded crimes ever committed in Kansas City."[85]

Redmond was no sooner released than he was picked up again for larceny. He made "leg bail" and headed north to the Windy City, where in August 1903 he was part of a gang that robbed the Chicago City Railway car barn of more than $3,000 and killed two men. He was quickly arrested, and Chicago's best sweated him for hours without breaking him. All they got was the smug admission, "I'm a thief. What of that? There are others in Chicago." Redmond could afford to take an attitude. He had an "ever-ready" alibi handy, something that had "many times saved him from the penitentiary and the gallows." Police had to let him go.[86]

He was a free man again, at least until police reopened the fourteen-year-old Pommeranz case. This time they found witnesses who would testify against him. He was convicted and sentenced to fourteen years in the penitentiary. It was little comfort to the friends and family of Emma Schumacher, but the law had finally caught up with James Redmond.

DANIEL COUGHLIN, wanted at Chicago, Ill., for Attempt to Bribe a Juror and Conspiracy to Do an Illegal Act Injurious to Public Justice; under two indictments in Cook County, Illinois; forfeited his bonds July 13, 1899.

Five Hundred Dollars Reward

offered by Cook County Board for his apprehension.

DANIEL COUGHLIN, EX-CONVICT AND FUGITIVE.

[From photographs taken at Joliet while Coughlin was serving time for the murder of Dr. Cronin. These show how he looks with a clean-shaven face.]

DESCRIPTION from Illinois Penitentiary Records as follows: Age at present 39; height 6 feet 1 inch; hair blond; eyes blue; sandy red mustache; complexion light; large mole on right cheek; his picture taken Jan. 14, 1890, at the Penitentiary is printed hereon; his weight is about 225; has somewhat sloping or stoop shoulders and appears large and strongly built; his eyes are considered by some to be grayish blue and by others as approaching a brownish hue; they are deepset under eyebrows well shown by his picture; they are small and flinching; was engaged in saloon business at time of becoming a fugitive from justice; had previously been a Chicago policeman; is noted for his connection as a defendant in the case of the murder of Dr. Cronin at Chicago; is of pleasant manner; rather reticent but genial in conversation.

Address all information to

JOSEPH KIPLEY, *Chief of Police, Chicago, Ill.,*
or CHAS. S. DENEEN, *State's Attorney, Chicago, Ill.*

DANIEL COUGHLIN

Gene Allen Smith

Sitting with stooped shoulders and looking into the lens with his grayish-blue deep-set eyes, thirty-nine-year-old Daniel Coughlin posed for his prison mug shot at the Illinois State Penitentiary in Joliet on January 14, 1899. A large man for the day, standing six-foot-one and weighing in at about two-hundred-twenty-five pounds, the burly former police detective had blond hair, a light complexion, a sandy red mustache, and a large mole on his right cheek. After having been issued a prison uniform and being photographed, Coughlin started working in the stone yard, an appropriate job for someone of his size. Despite his appearance of strength, however, Coughlin's wanted poster bearing a sketch based on his mug shot indicated that he was a reticent but pleasant man and genial in conversation. Could this gentle giant be responsible for the murder of Dr. Patrick Henry Cronin?

Daniel Coughlin was an Irishman first and foremost, and he found himself caught in the power struggle of the secret organization Clan-na-Gael, the Irish successor group that emerged after the Fenian Brotherhood's failed 1866 invasion of Canada. With a national membership of more than ten thousand, the United Brotherhood, as it was known to the members, developed chapters or camps in every major American city and actively promoted Irish independence. At the 1881 convention in Chicago, the Clan-na-Gael formed a five-member executive committee to run the organization. Shortly thereafter, three of the board members—informally known as the Triangle—began working together to gain control over the organization. They also began funneling money and men to England for a campaign of terror against the British. The open support of violence against England badly split the organization. Dr. Patrick Cronin vocally supported peaceful opposition methods, becoming the spokesman against the Triangle's leadership and charging them with embezzling money for their own use.

The Clan-na-Gael leadership responded that Cronin was an English spy. They demanded he appear before a board of inquiry whose membership consisted of the organization's most ardent members, including Coughlin. The inquiry rendered Cronin guilty, and the committee expelled him from the Clan-na-Gael. Cronin's vocal stance against the corruption of the Triangle, however, had won for him a strong following within the organization, and with his departure thousands of members resigned from Clan-na-Gael to form their own pro-Cronin camps. After some months of rancorous disagreements, leaders of the two fractious groups agreed to reconcile and promote a common goal of working to secure Irish independence; Cronin agreed to participate only if the Triangle were investigated. The resulting committee of six, which included Cronin, conducted the inquiry into the activities of the Triangle, but the final vote was four to two that the charges against them could not be proven. When Cronin threatened to make his notes of the proceedings public, one Triangle leader quietly suggested that the doctor should be removed.

At 7:30 p.m. on May 4, 1889, a carriage pulled by a white horse arrived at Dr. Cronin's house. The driver requested medical assistance for an employee at O'Sullivan's ice house. Cronin got in the carriage and was not seen alive again. His decomposing body was discovered eighteen days later in the catch-basin of a public sewer. During the following months the police conducted a lengthy investigation, which found among other things that Daniel Coughlin was intricately involved in the crime because he had rented the horse and carriage used in the abduction. The prosecution argued during the trial that Coughlin had also helped kill Cronin by stabbing him repeatedly in the back of the head with a sharp icepick-like object. The sensationalized trial lasted three and a half months, and closing arguments took two additional weeks. The verdict proclaimed that Daniel Coughlin and two coconspirators were guilty of first-degree murder in the "Crime of the Century." The court sentenced Coughlin and the other two to life in prison.

Facing such a dire future, Coughlin's attorneys appealed the verdict. The Illinois Supreme Court granted a new trial on the grounds that two of the jurors had been prejudiced against Coughlin. In late January 1893, Daniel Coughlin was acquitted and released. He returned to Chicago and opened a saloon with former policeman and partner William Armstrong at 123 Clark Street (now 326 North Clark Street). He also often did private detective work for the Illinois Central Railroad. In 1899, Coughlin was indicted again. This time he was accused of attempting to bribe juror James F. Taylor in a lawsuit against the railroad for which Coughlin worked. Starting in the mid-1870s Coughlin had apparently built a reputation as an incorrigible jury briber. Arrested and later released on a bail of $30,000 (some $870,000 in 2016 dollars), Coughlin, accompanied by Armstrong, immediately left town. Coughlin reportedly remarked to a bar patron before he left, "I don't like indictments. . . . I don't like trials, you never know how they are going to come out."[87]

Authorities sent out Coughlin's wanted poster, hoping someone would recognize the fugitive. Coughlin successfully evaded authorities for eight years, ultimately making his way south to the Gulf city of Mobile, Alabama, where he assumed a new identity and life as "James M. Davis." But in early June 1907 local police recognized him from the poster and arrested him. While awaiting extradition to Illinois, Coughlin escaped. He quickly boarded a departing tramp steamer (a ship with no fixed schedule or published ports) for the short voyage to Central America, landing in Honduras. Reportedly, Coughlin settled in San Pedro, Honduras, and quietly worked on a banana plantation until he died during the winter of 1910.

Having been accused of the "Crime of the Century," the big blonde Irishman garnered attention even when incognito in a sleepy southern port. His poster unmasked "James M. Davis" as a wanted murderer, forcing him to flee from the country, perhaps the only way he could escape from life and death in prison.

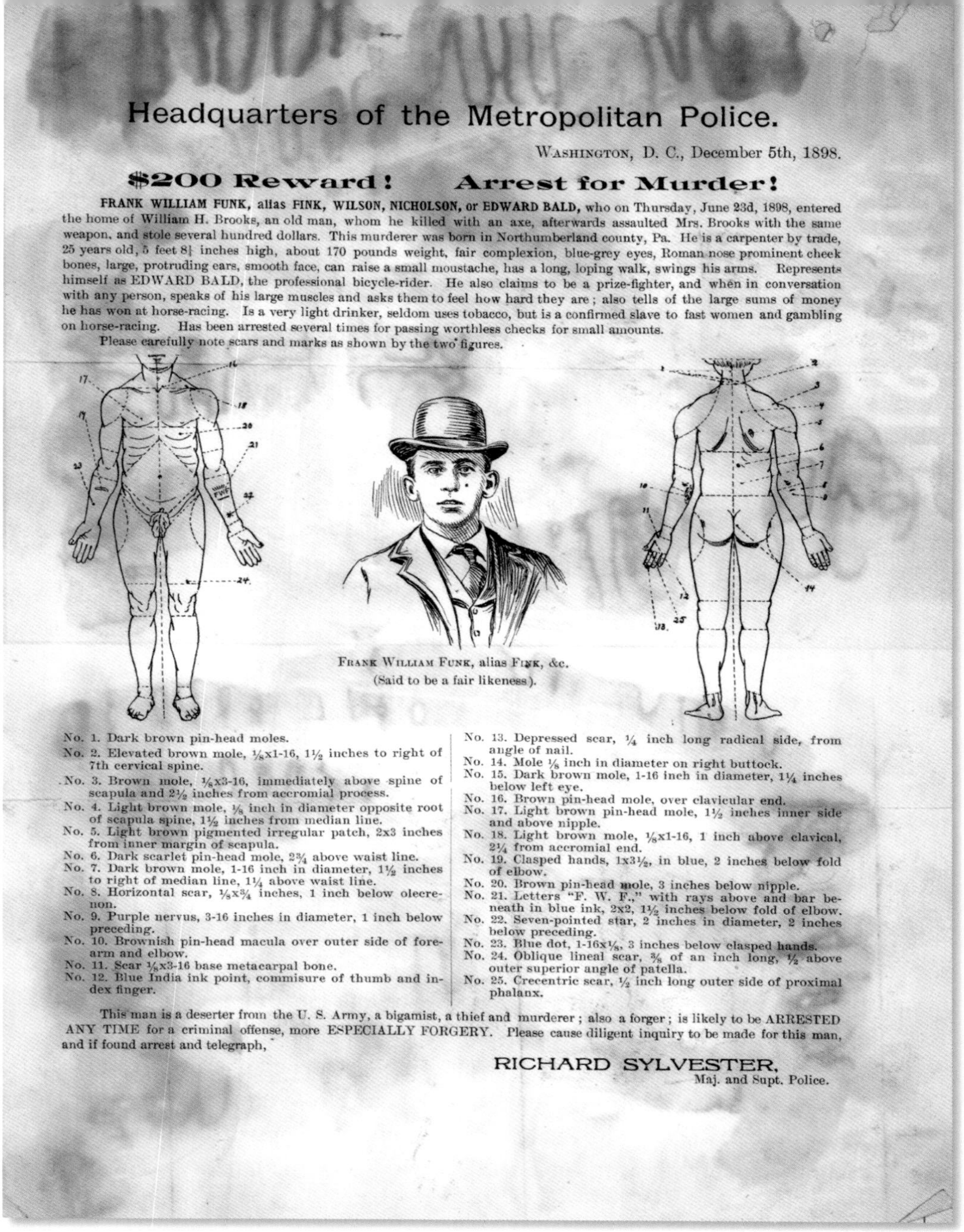

Headquarters of the Metropolitan Police.

WASHINGTON, D. C., December 5th, 1898.

$200 Reward! Arrest for Murder!

FRANK WILLIAM FUNK, alias FINK, WILSON, NICHOLSON, or EDWARD BALD, who on Thursday, June 23d, 1898, entered the home of William H. Brooks, an old man, whom he killed with an axe, afterwards assaulted Mrs. Brooks with the same weapon, and stole several hundred dollars. This murderer was born in Northumberland county, Pa. He is a carpenter by trade, 25 years old, 5 feet 8½ inches high, about 170 pounds weight, fair complexion, blue-grey eyes, Roman nose prominent cheek bones, large, protruding ears, smooth face, can raise a small moustache, has a long, loping walk, swings his arms. Represents himself as EDWARD BALD, the professional bicycle-rider. He also claims to be a prize-fighter, and when in conversation with any person, speaks of his large muscles and asks them to feel how hard they are; also tells of the large sums of money he has won at horse-racing. Is a very light drinker, seldom uses tobacco, but is a confirmed slave to fast women and gambling on horse-racing. Has been arrested several times for passing worthless checks for small amounts.

Please carefully note scars and marks as shown by the two figures.

FRANK WILLIAM FUNK, alias FINK, &c.
(Said to be a fair likeness).

No. 1. Dark brown pin-head moles.
No. 2. Elevated brown mole, ⅛x1-16, 1½ inches to right of 7th cervical spine.
No. 3. Brown mole, ⅛x3-16, immediately above spine of scapula and 2½ inches from accromial process.
No. 4. Light brown mole, ⅛ inch in diameter opposite root of scapula spine, 1½ inches from median line.
No. 5. Light brown pigmented irregular patch, 2x3 inches from inner margin of scapula.
No. 6. Dark scarlet pin-head mole, 2¾ above waist line.
No. 7. Dark brown mole, 1-16 inch in diameter, 1½ inches to right of median line, 1¼ above waist line.
No. 8. Horizontal scar, ⅛x¾ inches, 1 inch below olecrenon.
No. 9. Purple nervus, 3-16 inches in diameter, 1 inch below preceding.
No. 10. Brownish pin-head macula over outer side of forearm and elbow.
No. 11. Scar ⅛x3-16 base metacarpal bone.
No. 12. Blue India ink point, commisure of thumb and index finger.
No. 13. Depressed scar, ¼ inch long radical side, from angle of nail.
No. 14. Mole ⅛ inch in diameter on right buttock.
No. 15. Dark brown mole, 1-16 inch in diameter, 1¼ inches below left eye.
No. 16. Brown pin-head mole, over clavicular end.
No. 17. Light brown pin-head mole, 1½ inches inner side and above nipple.
No. 18. Light brown mole, ⅛x1-16, 1 inch above clavical, 2¼ from accromial end.
No. 19. Clasped hands, 1x3½, in blue, 2 inches below fold of elbow.
No. 20. Brown pin-head mole, 3 inches below nipple.
No. 21. Letters "F. W. F.," with rays above and bar beneath in blue ink, 2x2, 1½ inches below fold of elbow.
No. 22. Seven-pointed star, 2 inches in diameter, 2 inches below preceding.
No. 23. Blue dot, 1-16x⅛, 3 inches below clasped hands.
No. 24. Oblique lineal scar, ⅜ of an inch long, ½ above outer superior angle of patella.
No. 25. Crecentric scar, ½ inch long outer side of proximal phalanx.

This man is a deserter from the U. S. Army, a bigamist, a thief and murderer; also a forger; is likely to be ARRESTED ANY TIME for a criminal offense, more ESPECIALLY FORGERY. Please cause diligent inquiry to be made for this man, and if found arrest and telegraph,

RICHARD SYLVESTER,
Maj. and Supt. Police.

FRANK WILLIAM FUNK

Gene Rhea Tucker

In Washington, DC, around 6:00 p.m. on June 23, 1898, a friendly neighbor discovered seventy-three-year-old Civil War veteran William H. Brooks and his sixty-five-year-old wife Martha bludgeoned and bloody in a storeroom at the rear of their home at 914 Twenty-Second Street NW. The perpetrator had gashed their heads with several strokes of an ax, which was left at the scene. Mr. Brooks died as the doctor arrived, and the police conveyed Mrs. Brooks to the hospital in their patrol wagon. Surgeons performed risky operations on Mrs. Brooks, removing portions of her skull in the process, and gave her little chance of surviving. Their daughter Maggie Brooks, who was out of the house visiting friends, claimed that nearly two thousand dollars was missing from a locked kitchen drawer along with the money belt Mrs. Brooks normally wore around her waist.

The suspicion of officers and detectives soon fell on a man named Frank William Funk. Funk, a cash-poor carpenter hailing from Pennsylvania, had been to the Brooks home on several occasions. His sister was friends with another daughter of Mr. and Mrs. Brooks, Mrs. Sophia Brown. Funk was familiar with the family and aware of where they hid their money. On the day of the crime, he made appointments to meet the Brooks daughters at two different locations at 6:00 p.m. He failed to show at either meeting. This gave Funk time to commit the crime without the daughters present. Authorities found two blood-covered pencils on the floor next to Mr. and Mrs. Brooks. Detectives found the same brand of pencils in Funk's boardinghouse room. The lawmen further ascertained that Funk, dressed in dirty garb, bought a new suit and trousers from a clothing store shortly after the crime. He then purchased a pair of shoes, a hat, and a hotel room under the name of Harry A. Nicholson of Cincinnati. Funk paid for a train ticket under the name Edward Bald and set out for New York City that same night. The police later found Funk's bloody clothes in the hotel room.

Though doctors originally gave Mrs. Brooks a poor prognosis, she improved enough over the course of a few weeks to leave the hospital in the care of her daughters. Mrs. Brooks could not remember who had attacked her. Meanwhile, the police and press discovered that over the years Funk had had several run-ins with the law over charges that included assault and passing fraudulent checks. He had also enlisted in the army, then deserted after four months.

Police further discovered that Funk was a bigamist, married to Emma Whitmore of Laurel, Maryland, (with whom he had a daughter) and to Jennie Beederbeck of Philadelphia. He was a spendthrift too, throwing away his meager earnings on fine clothes, easy female companions, and gambling parlors. The police kept an eye on his family members and wives, but Funk didn't surface. The authorities mailed out wanted posters in June with a detailed description of Funk but offered no reward, as the fund for rewards had been exhausted. There were occasional reports of Funk's capture, but they all turned out to be false alarms.

Six months after Funk's flight, the police decided to circulate new wanted posters across the country, this time with a reward. The advertisements offered a detailed description of the location and size of various moles, marks, and scars on Funk's body. In the late nineteenth century, the military and law enforcement used such marks and measurements from the Bertillon system, so Funk's measurements were obtained from his army files. In addition to the particulars of his crime, the wanted poster included Funk's likeness, a description of his personality (calling him a "confirmed slave to fast women and gambling on horse-racing"), and a detailed delineation of his identifying marks. The authorities printed 170,000 posters and mailed them to 80,000 jurisdictions. One of those posters found its mark. In Columbia, Missouri, a man calling himself "William Conley" resembled the man on the circular, and the police picked him up on August 17, 1899. After identifying him based on his marks, he was extradited to Washington, DC. Funk proclaimed his innocence, claiming various other people had committed the crime.

Funk's trial began on December 11, 1899. The prosecution laid out its case, focusing on motive, opportunity, the bloody clothes and pencils, and Funk's guilty flight. Testimony also revealed that Funk's father tried to pay someone to provide his son with an alibi. After several days of testimony, the defense opened its case, eventually calling Funk himself to the stand. Funk's story was that Sophia Brown committed the crime with an accomplice, an African American bricklayer. Funk only stole the money from her, he claimed. In the process of spinning his story, he admitted to being at the scene of the crime around the time it was committed. On December 23, the jury found Funk guilty. After motions, the court sentenced Funk to be hanged on March 3, 1900. He appealed the decision and the punishment. The government postponed his original execution date, but the federal appeals court and the Supreme Court eventually rejected his claims. Funk's father sent letters to the Attorney General and President William McKinley requesting clemency, but in vain. On November 9, 1900, Frank William Funk was executed by hanging in the courtyard of the jail in Washington, DC. He admitted to the warden, "I have led an evil life, and am about to pay the penalty," but refused to confess to the murder of Mr. William H. Brooks, proclaiming his innocence to the end. Funk was buried in Baltimore's Holy Rood Cemetery.[88]

HENRY AND ROGERS GINGERY

Gene Rhea Tucker

In late 1899 and early 1900, an epidemic of smallpox was spreading across the state of Tennessee. By January 1900, with twenty-nine counties reporting cases, several deaths announced, and concern mounting, authorities across the state rigorously enforced the mandatory vaccination laws. In Lauderdale County, on the Mississippi River north of Memphis at the extreme western end of the state, authorities were under orders to arrest and inoculate any unvaccinated individuals. Reuben Gingery, an African American man living near the town of Durhamville, refused vaccination, and a warrant was sworn out for his arrest. Among the whites of the area "Gingery and his three brothers" were "negroes of bad reputation," so local constable W. D. Turner deputized Marvin Durham to assist him in the arrest.[89]

On the morning of January 9, 1900, the arrest went without a hitch, but Reuben's brothers, Henry Gingery and Rogers Gingery, decided to attempt a rescue. Gathering some horses and guns, they overtook the lawmen escorting their prisoner to the city of Ripley, the county seat. Henry and Rogers surprised Turner and Durham, shooting Turner in the back with a pistol and firing a shotgun at Durham. The Gingery brothers then beat the wounded and de-horsed officers to death. During the melee, Reuben Gingery was shot in the leg. While Henry and Rogers made their getaway, Reuben returned to Durhamville, just a half a mile away. Marvin Durham's father and two friends discovered the crime shortly after it occurred and recaptured the injured Reuben Gingery. He was locked up in a Durhamville store under armed guard.

As soon as the whites of Ripley learned of the tragedy, many closed their shops and left their work to join in the posse searching for the absconding Gingery brothers. Bloodhounds were called in, but rain soon destroyed the scent. Rumors spread that African Americans were arming themselves. During the tense hours that followed, the search party became a lynch mob. As the Nashville newspaper *The Tennessean* recounted,

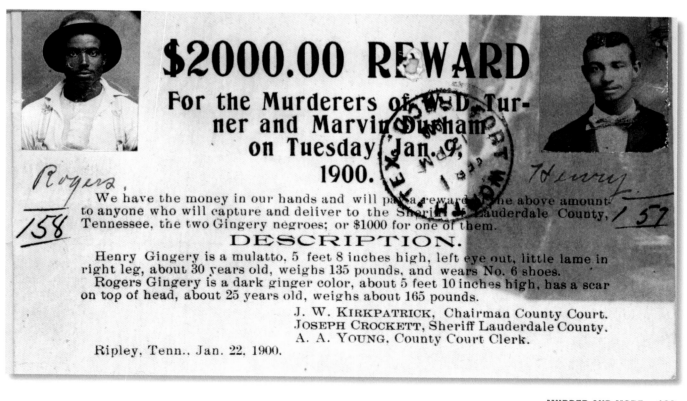

$2000.00 REWARD For the Murderers of W. D. Turner and Marvin Durham on Tuesday, Jan. 9, 1900.

Rogers,

158

We have the money in our hands and will pay a reward of the above amount to anyone who will capture and deliver to the Sheriff of Lauderdale County, Tennessee, the two Gingery negroes; or $1000 for one of them.

Henry,

157

DESCRIPTION.

Henry Gingery is a mulatto, 5 feet 8 inches high, left eye out, little lame in right leg, about 30 years old, weighs 135 pounds, and wears No. 6 shoes.

Rogers Gingery is a dark ginger color, about 5 feet 10 inches high, has a scar on top of head, about 25 years old, weighs about 165 pounds.

J. W. KIRKPATRICK, Chairman County Court.
JOSEPH CROCKETT, Sheriff Lauderdale County.
A. A. YOUNG, County Court Clerk.

Ripley, Tenn., Jan. 22, 1900.

a "lynching bee is in prospect." That night an armed crowd surrounded the place Reuben Gingery was being held and demanded him for punishment. Another group of whites went to the Gingery homeplace and carried off another brother, Frank Gingery, suspecting his complicity in the crime. The lynch mob then paraded Reuben and Frank Gingery to the scene of the crime and "informed the negroes that they must pay the penalty of death." The pair made no statements, were strung up to a gum tree beside the road, and hanged. The crowd affixed a placard next to the lynched men, stating "These bodies must be allowed to hang twenty-four hours." The riled-up mob considered lynching more members of the Gingery family, but law officers dissuaded them. The next day hundreds of spectators viewed the bodies. Some of the observers were local African Americans that whites now described as "quiet" without voicing "a protest or a criticism" of the lynching.[90]

As Henry and Rogers Gingery fled, hundreds of armed white men scoured the county searching for them. Other African Americans were targeted in the hysteria. In some towns in the region, posted notices warned African Americans to pack up and leave or face summary execution. Others were whipped and run out of their homes. On January 15 a lynch mob hanged another African American man, Anderson Gause, from the village of Henning, for supposedly aiding the runaway Gingery brothers. Mass meetings in Ripley raised a reward to which the Tennessee governor, Benton McMillin, added money. Meanwhile, authorities circulated wanted notices across the nation offering $2,000 for the capture of both Henry and Rogers. The notice sent to the Fort Worth Police Department was a postcard with thumbnail headshots of both men. "Henry Gingery is a mulatto," read the poster, "5 feet 8 inches high, left eye out, little lame in right leg, about 30 years old, weighs 135 pounds, and wears No. 6 shoes." "Rogers Gingery," the poster claimed, "is a dark ginger color, about 5 feet 10 inches high, has a scar on top of head, about 25 years old, weighs about 165 pounds."

The tense situation lingered in Lauderdale County for some time, but law enforcement never apprehended Henry Gingery or Rogers Gingery. A sheriff in New Madrid, Missouri, claimed to have caught the pair in April 1900, but no other evidence exists to substantiate that assertion. According to the 1900 and 1910 censuses, Henry's wife Caroline (née Dangerfield) and their children lived with her parents. Though Henry was not there, she still listed herself as married. The police dragged her in for questioning on numerous occasions. In March 1900, a lynch mob killed another black man, Louis Rice, for testifying in a court case. Other reported lynchings of African Americans in the county occurred in 1903, 1906, and 1917. The 1900 census of Lauderdale County, taken in June, showed two other Gingerys incarcerated in the county jail, fourteen-year-old Thomas Gingery and thirteen-year-old Jessie Gingery. As late as July 6, 1917, the local newspaper, *The Lauderdale County Enterprise*, reported that Henry and Rogers Gingery "have never been apprehended."[91]

CHARLIE PRINCE, MICH LAVERY, CHARLIE DENNIS, AND MAMIE WHEELER

Hollace Ava Weiner

The black dot, tattooed between the outlaw's thumb and index finger, was a mark of his profession—safecracking. Like the North Star, that dark dot on Charlie "Denny" Dennis's left hand focused his gaze and helped him line up numbers as he turned the dials to spring combination locks on steel vault doors. Presto! He was in.

Some safes—like the bank vault holding $20,000 at the Adams County Building and Loan in Illinois—had to be blown open with a stick of dynamite and liquid nitroglycerin. Jobs like that had cost Denny's partner Mitch Lavery the index finger on his right hand and had left Charlie Prince, the trio's ringleader, with an oblique scar his left thumb. Such were the liabilities in their line of business.

Dubbed the Prince Gang, these well-dressed gents with their gold pocket watches and diamond tie tacks were suspected of looting safes from Salt Lake City to Washington, DC. In Joplin, Missouri, police raided the burglars' rented rooms and found tools of the trade: skeleton keys, pry bars, and explosives.

The gang's preferred mode of looting a safe was not to blow it up but rather to quietly and gingerly turn the dials. The fingers of an experienced lock picker could sense a slight hitch when it was time to pause a dial and rotate a knob in the opposite direction. That was how the Prince Gang had emptied the vault at the Shukert Fur Company salon in Omaha the night of August 13, 1899. They pulled off that heist at midnight, with twenty-eight-year-old Prince standing lookout outside. On the inside were Lavery, age fifty-nine, who lacked a finger, and Dennis, age forty-five, the man with the dark dot.

They netted forty-five sealskin fur coats valued at $12,000. As quietly as the burglars entered the vault, they placed the garments into a steamer trunk, departed the premises, and walked to their rooming house two hundred yards south. Around 2:00 a.m., Denny strolled into Omaha Merchants Express Transfer Company and ordered a horse-drawn livery wagon to transport a very large trunk to the Union Pacific depot.

By noon the next day, when employees at Shukert's realized the vault was empty, the trunk with the stolen garments had arrived in Sioux Falls, Iowa, one hundred miles away, and had disappeared. Meanwhile, the thieves had checked out of their Omaha rooming house, crossed the state line into Council Bluffs, Iowa, and boarded a train headed north.

From mug shots, a cleaning lady and a night clerk identified the crooks. Two weeks later, a reward poster circulated picturing the trio along with Denny's wife, Mamie Wheeler, a convicted shoplifter with a reputation for selling stolen goods. Within seven days, the safecracking trio was spotted in the mining town of Joplin. Police confronted two of the gangsters in a hallway at the Keystone Hotel. Prince, the gang leader, entered the hotel just behind the cops, witnessed the arrests, and "turned on his heel," according to news accounts.

Back in Omaha, furrier Gustav E. Shukert offered a $3,000 reward for return of the sealskin coats, which had been in summer storage for customers. Itchy for the reward money, Omaha's chief of police offered the two jailed suspects a deal they couldn't refuse. If the furs were returned, he promised to drop the charges. Two of the gents' lady friends—both well-known pickpockets from Des Moines—negotiated with the chief by letter and telegram. They arranged to ship the stolen coats to Chicago, where the furrier and the chief traveled to retrieve them. Among the recovered goods were forty-one of the forty-five stolen coats. The furrier paid a proportionate reward of more than $2,700 to the Omaha police chief.

Now it was up to the chief to fulfil his part of the devil's bargain. The day of the suspects' preliminary hearing, witnesses who had previously identified the men from mug shots were either out of town or feigned amnesia. The jailed defendants were certain to walk free until the prosecutor introduced a surprise witness, the landlady who owned the rooming house. She fingered both culprits. The clerk at the transport station also identified Denny. Nonetheless, the police chief

$3,000.00 REWARD.

OMAHA, NEBR., AUGUST 25, 1899.

| CHARLIE PRINCE. | MICH LAVERY. | CHARLIE DENNIS. | MAMIE WHEELER. |

CHARLIE PRINCE, alias "Chuck." Age 28, weight 161, height 5 ft. 9¾ in., complexion medium florid, hair dark chestnut, thin on top, mustache dark chestnut, eyes azure blue. Blue ink anchor star on top above wrist of left arm front. Oblique scar first phalanx thumb of left hand rear. Index finger stiffened at first and second joints. Small pit scar one inch above inner point of right eye brow.

MICH LAVERY, alias "Mack." Age 59, height 5 ft. 8¼ inches, weight 150, complexion fair, hair gray, very bald, mustache gray, index finger right hand amputated. The above "photo" was taken seven years ago, but is a good likeness. Mustache cropped short while here.

CHARLIE DENNIS, alias Denny, alias C. L. West. Age 45, height 5 ft. 6 in., weight 135, complexion dark, hair dark, gray mixed. Has dot between thumb and index finger of left hand. Circular scar on right jaw. Smooth shaved when here.

MAMIE WHEELER. Age 30, height 5 ft. 1 in., weight 90, complexion medium.

On the night of August 13th, 1899, the above described men broke into the fur store of G. E. Shukert of this city and burglarized the vault of about 45 garments, consisting principally of seal-skin jackets, which were held in storage. The above amount will be paid for the arrest of the thieves and recovery of the property, or a proportionate amount will be paid for the recovery of any part of the goods.

The accompanying photograph of the woman is claimed to be the wife of Dennis, and is a notorious shop lifter, and may be found in company with him, or may try to dispose of goods for the party. Prince has served time in Salt Lake, Utah and Georgetown, Tex., for safe cracking. Dennis has only been out of the Jackson, Miss., penitentiary but a short time. Last winter Dennis and his woman Mamie Wheeler, and Prince's woman, (known as the Gorilla's former wife) were arrested in Kansas City, Mo., for shoplifting. Prince was also arrested in Beatrice, Nebr., in 1897-8, for safe blowing, and is well known to the police in Kansas City, Chicago, St. Paul, Minneapolis and Des Moines.

Lavery was arrested in Washington, D. C., in 1892, for safe blowing.

Officers are warned to be cautious in making arrests, as these fellows are all dangerous men.

Address all information to

MARTIN WHITE,
Chief of Police.

OMAHA FUR ROBBERS CAUGHT.

Wilson and Lavary Arrested by the Police at Joplin, Mo.

SPECIAL DISPATCH TO THE GLOBE-DEMOCRAT.

JOPLIN, MO., September 16.—James Wilson and Mich Lavory, two of the burglars who participated in the big fur robbery at Omaha last month, were caught here to-day. Last night the safe at Horn's grocery at Valley Heights, a mile east of Joplin, was skillfully cracked and robbed of its contents, 100 pennies. To-day the police, who had been watching these men, learned that they did not get into their rooms until 4 o'clock. They had the men's pictures and were waiting to catch them together, but this morning they concluded to arrest Wilson and Lavory. On them were found most of the pennies taken from the safe last night and $20 in bills. Wm. C. Prince, another of the fur robbers, was seen with Wilson and Lavory Thursday night, but the police have been unable to locate him since. The woman who helped these three men make the $10,000 haul, had been seen here. The men arrived last Monday, and have been living in retirement in an obscure lodging house. The police have no identification but the robbers' pictures, sent from Omaha. Even laundry marks on their linen were destroyed. Their grips contained only two pistols, some candles and a bottle of chloroform.

$25.00 REWARD

For one E. R. Drake, wanted for horse stealing. He stole the horse six miles northwest of Phillipsburg, Kan., on the 28th day of April, 1902, rode the horse to Orleans, Neb., and sold it; took the train to Oxford, Neb., got his hair cut and smooth shaved at Oxford; Drake is about 22 years old, weight about 150 or 160 pounds; large eyes, full faced, very thick lips, dark hair; has E. R. D. tattooed on one arm just above the wrist; is quite a fellow to talk; think he smokes cigarettes. If properly approached may admit his identity; 5 feet 8 or 9 inches high; will hang around saloons and billiard halls. The above reward will be paid for him in any jail in the United States.

H. N. YERTON, Sheriff.

PHILLIPSBURG, KAN., May 5, 1902.

took the witness stand to argue that nothing but circumstantial evidence linked the defendants to the crime. And so, Charlie "Denny" Dennis, who had served time for safecracking in Jackson, Mississippi, and Mich Lavery, who had once been jailed on similar charges in Georgetown, Texas, were released for lack of evidence.

The *Omaha Morning World-Herald* cried foul. The newspaper declared that the police chief "was more interested in the reward to be paid for the recovery of the goods than in the conviction of the thieves." The power of the press was no help to the prosecutor. The maxim that crime does not pay did not apply to Omaha's chief of police.[92]

Over the next several months, Midwest newspapers reported a crime wave, with safes, strongboxes, and bank vaults burglarized in Valley Heights, Missouri; Evansville, Indiana; and Galesburg, Freeport, and Quincy, Illinois. Each job replicated the modus operandi of the Prince Gang. On Saturday, January 27, 1900, three suspicious-looking figures checked into the Moecker Hotel in Quincy. Although the trio registered under aliases, the proprietor recognized their handwriting. He alerted police that several guests he had "suspected as being crooks" on an earlier visit had returned. Without a warrant, authorities searched the suspects' baggage and found "burglar tools" and explosives.[93]

Late that night, when one of the men stepped out of the hotel, a detective shadowed him. As the suspect walked toward another hotel, the officer "showed his star," according to the *Cleveland Plain Dealer*, and asked the out-of-towner to accompany him to the police station. With that, "the man drew a pistol and pointed it at the officer's heart, but as he did so the [detective] flashed his own pistol and fired four shots. . . . The [suspect] fell dead."[94]

Meanwhile, a dozen cops surrounded the Moecker Hotel. At 2:00 a.m., the other two suspects entered the lobby. Spotting uniformed police, the pair dashed into the hotel saloon, loaded their revolvers, and, with weapons flashing, raced down the corridors toward an exit. Police returned fire. One suspect died after a bullet went "crashing through his skull." A third man was shot on a staircase and "sank to the floor with a broken hip."[95]

"Disaster for Safe Blowers," declared Omaha's *Evening World-Herald*, adding that in each man's pockets were diamonds, "plenty of money," skeleton keys, and letters that revealed a variety of assumed names. Among the dead was gang leader Charlie Prince, described in news accounts as one of the "best safe crackers in the country," a con man "handy with his fists or his gun." There was confusion, however, over the identity of the other two men. Each carried documents with multiple aliases. Positive identity lay not in their fingerprints—a forensic science in its infancy—but literally in their fingers. Neither of the men was Mich Lavery, the con man with the amputated index finger. Police learned via telegraph that he was three hundred miles away in an Evansville, Indiana, jail. Neither of the men was Denny, for there was no telltale dark dot tattooed on either of the suspects' hands.[96]

But with Prince dead and Lavery jailed, two faces on the wanted poster were marked captured. Only the mugs of Denny, the safecracker with the dark-dot tattoo, and his wife Mamie would remain.

RUSH H. BEELER

Brooke Wibracht

The coroner's inquest into Otto Goette's murder revealed a gruesome death. Goette's body was found on his ranch in Byers, Colorado, about forty miles east of Denver, on April 23, 1899. Goette's neighbors, who were searching for him, found his body and recognized him by his clothing. The body lay face down in a small cavity along the bank of a stream within a few hundred yards of his cabin. It had been concealed by grass and dirt, but spring rains had washed the away the debris. Scavenging animals had found the remains and eaten the exposed flesh from the corpse. The coroner's examination revealed that the killer had crushed Goette's skull with repeated blows from an ax or a pick, leaving half a dozen fractures. In addition, he had been shot several times, sustaining wounds in his side and in his head. One of the bullets left a hole at the base of the skull the size of a closed fist. After the coroner completed his investigation, Goette was buried in Evergreen Cemetery in Deer Trail, Colorado.

Goette lived an irregular life. People who knew him said he was a "queer, eccentric, cross-grained man at almost all times and [he] resented any visitors or trespassing on his ranch." Supposedly he had fled from his home in Prussia and moved to Pennsylvania before taking permanent refuge on his Colorado sheep ranch. The herdsman was not a frequent visitor to Byers, but when he did come to town he spent time in local saloons, drinking beer and conversing with local ranchers and townspeople. Discussions with Goette usually turned to the topic of his religious practice of spiritualism and the séances he held with well-known mediums in the area. He explained that these intermediaries told him to shun luxuries and live in isolation on his ranch. He followed their advice and intentionally kept away from his neighbors. His desire to protect his secluded life made him combative. Any rancher in the area knew that if they stepped onto his ranch without his approval they would be greeted with gunfire. Supposedly, Goette was fond of gun play and target practice that left his cabin riddled with bullet holes. He was so fond of his firearms that when the police found his 45-calibre Colt revolver in his stolen wagon, they knew he was not likely to be found alive. Byers ranchers

expressed the opinion that the man who took Goette's gun away must have killed him first because he would not have given the gun up easily.[97]

The previous fall a neighbor had seen a masked man driving Goette's wagon, saddle horse, and about two thousand sheep bearing Goette's brand toward Corona, Colorado. Law enforcement following up on the lead discovered that when the thief and potential murderer arrived in Corona, he claimed to be R. H. Beeler. He sold and shipped the livestock to the firm of Cox, Jones & Co., in Omaha, Nebraska. The firm paid him part of the money up front and deposited the balance to his credit at the Colorado National Bank in Denver. The bank would not issue the balance of $2,800 without positive identification from a witness, however. To complete the deal, "Beeler" traveled to Denver and paid a man named Joseph Brewer, an employee of the Western Union Telegraph Company, to identify him as Beeler at the bank. The authorities arrested Brewer as an accessory in the theft of Goette's flock and his murder. After several days in jail, Brewer fingered Rush H. Beeler as the perpetrator. Beeler was a sheepman who used various aliases, including Tom Beeler and C. F. Newton or Newlin.

Once the police knew Beeler's name, they sent a detective to find him in Wyoming, where they believed he was hiding. In their effort to locate him, the detective and the sheriff unwittingly shared some information about their mission with local ranchers who knew and worked with Beeler. They found the fugitive first and warned him that the police were closing in on him. Beeler evaded the officers in Wyoming and led them on a chase through Utah and Colorado.

As the case evolved and the police failed to arrest the accused thief and murderer, several theories developed as to Beeler's whereabouts. Some newspapers reported that he was in San Francisco. Others suspected he was hiding out in Nevada. One particularly sensational theory claimed that Beeler eluded police and made it safely back into his group of friends, the Hole-In-The-Wall gang, known for famed members Butch Cassidy and the Sundance Kid. This was only

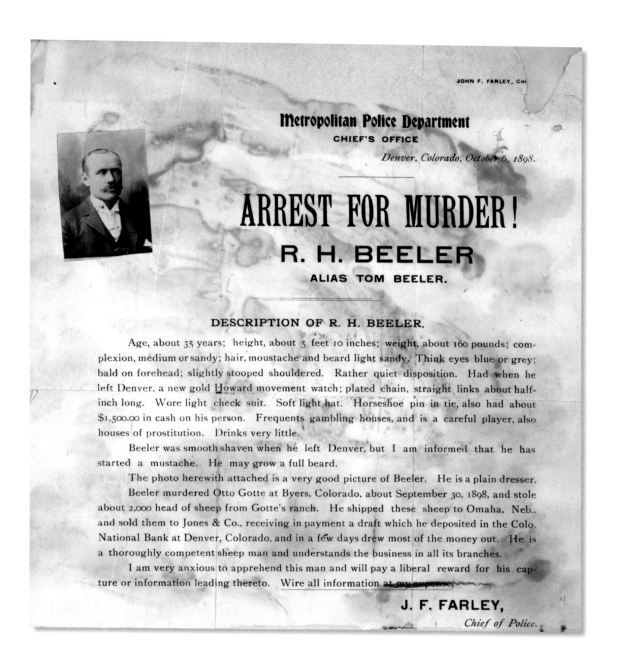

JOHN F. FARLEY, CHI

Metropolitan Police Department
CHIEF'S OFFICE
Denver, Colorado, October 6, 1898.

ARREST FOR MURDER!
R. H. BEELER
ALIAS TOM BEELER.

DESCRIPTION OF R. H. BEELER.

Age, about 35 years; height, about 5 feet 10 inches; weight, about 160 pounds; complexion, medium or sandy; hair, moustache and beard light sandy. Think eyes blue or grey; bald on forehead; slightly stooped shouldered. Rather quiet disposition. Had when he left Denver, a new gold Howard movement watch; plated chain, straight links about half-inch long. Wore light check suit. Soft light hat. Horseshoe pin in tie, also had about $1,500.00 in cash on his person. Frequents gambling houses, and is a careful player, also houses of prostitution. Drinks very little.

Beeler was smooth shaven when he left Denver, but I am informed that he has started a mustache. He may grow a full beard.

The photo herewith attached is a very good picture of Beeler. He is a plain dresser.

Beeler murdered Otto Gotte at Byers, Colorado, about September 30, 1898, and stole about 2,000 head of sheep from Gotte's ranch. He shipped these sheep to Omaha, Neb., and sold them to Jones & Co., receiving in payment a draft which he deposited in the Colo. National Bank at Denver, Colorado, and in a few days drew most of the money out. He is a thoroughly competent sheep man and understands the business in all its branches.

I am very anxious to apprehend this man and will pay a liberal reward for his capture or information leading thereto. Wire all information at my expense.

J. F. FARLEY,
Chief of Police.

conjecture and never proven. The final predominant theory—despite the corpse that had been found on the ranch—implied that Goette was not murdered at all, but simply left his ranch to find his sweetheart, Anna Glutz. She gave an interview with the *Denver Evening Post* several weeks after his disappearance and told her version of the story. She denied reports that the two were engaged. Glutz stated that they met in the late 1880s, and though the sheep rancher was enamored with her, she did not share the same feelings. They had remained friends over the years, however, in spite of their one-sided romance. She added that she knew Goette by another name, Otto Brown, and like his Colorado neighbors, she thought he was a peculiar man. She said that he talked often about unknown persons

who he believed wanted to kill him and steal his sheep. The circumstances of his death suggest that his claims might have been more than simple paranoia.

The authorities did their best to solve Goette's murder, but they encountered many hurdles. The sheepman's lifestyle as an eccentric and well-armed recluse inspired great curiosity among locals, yet it rendered few persons able to give clues to the crime. Meanwhile, Beeler's friends hindered the investigation by helping him avoid arrest. Despite lengthy, multi-state investigations by law enforcement agencies across the West, no one ever found R. H. Beeler, which left Goette's neighbors, contemporary officials, and present-day researchers with many unanswered questions as to the relationship of the two men and the motive of the killer.

ACKNOWLEDGMENTS

This book is the result of a cooperative effort between the Tarrant County College Archives and the Center for Texas Studies at TCU. On behalf of myself and my coeditor, LeAnna Schooley, the executive director of the Center, we extend our deepest gratitude to the professors, public historians, graduate students, librarians, archivists, and journalists who contributed their time and creative talents to the essays in this volume. We could not have published *Wanted in America* without your hard work. Thank you!

The TCC Heritage Room, where the Fort Worth Police Department collection of wanted posters is housed, was the brainchild of Duane Gage, a history teacher on the northeast campus. History students from that campus and volunteers from various Tarrant County local history and genealogical societies gathered the first archival materials, including items from Jenkins Garrett. After Gage's retirement, J. Paul Davidson, a librarian in the J. Ardis Bell Library, worked diligently for many years to maintain the archive and protect its valuable collections. I am profoundly grateful to these two gentlemen.

Dr. Gene Allen Smith, director of the Center, initiated this project. Aside from a handful of local historians and scholars, the scrapbooks of wanted posters were unknown to the general public. He understood the significance of the collection the moment he saw it. We both knew it deserved a wider audience and began planning to publish. The structure of this book—wanted notices accompanied by explanatory essays—was essentially his idea.

Without the unwavering support of Rick Heyser, Director of Technical Support Services, and Nigel Parker, Director of Records Management and Archives, *Wanted in America* would not have been possible. Nigel let me set aside other projects when I needed time to work on this project. I am especially grateful to Rick for dropping by every once in a while to check for a pulse and for the excellent breakfast and brunch meetings he provided for his staff over the course of each semester. Rick retired in the spring of 2019 to my great sorrow and will be greatly missed.

My coeditor did more than her fair share of editing and struggled almost single handedly with the minutia of formatting, footnoting, and checking sources. She did this all this while completing her doctoral dissertation, and came through the process with her sanity intact, mostly.

The effort to make the wanted poster collection available to the public goes beyond this book. Two of our TCC library catalogers, Ann Kutulas and Krista English, are busy building a digital archive of the entire collection. Digitization has been a goal of mine since I arrived at TCC and Krista and Ann took the initiative to create the basic architecture for the website. By the time you read this, all of the posters in this volume will be available online. Eventually, we plan to add between 1,500 and 2,000 items to our digital wanted notices archive. Krista and Ann deserve the credit for this substantial undertaking.

Several of our student workers played an essential role in the nuts-and-bolts work required to organize and document a project like this. Elbanie Totten, Leo Parrish, and Payton Parrish all contributed to the task of basic archival processing. I am grateful for their perseverance and attention to detail.

Finally, with love and gratitude, I'd like to dedicate my own efforts in this project to my wife Shelley. Her love, support and patience is what really make my career possible after what can best be described as an epically misspent youth. Thirty-three years of marriage, and she still hasn't changed the locks.

TOM KELLAM

NOTES

1. "Mrs. Anna Zimmerman," *New Holland Clarion* (PA), May 26, 1917.

2. Saqui Smith, "The Kidnapped Child—Marion Clarke," *Leslie's Weekly*, June 22, 1899, 486, 496.

3. Smith, "The Kidnapped Child—Marion Clarke," 486.

4. Louis Pizzitola, *Hearst over Hollywood: Power, Passion, and Propaganda in the Movies* (New York: Columbia University Press, 2002), 83.

5. Smith, "The Kidnapped Child—Marion Clarke," 487.

6. *San Francisco Call*, December 31, 1900.

7. "How and Why I Kidnapped the Cudahy Boy," *Philadelphia Inquirer*, April 1, 1906.

8. "Winold is Arrested," *Lexington Morning Herald* (KY), April 11, 1900.

9. "Winold is Arrested."

10. Quote 1, "Alleged Poisoner Arrested," *New York Times*, April 11, 1900; quote 2, "Charged with Kidnapping," *Baltimore Sun* (MD), April 11, 1900.

11. "Winold Confronted," *New York Times*, April 14, 1900.

12. "Profound Mystery," *Arkansas City Weekly Republican-Traveler* (KS), August 18, 1898.

13. "25-year-old Niles Mystery is Still Without a Solution," the *News-Palladium*, (Benton Harbor, MI), January 1, 1933.

14. "Valuable Rings Recovered," the *Evening Star* (Washington, DC), February 5, 1904.

15. "Valuable Rings Recovered."

16. Quote 1, "Phillips Leaves; Tragedy Averted: Prominent City Ward Physician Skips Out of Atlanta, Mrs. Jack Garner Has Also Disappeared," the *Atlanta Constitution*, January 23, 1901; quote 2, the *Watchman and Southron* (Sumter, SC), January 30, 1901; quote 3, "Phillips Leaves; Tragedy Averted: Prominent City Ward Physician Skips Out of Atlanta, Mrs. Jack Garner Has Also Disappeared."

17. "Husband and Wife Now Reconciled: Mrs. Jack Garner Made Statement Regarding Her Absence," the *Atlanta Constitution*, February 8, 1901.

18. "Denver Police Let Boston Crooks Go," *Denver Post*, July 28, 1901.

19. Quote 1, "Denver Police," *Denver Post*, July 28, 1901; quote 2, "Epworth League California Excursions," the *School Journal*, June 8, 1901, ix.

20. "Denver Police."

21. Frank D. Loomis, "My Pickpocket's Day in Court," the *North American Review* 228 (October 1929): 500.

22. Loomis, "My Pickpocket's Day in Court," 507

23. "Say They Hold 'Paddy Irish," *San Francisco Call*, February 15, 1905.

24. "Demand $34,000 of Graham," *Chicago Daily Tribune*, July 26, 1899.

25. "Plead for W.A.S. Graham," *Chicago Daily Tribune*, May 22, 1902.

26. "School Board in a Fix," *Chicago Daily Tribune*, January 5, 1905.

27. "Betrayed by His Statute: American Banker's Singular Capture," the *Daily Mail*, December 18, 1901.

28. "St. Louis Boodlers," *Indianapolis Journal*, September 10, 1902.

29. "What Folk Has Done," *Moberly Weekly Monitor* (MO), February 21, 1908.

30. "Eighteen New Indictments Charge Municipal Boodling; Fugitive J. K. Murrell Returns to Four Courts Disguised," *St. Louis Republic*, September 9, 1902.

31. "Big Criminals in St. Louis," *Seattle Daily Times*, April 24, 1902.

32. "Husband Takes Sweet Revenge," *San Francisco Call*, January 23, 1902.

33. "General White's Scandal," the *Grand Rapids Press* (MI), August 28, 1903.

34. "General White's Scandal."

35. "Second-Hand Stores," *Grand Rapids Herald* (MI), December 20, 1899.

36. "Is Wanted But Cannot Be Found," *Grand Rapids Herald*, January 3, 1900.

37. "It Staggered Him," *Grand Rapids Herald*, December 4, 1900.

38. "Inquiry Awaits All Detectives," *Chicago Daily Tribune* (IL), August 30, 1901.

39. "Inspector Douglass is Foiled," *Boston Herald* (MA), November 17, 1901.

40. Quote 1, "Tax Collector's Disappearance," *Evening Sentinel* (Santa Cruz, CA), November 29, 1898; quote 2, "Warrant Out for Findley," *Evening Sentinel*, December 3, 1898.

41. Quote 1, "Absconding Tax Collector," *Santa Cruz Sentinel*, June 18, 1899; quote 2, "Will Return for Trial," *Evening News* (San Jose, CA), May 12, 1899; quote 3, "Samuel Findley…," *San Francisco Call*, May 14, 1899.

42. "Findley's Finish," *Evening Sentinel*, April 4, 1900.

43. "A Convict's Promise," the *New York Herald*, December 23, 1878.

44. "Death Tells the Secret of the Train Robbery," *New Orleans Daily Picayune*, December 19, 1900.

45. Annual Report of the Executive Department of the City of Boston, For the Year 1895: Part II (Boston: Rockwell and Churchill, 1896), 129-130.

46. Annual Report of the Executive Department of the City of Boston, For the Year 1896: Part II (Boston: Municipal Printing Office, 1897), 439.

47. "Shooting on Caddo," *Daily Ardmoreite* (OK), May 23, 1897.

48. Letter from City of Fort Worth Police Chief William Rea, March 4, 1901. Name Index to Inmate Case Files, 1895-1931 (Record Group 129), National Archives, Kansas City Branch. Sam Vaughn, #1470.

49. Genie Vaughn vs. Sam Vaughn, District Court, Tarrant County, TX, file docket 77, p. 240 (1909).

50. International Association Chiefs of Police, Annual Convention, "Train Robberies, Train Robbers and The Holdup Men," speech by William A. Pinkerton, November 1907.

51. "Kill for Naught," the *Oregonian* (Portland), April 2, 1904.

52. "The Railroad Bandits: Advised Woman to Kill Her Husband by Giving Him Rough On Rats," the *Corvallis Times* (OR), May 14, 1904.

53. *Dallas Morning News*, November 26, 1898.

54. "Escape on Engine," *Topeka State Journal* (KS), April 21, 1910.

55. Kenneth M. LaMaster, *U.S. Penitentiary Leavenworth* (Charleston, SC: Arcadia Publishing, 2008), 46.

56. "Police Capture a Pair of Dynamitards: Four Arrests Made on Dr. A. V. L. Brokaw's Information," *St. Louis Republic*, August 13, 1900.

57. "Police Capture a Pair of Dynamitards: Four Arrests Made on Dr. A. V. L. Browkaw's Information."

58. "Murderer Still at Large," *Rock Island Argus* (IL), August 19, 1898.

59. Quote 1, "Murderer Still at Large"; quote 2, "Strange Mixing of Identities," *St. Louis Republic*, November 26, 1898; quote 3, "Is the Accused Murderer Herman Wendt, or is he Herman Wendt's Double?" *Seattle Post Intelligencer*, December 16, 1898.

60. "Innocent," *Cincinnati Enquirer*, September 8, 1898.

61. "Mrs. Schaedlich Acquitted," *Mexico Ledger* (MO), October 26, 1899.

62. "Hettrick's Tale of Kraus Murder," *Trenton Evening Times* (NJ), February 26, 1902.

63. "Not Guilty is the Verdict in Green's Case," *Buffalo Evening News* (NY), October 16, 1902.

64. "Arrested," *Boston Morning Journal*, October 2, 1898.

65. "O'Hagan Here," *Boston Journal*, October 13, 1898.

66. Donna B. Ernst, *The Sundance Kid: The Life of Harry Alonzo Longabaugh* (Norman: University of Oklahoma Press, 2009), 112.

67. Ernst, *The Sundance Kid*, 112-113.

68. "Slayers of Adams and Kirkley Together with Their Pals Make a Daring Attempt to Break Jail," *Birmingham Age Herald* (AL), January 3, 1901.

69. "Paid Penalty," the *Daily Herald* (Biloxi, MS), June 29, 1901.

70. "Frank Duncan Feels Hopeful," *Montgomery Times* (AL), October 25, 1904.

71. "Duncan Drops," the *Town Talk* (Alexandria, LA), November 26, 1904.

72. "Tragedy and Pathos are Mingled in This Story Which Has Shaken Indiana," *St. Louis Post-Dispatch*, December 11, 1898.

73. "Riddled to Death with Bullets," *Courier-Journal* (Louisville, KY), October 10, 1898.

74. "A Shocking Incident," *Courier-Journal*, October 12, 1898.

75. "Where Good Work May Be Done," *Courier-Journal*, October 23, 1898.

76. *The Southwest Reporter* 50, April 10 – May 29, 1899, Permanent Edition (St. Paul: West Publishing Company, 1899), 375-378.

77. "Briscoe Arrest Just a Blunder," *Chicago Tribune*, February 2, 1905.

78. "Murderer Content with Fate," *Chicago Tribune*, September 30, 1902.

79. "Shippy Gets Another," *Kalamazoo Gazette* (MI), January 29, 1905.

80. "Double Murder in Limestone," *Birmingham Age-Herald* (AL), January 25, 1900; "Double Tragedy," *Florence Herald* (AL), January 25, 1900.

81. "Determined to Kill Them," *Columbia Herald* (TN), February 2, 1900.

82. "His Love Spurned, He Tried to Kill," *Boston Sunday Post*, October 6, 1901.

83. "It is Murder," *Lowell Sun* (MA), October 7, 1901.

84. "Cooley Case Becomes as Exciting as Blondin," *Lowell Sun*, October 18, 1901.

85. *Taney County Republican* (MO), January 14, 1904.

86. *Marshalltown Evening Times-Republican* (IA), September 9, 1903; *Taney County Republican*, January 14, 1904.

87. Gillian O'Brien, *Blood Runs Green: The Murder That Transfixed Gilded Age Chicago* (Chicago: University of Chicago Press, 2015), 204.

88. "The Execution of Funk," *Washington Times* (DC), November 10, 1900.

89. "Ripley Mob: Brother of Durham Tells the Story of the Killing," the *Tennessean* (Nashville), January 15, 1900.

90. Quote 1, "Lynching Bee is in Prospect," The *Tennessean*, January 10, 1900; quotes 2 and 3, "Bodies Swinging with the Breezes," the *Tennessean*, January 11, 1900; quote 4, "Excitement Still High," *Dallas Morning News*, January 11, 1900.

91. Tiffany, "More Tragedy for the Gingery Family—A Follow Up," *Black Ripley* (blog), March 11, 2014, accessed July 27, 2016, https://blackripley.com/2014/03/11/more-tragedy-for-the-gingery-family-a-follow-up/.

92. "Twelve Statements and Twelve Queries," *Omaha Morning World-Herald* (NE), October 18, 1899.

93. "Police Killed Safe Blowers; Desperate Fight Occurred in a Quincy, Ill., Hotel Corridor; Two Men Shot, Third Badly Wounded," *Cleveland Plain Dealer*, January 27, 1900.

94. "Police Killed Safe Blowers; Desperate Fight Occurred in a Quincy, Ill., Hotel Corridor; Two Men Shot, Third Badly Wounded."

95. "Police Killed Safe Blowers; Desperate Fight Occurred in a Quincy, Ill., Hotel Corridor; Two Men Shot, Third Badly Wounded."

96. "Disaster to Safe Blowers," *Omaha Evening World-Herald*, January 29, 1900.

97. "Remarkable Disappearance of Otto Goette," *Denver Evening Post*, September 28, 1898.

CONTRIBUTORS

SHIRLEY APLEY worked in the Genealogy, Local History, and Archives Unit of the Fort Worth Public Library. After her work there she returned to her native state to become the director of the Huron Public Library in Huron, South Dakota. Finding lost souls within old documents is her passion and hobby.

LINDA BARRETT is a native of Fort Worth, Texas. She holds a Master of Library and Information Science degree from the University of North Texas. Linda is the Manager of Genealogy, Local History, and Archives Unit and the City Archivist at the Fort Worth Public Library.

JENSEN BRANSCOMBE completed her dissertation at TCU in 2013. She is currently an assistant professor in the History Department at Tarleton State University, where she teaches in the fields of modern US and early US history, women's history, and Modern Latin America, with concentrations in US immigration history, women and immigration, and the US borderlands.

O.K. CARTER is a writer and historian with a long history as a *Fort Worth Star-Telegram* journalist, where he was a columnist, editorial writer, and former editor and publisher for the paper in Arlington. He is also a former Tarrant County College trustee (2010-17) and an adjunct professor in communication at UT Arlington.

BRIAN CERVANTEZ is an associate professor of history at Tarrant County College, where he has taught since 2005. A Fort Worth native, Cervantez is the author of *Amon Carter: A Lone Star Life*.

KENDRA DEHART received a BA in History from Southwestern University and an MA in Public History from Texas State University—San Marcos, Texas. She is a doctoral candidate writing her dissertation for TCU. She currently teaches US History at Sul Ross State University in Alpine, Texas.

KEVIN FOSTER is a veteran police officer of the Fort Worth Police Department who retired after twenty-nine years on the force. Originally from Fort Worth, he currently resides in Weatherford, Texas, and is a supervisor with the TCU Police Department.

RENE GOMEZ, a Fort Worth native, has a degree in Radio and Television Production from UTA and a Masters in Library Science from the University of North Texas. He has been the unit supervisor at the Genealogy, Local History, and Archives Unit at the Fort Worth Public Library since 2001.

RICHARD J. GONZALES published *Raza Rising: Chicanos in North Texas*, in March 2016, and in July 2017 published a novel titled *Deer Dancer*. He was a *Fort Worth Star-Telegram* op-ed columnist for six years and has published short stories in the *Americas Review*.

MICHAEL GREEN is a PhD Candidate in History at TCU. Originally from Greenville, Texas, he completed his BA at Texas A&M—Commerce before moving to Fort Worth to attend TCU. He is currently writing a dissertation on the history of intellectual disabilities, deinstitutionalization, and the welfare state in post-1945 Texas.

PETER R. HACKER teaches US and Texas history at Tarrant County College. A native of Southern California, Hacker received his BA from UCLA and his MA from TCU.

GAYLE HANSON is a historian, genealogist, lecturer, and researcher for Texas Historical and Ancestry Researchers (THR) in Arlington, Texas. Ms. Hanson's current projects include research on the WPA Federal Writers Project Ex-Slave Narratives of Tarrant County, and a book on the Early Negro Schools of Tarrant County and the Jeanes Supervisors of Texas.

JAMALIN R. HARP is a native of San Antonio, Texas. She received her BA in history and English from Abilene Christian University and her MA and PhD in history from Texas Christian University. She is a lecturer at the University of Texas Rio Grande Valley.

HARRY MAX HILL, a Fort Worth native, worked for the Fort Worth Public Library for nearly twenty-nine years before his retirement in 2005. He served as assistant manager of the Genealogy, Local History, and Archives Unit for the last thirteen years. His current research interests are Fort Worth nightclubs, golf courses, and historic movie censorship in the city.

JODY HOKS has worked as an Assistant Archivist for the Bernard Rapoport Legacy Project at the Briscoe Center for American History and as Digital Archivist at the Fort Worth Public Library. She currently resides in Chicago.

MEREDITH MAY is a native of Huntington, Texas. She graduated with her BA from Stephen F. Austin State University and pursued graduate work in Texas and women's history at Texas Christian University. She obtained her MA in 2012 and her PhD in May 2017. She is currently on the faculty at Kilgore College.

QUENTIN MCGOWN is a sixth generation Texan and fourth generation Fort Worth attorney with a lifelong interest in history. McGown now serves as Associate Judge in Tarrant County Probate Court Number One. He teaches courses on Fort Worth history and has published three books on the topic.

BRYAN MCKINNEY is a native Dallasite from Oak Cliff who received his BA from UTA and a Masters in Library Science from UNT. He worked in the archives departments of both the Dallas Public Library and the Fort Worth Public Library.

KEVEN MCQUEEN is from Richmond, Kentucky. He is the author sixteen books on historical true crime, biography, history, natural disasters, ghostlore, and other strange topics. He is an instructor in the Department of English at Eastern Kentucky University.

WILLIAM MEIER is Associate Professor and Chair of History at TCU, where he teaches courses on Britain, Ireland, and empire. He is the author of *Property Crime in London, 1850-Present* (Palgrave Macmillan, 2011) and is currently writing a history of terrorism in modern Britain.

AMANDA MILIAN is a Doctoral Candidate in History at TCU. Her dissertation *Dining at the President's Mansion: Material Worlds of the Early Republic, 1790-1840* analyzes the entertaining habits and material culture of the first seven presidents and their respective first ladies. She currently serves as project archivist at the Tarrant County Archives.

ELIZABETH SODEK MOCZYGEMBA is originally from Houston and currently resides in Austin. She earned her PhD in American History from TCU in 2014, focusing on women's history and public history. After working in the museum field for ten years, Elizabeth is currently employed by her active toddler.

ROBERT OLIVER holds a BS in business administration from the University of Texas at Dallas and spent thirty years in technology sales and management. Following a career in business, Bobby returned to school to pursue his passion, history, receiving an MA in History from TCU, where he is also pursuing his PhD.

MICHAEL H. PRICE settled into the newsroom during the late 1960s as a crime-and-politics reporter and courtroom portraitist, then became city editor of the *News & Globe–Times* at Amarillo. Price has dealt primarily in art and film criticism since 1980, as author of the *Forgotten Horrors* series of movie-genre encyclopedias.

BRENNAN GARDNER RIVAS received her PhD in history at Texas Christian University in 2019. She specializes in nineteenth-century Texas history. Brennan is a longtime resident of North Texas and currently lives in Fort Worth. She is a lecturer in history at TCU.

ESTHER RIVERA serves as program coordinator for the Holdsworth Center in Austin. She received her BA from the University of Texas and her MA in history from Texas State University, where she cultivated her passion for public history. Her career includes work in history and art museums, as well as in educational non-profits in Texas.

RICHARD SELCER is a Fort Worth author and historian who also calls the city home. He has taught for forty-five years, both in the US and overseas, on every level from high school through university, and to date has published eleven books and more than fifty articles. In his spare time he leads walking tours of historic Fort Worth.

GENE ALLEN SMITH is a professor of history at TCU specializing in American naval/maritime history, Gulf territorial expansion, and the War of 1812. He is a cofounder of the Center for Texas Studies at TCU and has served as its director since 2003.

GENE RHEA TUCKER, originally from Killeen, Texas, earned his BA and MA in history from Tarleton State University and his PhD in transatlantic history from the University of Texas at Arlington. He is an assistant professor of history at Temple College in Temple, Texas.

JESSICA WEBB is a PhD Candidate at Texas Christian University. She is currently writing her dissertation on the red-light districts of Fort Worth and San Antonio at the turn of the century. Her interest in Texas history stemmed from being born and raised here, and she hopes to continue researching and telling the stories of the Lone Star State.

HOLLACE AVA WEINER, a journalist turned historian, covered criminal courts in Baltimore many years ago and was happy to return to that milieu to investigate the stories behind the faces on a wanted poster. Weiner has written four books on Texas Jewish history and Fort Worth history. She is director of the Fort Worth Jewish Archives.

BROOKE WIBRACHT received her PhD in history from TCU, where her dissertation focused on modernizing research into the Texas Fence-Cutting Wars by including race, class, and gender. Wibracht graduated from Texas A&M University with her BA in 2004 and from Loyola University Chicago with her MA in 2011.

Coeditors

TOM KELLAM is a native of Fort Worth with degrees in philosophy, history, and library science. He worked in the Genealogy, Local History, and Archives Unit at the Fort Worth Public Library for twenty-three years. He is currently the district archivist for Tarrant County College.

LEANNA S. SCHOOLEY is executive director of the Center for Texas Studies at TCU, where she received her PhD in 2017. She has spent her career working in museums and public history organizations including the W.K. Gordon Center for Industrial History of Texas, the Texas Historical Commission, and the Fort Stockton Historical Society.